Ethics and Communication

Ethics and Communication

Global Perspectives

Edited by
Göran Collste

ROWMAN & LITTLEFIELD
INTERNATIONAL

London • New York

Published by Rowman & Littlefield International Ltd
Unit A, Whitacre Mews, 26-34 Stannary Street, London SE11 4AB
www.rowmaninternational.com

Rowman & Littlefield International Ltd. is an affiliate of Rowman & Littlefield
4501 Forbes Boulevard, Suite 200, Lanham, Maryland 20706, USA
With additional offices in Boulder, New York, Toronto (Canada), and Plymouth (UK)
www.rowman.com

British Library Cataloguing in Publication Data
A catalogue record for this book is available from the British Library

ISBN: HB 978-1-7834-8597-0
    PB 978-1-7834-8598-7

Library of Congress Cataloging-in-Publication Data
Names: Collste, Göran, 1950- editor.
Title: Ethics and communication : global perspectives/edited by Göran Collste.
Description: London; New York : Rowman & Littlefield International Ltd. is an affiliate
    of Rowman & Littlefield [2016] | Includes bibliographical references and index.
Identifiers: LCCN 2016015678 (print) | LCCN 2016016396 (ebook) |
    ISBN 9781783485970 (cloth : alk. paper) | ISBN 9781783485987 (pbk. : alk. paper) |
    ISBN 9781783485994 (electronic)
Subjects: LCSH: Ethics. | Communication.
Classification: LCC BJ1031 .E758 2016 (print) | LCC BJ1031 (ebook) | DDC 170—dc23
LC record available at https://lccn.loc.gov/2016015678

♾ ™ The paper used in this publication meets the minimum requirements of American
National Standard for Information Sciences—Permanence of Paper for Printed Library
Materials, ANSI/NISO Z39.48-1992.

Printed in the United States of America

Contents

1 Introduction: Ethics and Communication – Global Perspectives   1
Göran Collste

PART I: THEORY   21

2 Global Ethics: A Framework for Thinking about Communication   23
Nigel Dower

3 Treacherous Tropes: How Ethicists Communicate   43
Maren Behrensen

PART II: ETHICS ACROSS RELIGIOUS AND CULTURAL BORDERS   61

4 'Western' versus 'Islamic' Human Rights Conceptions? A Critique of Cultural Essentialism in the Discussion on Human Rights   63
Heiner Bielefeldt

5 Peng Chun Chang, Intercultural Ethics and the Universal Declaration of Human Rights   95
Hans Ingvar Roth

6 Critical Thinking and Culture: Shared Values, Different Guises   125
Soraj Hongladarom

7 Religious Transcendence: Hope for Global Communication Ethics   143
Peter Gan

Contents

PART III: ETHICS AND COMMUNICATION: CASE STUDIES   **161**

8   Communication Ethics in Japan: A Sociocultural Perspective
     on Privacy in the Networked World   163
     Kiyoshi Murata and Yohko Orito

9   What is the Critical Role of Intercultural Information Ethics?   181
     Elin Palm

Bibliography   197

Index   215

Notes on Contributors   223

Chapter 1

Introduction

Ethics and Communication – Global Perspectives

Göran Collste

Ethics requires empathy and communication. Why should we bother about what is right and wrong if we have no idea of how other people feel and sense? Our ability to identify with other people is an important starting point for ethics. A morally conscious person cannot remain indifferent and passive when human beings are exposed to suffering. There is a tacit demand to intervene when we encounter other peoples' needs and suffering (Løgstrup 1997). A blunting of moral sensibility or cold-heartedness implies that a person lacks the ability to see and judge events from a moral perspective.[1]

A person does not live his or her life in a moral vacuum. By our very existence, we are included in morally relevant relationships, and communication is thus a fundamental existential category. As humans, we are dependent on other people in various ways and on the natural world around us. Our actions – or our failures to act – affect in various ways other people; we can harm or succour. The aim of morality is to guide our actions so that we can take responsibility for our way of living and acting.

This view of moral responsibility seems to presuppose that ethics requires nearness between individuals. We must experience the other person's vulnerability and suffering. What is then the impact of globalization for our moral responsibility? Globalization means that we are linked to people at a distance. Does distance exclude moral relations with the Other as some communitarian philosophers seem to assume?

Globalization implies that our actions have far-reaching reverberations. The dissemination of greenhouse gas leading to global warming is one example of this. Globalization also means that we are better informed about living conditions in different parts of the world; of wars, oppression, natural catastrophes and other things which challenge people's lives at a far distance. This information can lead to involvement and commitment. The worldwide

1

shockwave following the publication of the picture of the three-year-old Aylan Kurdi's dead body at the shore of Turkey in 2015 shows that empathy can transcend national boundaries. We can identify with a distant victim, which inspires our moral engagement.

But how can we communicate our moral views across cultural and national borders? The aim of this book is to discuss and provide answers to this question. 'Global Perspectives' in the book title means that the book focuses on ethics and communication in an age traced by globalization. But it also means that authors with various cultural backgrounds coming from different parts of the world contribute in the search for answers.

In the wake of globalization, social practices such as politics, research, (social) media, health care, information and communication, education and business increasingly include actors from different parts of the globe. Ethics is of crucial importance for these practices, and hence, the question of how to communicate ethics across borders becomes acute.

How then is ethics communicated in an age of globalization? Is it possible to overcome cultural differences and agree on values and ethical principles across cultural borders? The overarching aim of this anthology is to respond to these questions. Comparative value surveys are often researched empirically with the help of sociological methods or pursued within communication studies (Ingelhart and Welzel 2005, Hall 2005). However, this anthology's disciplinary point of departure is philosophy, and in particular ethics. Studies of ethics and communication entail both the classical question of the universality or contextual limits of ethics and values, but also new challenges for communication; how are values and norms communicated, shared and perhaps transformed in global interactions?

Ethical issues raise controversies in various fields. Through e-medicine, medical information and consultation are provided globally via the Internet. But ethical norms of medicine and health care are embedded in local health care institutions. The ethical principles guiding health care in Europe and United States, such as the four principles of patient autonomy, non-maleficence, beneficence and justice may be contested in other parts of the world (Beauchamp and Childress 2013; Fu-Chang 1999). So, which principles should guide globalized e-medicine?

Research is another social practice that has turned global. Established guidelines for research on human beings include principles of health, human dignity, integrity, right to self-determination, privacy and confidentiality of personal information of research subjects, and the conduct of research is based on ethical principles of integrity, honesty and trust (Helsinki Declaration 2013; Singapore Statement 2010). There are controversies of how to balance and prioritize principles of research ethics and challenges for participants in global research projects to come to agreements.

Gender equality is one of the basic goals for Swedish foreign aid. But is this goal interpreted in the same way by Swedish donors and the receiving countries? Global warming illustrates how we are globally connected and how our collective actions have increasingly global reverberations. In order to come to grips with climate change, shared ethical principles have been articulated (UNESCO 2010), but it has also raised controversies regarding what is a just distribution of the burdens to limit climate change.

Questions of justice are also raised by migration from the global South to the global North. What are the rights of migrants and refugees and what duties do the wealthy countries have to open their borders?

These examples illustrate that globalization requires communication of ethics and new arenas for discussions of ethical issues. But are not cultural boundaries and traditions obstacles to communication and do perhaps conflicting social and economic interests stand in the way of global ethics?

According to *Encyclopedia Britannica*, 'communication is the exchange of meanings between individuals through a common system of symbols'. An 'exchange of meanings,' in our case an exchange of ethical ideas (values, norms, rights, principles etc.), requires that the ideas are comprehensible for the receiving partner of the exchange. Otherwise, no exchange of meanings takes place, and agreements on ethical issues will be either illusory or based on misunderstandings. Hence communication requires first the possibility of mutual understanding. Second, communication also requires reciprocity and a willingness to listen. If the potential receiver of a message is not willing to listen, there will not be any exchange of meanings. This requirement becomes clear when we look at the etymological root of the word 'communication'. Commmunication comes from the Latin word *communis* which means 'common' and 'community'. So, communication requires a community, a shared social understanding and reciprocity.

Both requirements for communication – shared understandings and reciprocity – are contested. The possibility of a shared understanding of values and norms across cultures has been questioned by influential theories in philosophy and political theory. Reciprocity in communication is challenged when globalization implies economic and ideological domination of powerful actors and marginalization of weak voices, what Rajeev Bhargava calls 'epistemic injustice' (Bhargava 2013). In the following I will elaborate on these two requirements for the communication of ethics.

IS COMMUNICATION OF ETHICS POSSIBLE?

What then are the prospects for communication of values, norms and ethical principles in a globalized world? As we noted, communication of ethics requires that a receiver understands the moral language used by a sender, but is such a shared understanding feasible? Is communication of ethics across cultural borders really possible or are the moral languages so different that translation and mutual understanding are unattainable?

Before I discuss some theoretical approaches to the question of communication across cultural borders, a note on different levels of ethical thinking would help. We can distinguish between different levels of ethical thinking and ethical decision making. First, we have a specific moral view justifying a particular course of action, for example 'do not secretly monitor Mr. Jones'. The next level is a norm that specifies a kind of action, for example 'do not violate people's privacy'. This norm is a premise in the argument for the specific moral view. It can, in turn, be warranted by a more general ethical principle, for example the 'principle of human dignity'. Then, the principle of human dignity implies the norm to respect people's privacy.

Communication of ethics can start on all levels of the moral discourse and we might agree or disagree on the different levels: the specific view, the norm or the principle. However, it is also possible that we agree on the specific view, for example that political authorities should not secretly monitor Mr. Jones. But we might disagree about which norm or principle that supports this view. On the other hand, we might also agree on the norm 'do not violate people's privacy', but disagree on its application. For example, we might balance the norm 'do not violate peoples' privacy' and the norm 'protect public security' differently, which will imply different positions with regard to the secret monitoring of Mr. Jones.

Some would argue that a particular moral case is the best starting point for ethical communication. According to moral particularism, each moral situation is unique and communication should be case based. Ethical communication is, according to this view, best achieved through narratives of specific cases.

But is really each moral situation unique? Yes, of course regarding time and situation-specific characteristics but not regarding the ethical aspects. Let me illustrate this with two cases. In the first case, a patient faces a choice of two different treatments for cancer. The patient is informed about the pros and cons of the treatments and she can then choose one. In the second case a person is asked to participate in a psychological experiment. She is informed about different aspects and can, based on the information, chose whether to participate or not. These cases are very different but they both actualise the same ethical principle, namely the principle of informed consent. The patient is informed about the treatments and has the right to choose one of them. The person facing the psychological experiment is similarly informed about the experiment and has the right to decide whether to participate or not. In conclusion the situations are unique but the ethical principle of informed consent is relevant for both.

Is then communication of ethics across cultural borders easier regarding specific moral cases or regarding ethical principles? Let us assume that doctors in India, Africa, Saudi Arabia and Europe are to decide on the interruption of a lifesaving treatment. Should the conversation between them start with the case or with the relevant ethical principles? Perhaps it is for pedagogical reasons better to start with the particular case to get a common understanding and agreement. However, the discussants will immediately face the questions of the salient moral aspects of the case. Why is it a moral problem at all? The answer depends on views on the other levels of the moral discourse; perhaps one discussant focuses on the dignity of the person, and another on the amount of pleasure or pain that the decisions will imply. For the first, the question of life-saving treatment is a moral question because a human life it at stake; for the second because it is about a human being's pain and pleasure. Hence, ethical principles, for example the principle of human dignity or the principle of utility, are inherent in ethical argumentation.

The above reasoning could also be applied to virtue ethics, that is, ethical theories focusing on personal characters and practical wisdom. People with different cultural backgrounds could agree on what a virtuous person should do in a particular situation but they could still disagree on which virtues are cardinal and on the ranking of virtues.

The theoretical discussion on the possibility of the communication of ethics across cultural borders is multifaceted, and I will now present some different views.

THE INCOMMENSURABILITY THESIS

One of the most influential and controversial contributions to the modern discussion on religious and ideological pluralism is Samuel Huntington's book *The Clash of Civilizations and the Remaking of World Order* published in 1996. Huntington warns of a post-Cold War development characterized by conflicts rather than communication between the civilizations of the world.

What, then, is a 'civilization' according to Huntington? 'Both civilization and culture refer to the overall way of life of a people, and a civilization is a culture writ large,' writes Huntington (Huntington 1998: 41). Common language, history, religion, values and institutions are among the defining characteristics of a civilization, and a civilization provides a basis for the subjective identification of peoples; 'Civilizations are the biggest "we" within which we feel culturally at home as distinguished from all the other "thems" out there,' Huntington writes (Ibid: 43). Among the major civilizations are

'Western' Christianity, Orthodox Christianity, Confucianism, Hinduism and Islam.

While civilizations differ when it comes to deep and fundamental social values and most people tend to identify with their civilization, clashes of civilizations are 'interminable' and endless, Huntington maintains (Ibid: 291). Are there then ways to avoid clashes and enter into dialogues and harmonious relations? Yes, Huntington argues, while civilizations also interact and 'overlap' (Ibid: 43), 'peoples in all civilizations should search for and attempt to expand the values, institutions and practices they have in common with peoples of other civilizations' (Ibid: 320).[2] This is, according to Huntington, the only way to avoid a clash of civilizations.

While Huntington stresses the conflicts of 'civilizations' from the perspective of political theory, philosopher Alasdair MacIntyre argues for a contrast thesis from a philosophical point of departure. According to MacIntyre, there are serious obstacles for cross-cultural understandings of values and norms due to the contrasts between moral and cultural traditions. Today's disagreements on moral issues are, according to MacIntyre, explained by underlying different conceptions of justice and rationality. There are 'rival theories of justice' and 'rival rationalities' (MacIntyre 1988: 1–2). He writes: 'Doctrines, theses, and arguments all have to be understood in terms of historical context' (Ibid: 9). Hence, there is little room for dialogue and mutual understanding between representatives of different traditions. As evidence for and illustration of his argument, MacIntyre refers to the differences between the classical traditions Hebraism, Platonism, Aristotelism and Augustinism. It is a failure of the post-Enlightenment 'liberal individualism' to assume first that its own point of view is neutral and not 'imprisoned by a set of beliefs which lack justification in precisely the same way and to the same extent as do the positions which they reject ...' and to assume second that there is a shared rationality across cultures and traditions (Ibid: 396).

Is there then, according to MacIntyre, any way to overcome differences between traditions and achieve a shared understanding of moral issues? Yes, but it requires first that one is cognizant of one's own tradition and 'first language,' and second, that one through 'empathetic conceptual imagination' becomes so familiar with a rival tradition that it is mastered as a 'second first language' (Ibid: 394). 'Understanding requires knowing the culture, so far as is possible, as a native inhabitant knows it, and speaking, hearing, writing, and reading the language as a native inhabitant speaks, hears, writes, and reads it' (Ibid. 374). So, according to MacIntyre, intercultural ethics is possible but requires the toilsome process of putting oneself in the other's shoes.

As we see, MacIntyre emphasizes the uniqueness of different traditions and the difficulties of translations. Let me take two examples from religious ethics that may illustrate his point but also why it is problematic. The two examples are the *ahimsa* norm in Indian tradition and the *agape* norm in Christian ethics.

Ahimsa means non-harming of sentient beings. It is a view prevalent in Indian religions and in particular in Jainism. Its ground is the idea that all living is conscious, and, thus, that one should not harm or kill any sentient being. The norm of *ahimsa* is particularly radically interpreted in Jainism. To avoid killing any living being, Jainist monks strain water to avoid drinking any creatures and cover their mouths so that they can avoid inhaling any insects. *Ahimsa* is a moral norm based on a doctrine not found in other moral traditions (Bilimoria 1991).

Agape, love, is another moral norm tightly connected to a religious doctrine. *Agape* is the Greek word for love, and is according to some interpretation of Christianity a unique Christian idea of love. *Agape* means God's self-giving, altruistic love and has as its pattern Jesus' life and death and his commandment to love your enemy. According to theologian Anders Nygren, *agape* is an interpretation of love which is contrary to the idea of love (*eros*) in other religions and world views. For example, in Indian religions love means, according to Nygren, that man is trying to unite with the transcendent, but in Christianity, love means God's love of human beings (Nygren 1982).

Both *ahimsa* and *agape* are examples of moral norms that are tightly connected to metaphysical and religious beliefs. In order to understand their meaning and prescriptive force, one must know something about the doctrinal backgrounds. These examples of two moral views embedded in religious traditions illustrate also a problem with MacIntyre's incommensurability thesis. In contrast to what MacIntyre assumes, both norms are understandable even if not shared by non-believers.

Huntington speaks of 'civilizations' and MacIntyre of 'traditions', but they basically seem to refer to similar entities, with Huntington analysing them from a political point of view and MacIntyre from a philosophical. They have in common the emphasis on the contrasts between civilizations and traditions and the difficulties of communicating ethics across cultural borders, even though they also acknowledge that there are ways to overcome the differences.

OVERLAPPING CONSENSUS

By introducing the concept of 'overlapping consensus' John Rawls demonstrates a way to overcome boundaries between traditions, or 'comprehensive doctrines' as is the term he uses. Comprehensive doctrines refer to world religions as well as to philosophical doctrines.[3] Rawls wants to avoid 'parochialism', that is, assuming one particular point of view, for example, the Western or the liberal, as being universal. According to Rawls, a 'political conception of justice' must be endorsed by all citizens irrespective of cultural belonging. This is possible through an overlapping consensus. Rawls's argument is developed within political theory but the idea of overlapping consensus could also be used as a metaphor outside of the domain of political institutions. For example, Martha Nussbaum argues that her notion of 'capability' as a measure of human well-being can be an object of an overlapping consensus across cultural and religious borders (Nussbaum 2006). As Hans Ingvar Roth points out in his chapter in this book on Peng Chun Chang, one of the authors of the Universal Declaration of Human Rights, the authors of the Declaration thought that it would be accepted worldwide through something like an overlapping consensus.

What then does overlapping consensus mean? Rawls writes, 'Justice as fairness', a conception of justice entailing political values and principles of justice, 'fits into and can be supported by various reasonable comprehensive doctrines that endure in the society regulated by it', and they are justified from the point of view of different comprehensive doctrines (Rawls 1993: 145). Thus the same political principles, for example principles of liberty and equality, can be justified by different comprehensive doctrines. The principles are overlapping, but the justifications of the principles are different.

Rawls mentions the support for the so-called 'difference principle' – his own preferred principle of just distribution – as one example of an overlapping consensus of different comprehensive doctrines. The difference principle states that 'social and economic inequalities are to be arranged so that they are ... to the greatest benefit of the least advantaged' and it can be supported by different comprehensive doctrines (Rawls 1971: 302). According to Rawls, Kantian support for the difference principle could refer to Kant's example of the duty of beneficence, Christian support could refer to the parable of the Good Samaritan in Luke 10, and – one may add – Muslim support could refer to the duty of *zakat*, alms (Rawls 1999: 155). So, Rawls's point is that there are ways to bridge diverse comprehensive doctrines in order to achieve support for principles of justice. In a similar way, 'overlapping consensus' could be used as a bridging notion with respect to other value differences between moral traditions.

THE POSSIBILITY OF COMMUNICATION

We have so far encountered three theories of how to understand differences between traditions and communication of ethics. Traditions (or for that sake ideologies, religions, 'comprehensive doctrines', world views etc.) are typically not all-embracing, delimited and mutually exclusive. Normally, a tradition has developed from, and in dialogue with, other traditions. For example, Christianity was influenced by Hellenism and Judaism, Islam by Judaism, Christianity and Hellenism, Buddhism by Hinduism and Confucianism etc. Thus a tradition entails views from previous traditions and as a consequence, within each tradition there is room for different and conflicting moral views and values.

Seeing traditions as comprehensive and delimited entities invites to use stereotypes like 'Eastern values', 'Western values' etc. But, obviously, both the West and the East are homes for diverse ideologies and world views. Catholicism, Protestantism, the humanism of the Enlightenment, Liberalism, Marxism and Fascism originate from the West, and Confucianism, Taoism and Buddhism from the East. But within these ideologies, religions and world views there are a variety of moral views. In line with this, cultures should be seen as open, changing and porous, in contrast to bound and systematically structured (Li 2006). So, there are conflicting views on moral issues, like for example justice and gender equality, within cultures, and there are similar views on these issues between adherents of different traditions. The inner diversity of cultures and traditions opens up for the possibility of communication and shared understandings across borders.

Is freedom, for example, a typical Western value without relevance and foundation in other cultures, such as China and Japan? In his book *Development as Freedom* (1999), Indian philosopher and economist Amartya Sen examines the relation between development and freedom. He argues that 'substantive individual freedom' is the corner stone of social and economic development, and further that freedom is a universal value relevant in all parts of the world and internal to all major moral and cultural traditions. But, one may ask, is not individual freedom a Western, liberal concept? Does it really have any relevance in Asia?

Sen argues against a characterization of values based on culture, exemplified in the distinction between 'Asian values' and 'Western values'. He emphasizes instead the inner diversity of cultures and traditions. One can, for example, find authoritarian as well as liberal ideas in both the Eastern and the Western traditions. The respective founding fathers Confucius and Plato are examples of authoritarian heritages. But one also finds 'components' of the comprehensive notion of political liberty in the different traditions. Individual freedom is indeed a value that is important in present-day Western political and philosophical discourse. But it is not therefore a *unique* Western value. To show that it is not, Sen points at empirical examples from the history of Asian traditions (Sen 1999: 231–248).

Buddhism is a highly influential tradition in Asia that, according to Sen, pays great attention to freedom and human choice. Islam is often seen as an anti-liberal and authoritarian religion, but Sen points at important historical examples of when Islamic rulers were guardians of freedom and tolerance. He concludes,

> The point to be seized is that the modern advocates of the authoritarian views of 'Asian values' base their reading on very arbitrary interpretations and extremely narrow selections of authors and traditions. The valuing of freedom is not confined to one culture only, and the Western traditions are not the only ones that prepare us for a freedom-based approach to social understanding. (1999: 241)

Hence, during certain historical periods, totalitarian values will be dominant, while during others freedom will prevail in both East and West.

Categorizations of values according to geographical, cultural or religious boundaries are based on the view that values are contextual. But what does it mean that a value in this sense is contextual? There are numerous possible interpretations. First, it can mean that a value has its *origin* in a specific culture. Then the focus is on history. A value is seen as contextual in the sense that its origin can be traced to a specific cultural, religious or philosophical tradition. Second, it can mean that different societies provide more or less *favourable cultural or political conditions* for the implementation of a value. For example, a value like freedom may be easier to implement in a democratic society than in a totalitarian (Li 1996). Third, it can mean that a value is *accepted* by a greater part of the population in one society than in another. Due to such factors as illiteracy and ignorance, a value that is widely supported in one society may not even be known by people in another society.

According to the first interpretation above, some values originate from a certain culture. For example, one could claim that human rights originates from the Enlightenment with a background in a Hebrew-Christian view of man as the 'image of God,' but nonetheless hold that due to globalization this is a historical fact with little relevance for characterization of cultural value differences today. According to the second interpretation, a value like freedom is not less important in a totalitarian society than in a democratic, but is just more difficult to realize, and according to the third interpretation, a value like informed consent, important as it is in research ethics, is more difficult to realize in certain countries due to such factors as illiteracy and ignorance. None of these interpretations exclude the possibility of cross-cultural understanding of, and support for, similar values.

What, then, are the differences between, for example, the East and the West when it comes to values and morality? This question invites generalizations and clichés. A common answer is that the West puts an emphasis on individuality and autonomy; the individual is taken as a point of departure for moral reasoning, as a basic object of concern and – normatively – individual autonomy is highly esteemed. In contrast, the East emphasizes community and social values. A second common answer is that the moral discourse in the West focuses on *criteria for a right action*; while in the East, on the question of how to be a *good person*, that is, virtue ethics. Ethics is in the West action oriented and in the East virtue oriented.

There might be some empirical backing for these dichotomies. In a recent value survey, Chinese respondents to a larger extent adhered to community values more than did the respondents in the West (Matthews 2000). However, the simplistic dichotomies must be modified. There is in the West a long tradition of communal thinking, for example in Marxism and social democracy, and there are in the East many activists struggling for human rights, which by nature are individual.

From a normative point of view, the contrast between autonomy and community seems to be artificial. Why should the value of autonomy conflict with the value of community? Don't we value both – in the West as well as in the East? Autonomy is valuable because it gives the individual possibilities to realize her wishes, and community is valuable because it gives the individual security and social relations (Griffin 2008).

Second, regarding the focus on the moral discourse, virtue ethics is not restricted to the East, but it is one of the main ethical positions in the West, today represented by influential scholars like Alasdair MacIntyre (MacIntyre 1981) and theologian Stanley Hauerwas (Hauerwas 1974). And, on the other hand, individual actions play an important role also in Eastern ethics. For example, in Buddhism, there is an emphasis on *both* individual acts – 'individuals create themselves with their moral choices' (Keown 2005), which leads, more or less, to *karma* and virtues.

So, there seem to be strong reasons to assume that shared understandings of values and norms across traditions are feasible. As philosopher Chandran Kukathas argues, globalization may even further facilitate this. In an attempt to explain moral variety and cultural differences, he refers to Adam Smith's theory of how sympathy is a basis of the development of moral standards. Smith argued in line with David Hume that morality begins with the human capacity for sympathy. As social creatures, we have a desire to be in accord with our fellow human beings. Thus, common moral standards develop in an urge for mutual understanding and commonality. Kukathas writes: 'Others, then, are crucial for the development of standards of moral self-evaluation … it is the process of self-evaluation by reflecting on the likely judgements of others that leads to the development of common moral standards' (Kukathas 1994: 13). When societies exist in isolation, they will develop their own moral standards. However, when there is interaction between individuals belonging to different societies and cultures, one can expect an interchange of moral norms and values. According to Kukathas, this will also lead to moral development while the norms and values in one society will be put on trial in the light of the standards of another. With globalization leading to increasing interactions across different societies and moral traditions, one could thus expect a convergence of moral standards towards universal values (Ibid: 20).

Kukathas' view is empirically validated by the global reach of human rights. As Xiarong Li argues: 'The globalization of the ideal of human rights remains an unpleasant fact for cultural relativists and moral sceptics who doubt the possibility of establishing the universal (cross-cultural) validity of human rights' (Li 2006: 124).

The incommensurability thesis is also challenged by the possibility of cross-cultural ethics teaching. Those of us who have taught ethics in countries far away or at international ethics programmes at home have experienced that it is, in fact, possible to overcome cultural gaps and discuss moral dilemmas with students with various cultural backgrounds.

However, there is also reason for caution when referring to globalization as a force behind universalization of values and norms. In the present time, globalization is not characterized by equality and reciprocity. Quite the opposite. Many facets of globalization mean the dominance of powerful economic organizations and multinational companies and a westernization of cultures and values. From this perspective, globalization could be seen as a continuation of colonialism. As its worst, globalization also implies colonization of cultures and minds.

COMMUNICATION, RECOGNITION AND THE ETHICS OF LISTENING

The discourse on ethics and communication should also be analysed from a power perspective; who has the power to speak and whose voices are not heard in the age of globalization? Global inequalities with relevance to questions of ethics and communication have different features.

The global implementation of intellectual property rights is an illustrative example of the globalization of parochial Western values. One aspect of the last decades' globalization is the global commercialization of all sorts of products, including pharmaceuticals, herbs and seeds. This was manifested by the TRIPS agreement (Agreement on Trade-Related Aspects of Intellectual Property Rights) in 1994. According to the TRIPS agreement, intellectual property (like pharmaceuticals and genetic material) should be globally protected and the TRIPS agreement was institutionalized when ratification of TRIPS became a condition for membership of the World Trade Organization (WTO).

TRIPS has been criticised for limiting access to life-saving medicines for poor people in developing countries due to the huge increase of prices following patenting and cheap generic medicines disappearing from the market (Collste 2011). Another controversial aspect of the global intellectual property regime (IPR) is the extension of property rights to cover traditional knowledge. In a number of cases, plants, herbs and other products used for ages by traditional communities and indigenous peoples have been patented by Western firms. Here, traditional knowledge and communal ownership come into conflict with privatization and property rights. This conflict is an example of when globalization means the dominance of Western interests at the expense of the interests and values of weaker communities and peoples. As a way of balancing the interests in favour of traditional communities and to achieve a less unfair sharing of benefits from the use of traditional knowledge, the United Nations agreed in 1992 on the Convention of Biological Diversity (Komparic 2015; Shiva 2001; Commission 2002).

From an Indian perspective, political theorist Rajeev Bhargava reflects on the process of colonization of culture, and he introduces the concept 'epistemic injustice'. He explains: 'Epistemic injustice is a form of cultural injustice. It occurs when the concepts and categories by which a people understand themselves and their world are replaced or adversely affected by the concepts and categories of the colonizers' (Bhargava 2013). Bhargava's analysis refers to Indian experiences of British colonization and postcolonialism. In a similar way, globalization implies epistemic injustice when the symbols, images and values of a dominating culture take over local cultures, which then become diffused and marginalized.

A Pakistani master's student gave a vivid example of epistemic injustice when responding in class to the question whether colonialism had left 'morally relevant traces' in the present. She said,

Yes, certainly! Everything Pakistani is today considered of less worth compared to the West: we consider our own history as shameful and we feel that we are still slaves under the British rulers. These feelings have also a cultural impact today; to be beautiful is to have blond hair, not black, to be civilized is to eat with knife and fork, not to eat in our traditional way and our traditional languages are superseded by English.

How then can we avoid 'one-directional' communication and cultural domination? How can we avoid stereotypes of the Other? How can we avoid 'epistemic injustice' in the wake of globalization? As Nancy Fraser and others have emphasized, 'recognition' is a central concept here. She writes: 'Misrecognition ... means *social subordination* in the sense of being prevented from *participating as a peer* in social life' (Fraser 2001: 24). As we noted above, many sides of 'social life' are globalized and, as a consequence, communication of ethics requires recognition of the distant other partner, an equal say in conversations and dialogues.

Listening to the Other follows from recognition. To listen is more than just to hear. Michael Purdy defines listening as 'the active and dynamic process of attending, perceiving, interpreting, remembering, and responding to the expressed (verbal and nonverbal) needs, concerns, and information offered by other human beings' (Purdy 1991). Listening is a crucial condition for communication and a requirement for reciprocity, that is, for 'fair terms of cooperation' in the age of globalization (Rawls 1993: 16).

By listening to the other, we will get lots of fruitful insights and perspectives. Think, for example, of the influence of Mahatma Gandhi on the global discussion of peace and war, the South African contributions through Desmond Tutu and others to the insights of reconciliation and conflict resolutions, the African idea of Ubuntu, that is, the insights of community and interdependence developed within African moral traditions. Consider also the Japanese Mottainai principles emphasizing respect for resources, no waste and reuse and the Peace Nobel laureate Wangari Maathai's contributions to the discussion of sustainable development, democracy and peace.

This takes us finally to the theory of Jürgen Habermas, the modern philosopher who more than anyone else has contributed to the modern discussion on ethics and communication. According to Habermas, communication, or 'communicative action' as is the term he uses, presupposes in contrast to 'strategic action', equality, mutual respect and sincerity. The aim of communicative action is shared understanding (Habermas 1990).

For Habermas, human communication and the justification of claims about what is right or wrong presupposes the possibility to understand others' moral views. He proposes the following criteria of justification: 'Only those norms can claim to be valid that meet ... with the approval of all affected in their capacity *as participants in a practical discourse*' (Ibid: 66). The *autonomy* and the *equality* of all affected in the discourse are two conditions for validity of norms and to achieve a *herrschaftsfrei* communication (Ibid: 71). The practical discourse in focus for this book on ethics and communication is global in scope, and the two conditions, autonomy and equality, do effectively rule out any kind of domination for the validation of norms.

THE CONTENT OF THIS BOOK

How can ethics be communicated in an age of globalization? Is it possible to overcome cultural differences and agree on common values and principles that cross cultural borders? The aim of this book is to contribute to the discussion on these questions. There is a need for pursuing questions of ethics and communication which entails both the classical question of the universality/ contextuality of ethics and values, but also new challenges for communication; how are values and norms communicated and shared over cultural and national borders? The book contains chapters dealing with theoretical questions of global ethics, ethical universalism and communication, chapters discussing ethics and communication with reference to world views and religions and chapters focusing on the challenges of globalization for ethical communication in particular social practices.

From the outset, there is a need for conceptual clarifications. In the second chapter, Nigel Dower presents various approaches to global ethics and their relevance for the theme of communication is discussed. Dower provides the reader with an overview and taxonomy of different positions in the modern discussion. For example, he distinguishes between the descriptive and normative meanings of communication of ethics; the first referring to the processes by which global values and norms are communicated across the world as a by-product of the globalization of ideas, and the latter by posing the question of whether global values should be more communicated or not, illustrated by the Parliament of World Religions report *A Declaration toward a Global Ethic* in 1993 which argued for some global core values. Dower also distinguishes between global processes of communicative dialogues, for example initiatives of communication between world religions, global ethics inquiring the nature, content and justification of theories of global ethics, how a universal ethics is related to global ethics and how internationalization is related to globalization.

Further, Dower makes an overview of various ethical theories which are universal in scope in contrast to theories emphasizing context and community, and different approaches to global justice by referring to, for example, human rights and capabilities and its opponents; relativism and communitarianism. He defends himself a 'solidarist pluralism', that is, a culturally sensitive internationalism.

Maren Behrensen focuses in the third chapter on academic ethics teaching, indeed an important form of communication of ethics! Ethics has lately become a popular academic discipline. Doctors, business people, engineers, politicians and others turn to professional ethicists for advice and ethics courses to get answers to complicated moral questions in the modern society. However, ethics as an academic discipline is in its present shape not really helpful according to Behrensen. She points at different related explanations for this. First, Behrensen argues that there is a cultural and social homogeneity among ethics teachers. They have a similar social, gender and ethnic background which tends to narrow their views on ethics. There are few female ethics professors and even fewer come from minority groups. The effect is that pedagogical examples and cases are distant from real life and today's moral challenges. A second reason is the established philosophical mode of teaching. Behrensen mentions three common pedagogical tricks; she calls them 'treacherous tropes' that tend to distance ethics teaching from reality. Hypothetical cases about 'baby lottery', torture and 'ticking bombs' – which have their horrifying equivalence in real life – are dangerous, Behrensen argues, 'in that they encourage a disregard for reality and in that they make things seem simple that are patently not so'. This way of teaching, transforming complex and tragic ethical challenges into quiz, distances the students from empathy and responsibility. Also the 'listicle ethics', reducing ethical analysis to the application of a set of principles, and 'empty dichotomies', simplifying real dilemmas, have similar consequences, Behrensen argues.

The Universal Declaration of Human Rights is the most important single document portraying a universal ethics, and it plays a crucial role in today's international politics. The Declaration has also become the *lingua franca* for communicating ethics across borders. It is often claimed that human rights originates from the Western Christian tradition. In contrast, some Muslim authors have developed an Islamic conception of human rights which they base on the Qur'an. Heiner Bielefeldt argues against both these 'encapsulations' of human rights, which according to Bielefeldt represents a flawed cultural essentialism. He shows with historical examples that there are as many Western religious and philosophical historical motifs in support of human rights as there are against. From a hermeneutic retrospective perspective one can perhaps find *analogies* between, for example, the Hebrew-Christian view of man as 'being an image of God' and human rights, but never the 'roots' or 'causes' of human rights.

There is an obvious tension between Islam and human rights, especially the equal human rights for women and the right to religious liberty. How then can Islam and human rights be reconciled? Bielefeldt refers to various Muslim scholars who criticize a legalistic view of *sharia* and instead want to liberalize and modernize Islam. This revision of Islam is based on a critical hermeneutics that sees *sharia* as an ethical rather than a legal concept, and instead of trying to apply legal principles from the seventh and eighth century, search for the intentions and motives behind. From this perspective and in relation to Rawls's idea of an overlapping consensus, Bielefeldt argues that both Christian and Muslim traditions entail ideas that cohere with human rights. This fact could serve as a basis for a constructive dialogue and agreement.

Against those who criticize human rights for Westernization in disguise, Bielefeldt argues that the basic tenet of human rights is the defence of diversity and pluralism. Rights to free speech, freedom of thought, conscience, religion or belief etc. can rather be seen as impediments to the imposition of, for example, Western ideas.

How was the construction of the Universal Declaration of Human Rights possible? What are the reasons for its success story? One factor is probably its transcultural and inclusive character. The Declaration does not presuppose any doctrinal beliefs in God or Nature. The Chinese scholar Peng Chun Chang was one of the key members of the committee who wrote the Declaration and Chang's prime mover was the aim to make the Declaration truly universal. The motives behind Chang's integration of Chinese and Western ideas are presented and discussed in Hans Ingvar Roth's chapter. The chapter also entails new information about the discussions between the authors of the Declaration that has never been published before.

Chang represents some important ideas which were crucial for the Declaration and probably also for any efforts of communicating ethics across borders. One he calls 'liberated inventiveness', implying liberation from formulated inertia and cultural dogma, and another as traditional Chinese philosophical insights of pluralistic tolerance.

Soraj Hongladarom takes critical thinking as his point of departure for the discussion on ethics and communication. Critical thinking is a basis for rational argumentation. According to a prevalent belief, ethical reasoning and critical thinking is lacking in Asian philosophy. This would then be an obstacle to a cross-cultural ethical discussion and argumentation. However, as Hongladarom shows, there are Asian traditions of logic and critical thinking that go back in history as long as the European philosophical tradition, and Hongladarom illustrates his argument with ideas from Mohism and Buddhism.

In spite of this common background, how come that the Thai cultural and educational standards are today far behind the Western, Hongladarom, who himself is a Thai, asks. The reasons are, Hongladarom argues, first that Thailand imported technical skills but not the values of freedom and creativity from the West, and, second, that the Asian tradition of critical thinking fell in the background.

The title of Hongladarom's contribution is 'Shared values, different guises', and he argues that universalism is untenable in the sense that there is one particular set of values that is the only true one, but instead in the sense that there are some shared values between the East and the West, but that they are expressed in different ways. The possibilities of communicating ethics across cultures lie precisely in finding the common core behind the different representations.

What role does religion play in ethics and communication? Can religions facilitate communication or do religions rather contribute to conflicts, mutual disrespect and misunderstandings? These questions are not least important for the reflections on global perspectives on ethics and communication in an era characterized by the revival of religions. Peter Gan starts from the common religious notions of transcendence, infinity and hope in his reflections on the relations between religions and the communication of ethics. According to Gan, transcendence is a shared denominator for religions, and the phenomenon of hope is a vital expression of this transcendence. The notion of 'absolute hope', implying the conviction that change is possible and an openness to whatever the future offers, is found in most religions and this conviction can be a source of inspiration for moral responsibility. However, as Gan notices, religions take many forms in today's world; there are religious fundamentalists, universalists, liberals etc. and the possibilities of communication varies accordingly. And as multiple examples from history and the present show us, adherents of fundamentalist religions, assuming as they do that they represent the one and only truth, are impediments to mutual understanding and communication. On the other hand, religions have a great potential of promoting the communication of ethics, Gan argues. The intrinsic value of human beings and other living creatures, universal love, empathy as a moral resource and the notion of a universal community are some religious sources for the communication of ethics.

In their chapter, Japanese ethicists Kiyoshi Murata and Yohko Orito discuss the case when traditional Japanese sociolinguistic tradition is confronted with globalized information- and communication media, and in particular Facebook. The traditional Japanese culture has cautious rules when it comes to communicating matters of privacy. The apparent openness to others in sharing space and private information is balanced by social norms and informal regulations. The traditional Japanese social norms also regulate what kind of personal information is shared with closely affiliated persons (*uchi*) and which is shared with anyone (*tanin*). These social norms presuppose that Japanese can identify vertical relationships in a social context, but when they use Facebook and other social media, the old norms do not fit. As a consequence, many Japanese put private information traditionally limited to *uchi*, on Facebook. The new Act on the Protection of Personal Information, with the aim of protecting privacy in Japan is according to Murata and Orito neither applied nor understood by most Japanese. The challenge remains: globalization makes it necessary to communicate ethical norms like privacy globally. But how can this be done in Japan – and in other societies – where social norms of communication are traditionally regulated? Murata's and Orito's chapter illustrates the potential conflicts between global and traditional norms and rules for behaviour. It also emphasizes that ethical guidance of global practices like social media must be culturally sensitive.

Murata's and Orito's chapter on the conflict between the new global social media and traditional Japanese understanding of privacy leads nicely over to Elin Palm's critique of the new research area Intercultural Information Ethics (IIE). Information- and Communication Technologies (ICT) originates in the West but are spread all over the world. ICT are both technological and social systems, leading to new forms of social media, chat rooms and advisory channels. A classical question in IIE is whether values embedded in the usage of ICT are culture specific or universal and the aim of IIE is to critically assess the cultural parochialism of this development. However, as Palm points out, the IIE has so far used a simplistic and naïve notion of culture and has identified culture with a nation or a geographical area; West versus East. She shows that both the West and the East contain a multitude of different cultural views and it is a mistake to talk of a 'Western' view of privacy or autonomy.

As an alternative path, Palm suggests that, IIE needs a more nuanced view of culture and of differences within cultures. Both domination and stereotyping must be avoided. Further, it is necessary that IIE scholars listen to the views of marginalized people to develop more inclusive ICT systems.

NOTES

1. A thanks to the participants of the advanced seminar in applied ethics at Linköping University for valuable comments.

2. A problematic aspect of Huntington's argument is that he does not distinguish between civilizations and the politics of states. This is obvious in his discussion on human rights. 'The West' are according to Huntington united behind respect for human rights but Confucian and Muslim civilizations are against. The pieces of evidence are discussions at the World Conference on Human Rights in Vienna 1994 over the priority of political or economic rights, interventions, economic assistance to states etc. (Ibid: 195–196). However, these controversies are better explained by the conflicting interests between states than by opposing values and world views.

3. Rawls's concept 'comprehensive doctrine' may misleadingly suggest that religions and other world views appear articulate and concise in the real world.

Part I

THEORY

Chapter 2

Global Ethics

A Framework for Thinking about Communication

Nigel Dower

GLOBAL ETHICS AND COMMUNICATION

This chapter explores the nature of global ethics, and examines how the different approaches to global ethics inform how one sees the ethical issues in relation to communication in a modern globalized world.

The account of global ethics I shall give is as follows: global ethics is thinking ethically about global issues, and central to this is enquiry – usually critical and sustained – into the nature, justification and application of a global ethic. A global ethic is a set of norms and values held by an individual or a group which are thought to be in some sense universal or universally applicable. Although 'values' could include the whole field of ethics, here I am referring to conceptions of 'good' and of virtue in contrast to norms which cover duties/obligations and rights. And usually included are norms about global, that is, transboundary responsibilities.

That said, there are two distinct ways in which such an ethic may be said to be 'global': the norms and values are global in content: that is, what that person or group thinks, whatever others may think, has a certain content; it is *about* what that person or group thinks; for instance she may think that everyone has a right to food or that capital punishment is always everywhere wrong (the latter claim being one that clearly many do not endorse). Or they may be said to be global because they are shared across the globe; they are global in the scope of acceptance. There may be in this sense competing global ethics (plural of global ethic). Whether there is (or will be or should be) *a* global ethic that is universally (or near-universally) shared is another more controversial question.

As this last remark brings out, someone doing global ethics could actually adopt a critical approach towards the possibility of a global ethic: this

scepticism might derive from questioning whether a global ethic, as something shared by all, though a conceptually coherent idea, either exists or is
likely to exist; but it could also derive from a deeper questioning of whether
the idea of universal norms and values applicable to all is even coherent,
whatever some people might believe.

Before expanding this account, I want to relate this to the question that is
central to this book, namely communication in a global era. If one takes the
three terms that are central – global, ethics and communication – one realizes
that there are at least three significant ways of combining them. First there is
the global communication of ethics, then the communication of global ethics
and finally the ethics of global communication.

The first two should be treated as a pair in contrast to the third. But they
are not the same. The first refers to the phenomenon, whereby ethical norms
and values are communicated across the world. These norms and values vary
considerably in content, but more to the point they may not be a global ethic
in the sense of being global in content. The person communicating them may
or may not think of them as universal or to be adopted universally; if the latter, he might be a relativist, but he still wants to communicate them either
because the recipient is already sympathetic to them or he wants the recipient
to accept his values. There is little doubt that these processes occur, but the
more interesting question concerns the communication of global ethics.

The communication of global ethics is more explicitly about the processes
by which certain values and norms that are global in content are communicated across the world – an aspect of the globalization of communities of
shared values. Whether there is or indeed there ought to be one set of norms
and values that are generally or widely accepted across the world is, as I said,
a further question (to be explored later). In the case of people being sceptical
of there being a global ethic, it is often this idea of a widely or universally
shared set of norms and values that is being questioned, rather than the existence of different global ethics (in plural) as sets of beliefs held by various
groups of people – in different kinds of emerging global communities – that
are global in content.

Another way of considering this, beyond asking whether the communication of global ethics is a process that is happening, is to ask the practical or
normative question whether and in what ways communicating global ethical
thinking can or should be made more widespread.

Implicit in the idea of the communication of global ethics is the point that
the communication itself is global. So perhaps we should see what we are
looking at as the global communication of global ethics.

This (global) communication of global ethics takes several forms: first,
the increase in global communications may mean that there is an increase in
globally shared content in ethical norms and values, and these may be caused

by many processes – Internet, broadcasting, social media, capitalism, advertising and so on. In this sense such increases are a by-product of the globalization of ideas. As a distinct part of this there may be more of a sense of global responsibility across borders, as people are exposed, for instance, through the media to what is happening in other parts of the world.

But there are also, alongside these broad processes, more self-conscious developments in the process of communicative dialogue, which are valuable in themselves, but at the same time promote globally shared values and norms. Consider such examples as the Parliament of World Religions which, while claiming to describe a pre-existing but less self-consciously articulated coincidence of core values amongst all the major religions, was, by promulgating *A Declaration toward a Global Ethic* in 1993, deliberately attempting to spread its acceptance (Küng and Kuschel 1993). The authors of *Our Global Neighbourhood* attempted a similar thing in articulating its 'global civic ethic' (CGG 1995), as were the authors of the *Earth Charter* in 2000. As noted earlier, the norms include those of global responsibility, and often self-conscious dialogue and discussion occur to try to hammer out what our global responsibilities are (such as how to respond to the refugee crisis in 2015).

The third significant combination of terms, namely the ethics of global communication, is more about an ethical critique of how global communication occurs, involving issues in media ethics, the ethics of the Internet, privacy issues and so on. Where do such critiques come from?

If it is concerned with the character of communication anywhere in the world, it comes from some form of global ethic/ethical thinking. That is, it comes from an ethic which is global in content and is the ethic of some individual thinker or group.

The contrast between this and the earlier two ideas can be illustrated by looking at a very similar and indeed linked contrast: the globalization of ethics versus the ethics of globalization. The globalization of ethics is about the many different ways in which ethical thinking has become more global, and there being more acceptance of global norms and global responsibilities amongst more people. Ethics is itself one aspect of what is changing under globalization. By contrast the ethics of globalization is the critical assessment by thinkers, given their own normative positions, of the various processes that are going on in the world called globalization. Globalization is itself the subject matter for ethics. Such ethical critique could come from perspectives that are not global ethics; a communitarian might critique globalization because of its tendency to undermine or weaken local cultural values. But more commonly, and relevantly for the purposes of this chapter, critiques come from global ethics perspectives, such as Kantian, utilitarian or human rights critiques (these approaches, will be discussed more fully later). Consider for instance Singer's consequentialist criticism of globalization in his book *One World – The Ethics of Globalisation* (Singer 2002). Similarly and indeed as an aspect of globalization, one can do a global ethical critique of global communication. So we have, putting it more fully, the global ethics of global communication.

In order to frame our understanding of the two ways of looking at the relationships between global ethics and communication, we now need to step back and look at global ethics itself.

GLOBAL ETHICS

Global ethics is a field of enquiry into the character of ethical relations between people across the world. It covers the relations between people as individuals as well as relations between corporate bodies such as nation states or business companies. Global ethics as an enquiry is commonly focused on the nature, content, justification and application of ethical values and norms that make up what may be called a global ethic, generally understood as a set of universal values and norms including some norms to do with transboundary responsibilities. Someone doing global ethics (or world ethics as it used to be called sometimes) (Dower 1998, 2007) is usually comparing different normative theories such as human rights theory and utilitarianism in relation to global relations generally or some particular global issues such as climate change, war and peace, development issues or communication issues, and defending one of them. (In what follows, if the reader is more familiar with the language of world ethics/ethic, then she should substitute mentally this terminology for the terminology of global ethics/ethic in the text.)

There are however at least two other approaches possible under the general label of global ethics. First, someone interested in global ethics may be interested in more abstract theoretical or 'meta-ethical' issues about the nature of a global ethic, for instance, about what makes such an ethic possible in the face of diverse ethical approaches amongst individuals and between cultures. So it may be that an account has to be given of 'universality' that accommodates diversity. He might even take a sceptical view about the possibility of a global ethic, by questioning in general the universality of values or questioning the idea of significant obligations between different societies and states.

Second, a more descriptive or social science approach is possible. The global ethicist may attempt to map out different ethical approaches across the world (much as someone studying world religions is interested in the diversity of religions across the world). Or he may document the extent to which human relations are now informed by various, multiple globally shared ethics and/or are converging on *one* such shared ethic or fewer than before. That is, his interest is in what may be called the globalization of ethics (as distinct from the ethics of globalization, which is, as I remarked earlier, the ethical critique of aspects of what goes on in the world under the label globalization).

Although the main focus of the chapter is on global ethics in the first sense – the delineation of different theories of global ethics and how they are applied to global issues including some issues coming under communication – the concerns raised under the other ideas of global ethics will from time to time feature in the discussion, not least because they are all interrelated to one another.

There are at least three main sources of interest in global ethics in the modern world. First, there is the long trajectory of interest in the idea of a 'universal ethic' which is found in at least some of the ethical thought of all the major religious traditions. One source of this in the Western world was the thinking of the Stoics in the Graeco-Roman world. Their vision of cosmopolitanism (i.e. being a citizen of the world/universe) was of all humanity living in one large moral community in which a common moral law was acknowledged. This kind of thinking was reflected in the Catholic idea of the natural law applicable to all human beings and of the *ius gentium* – the moral law accessible to all peoples because it is based on rationality rather than faith. In the eighteenth century the idea of cosmopolitanism again came to the fore, particularly in the writing of Kant. This traditional dimension was part theological and part philosophical.

Second, it has become increasingly apparent, especially since the Second World War, how many of the problems that we have are global problems, where problems are caused in one country by the actions of other countries or corporate bodies such as transnational companies, and where solutions to common problems require cooperation and coordination between countries. Here a global ethic of collective self-interest comes to the fore.

Third, with increasing information and communications across the world – the globalization of knowledge and community – people are more aware of their global interconnectedness, their identities being more formed by relations across the world not merely local relations, and there is more recognition of common values, but equally of how much values differ. These all become important aspects of how the world is experienced. This increased awareness covers not only the development of new kinds of identity but also the development of a sense of global responsibility, for example, in responding to the challenges of world poverty or playing one's part in combatting climate change.

WHAT THEN IS A GLOBAL ETHIC?

There are two ways of approaching this question. First, one can think of it as an ethic accepted by an individual or a group which has a certain global *content*. It is that individual's or group's ethical view of the world. This view is likely to have two main elements: first, some set of values and norms that are believed to be universally valid that is applicable to human beings anywhere though they may not be accepted by everyone; second, some view about our obligations or responsibilities, again seen as universally valid, towards people anywhere in the world, for instance that the wealthy of one country have some obligations to help alleviate extreme poverty in other countries. Various ethical theories, some of which will be discussed more fully shortly, drawn from philosophy and theology, present and defend a global ethic in this sense.

Second, we can think of an ethic as global in the sense of being *globally accepted*, is, that there is a set of values and norms that are accepted by people all over the world – perhaps by people, for instance, who share a particular religious faith, or by the community of international diplomats (or people in business companies) worldwide. In this sense there could be a number of different 'global ethics'. What is of interest to some thinkers is whether there is a core set of values that can be said to be actually universally shared (or at least nearly universally shared since although these may be shared in all societies, there will always be a few people, especially in liberal societies, who may have unusual, not to say, strange values). This could then be seen as *the* global ethic that is almost universally shared.

An example of this last idea is the *Declaration towards a Global Ethic* of the World Parliament of Religions in 1993, which seeks to articulate the common moral core to all the major religions – reflecting the approach of one of its key advocates, namely Hans Küng (Küng and Kuschel 1993). Bhikhu Parekh presents the idea of a global ethic as one which is both consented to and assented to – consented to through the process of intercultural dialogue, but at the same time assented to because each person or group of people have their own reasons for assenting to it (Parekh 2005: 27). The relevance of these ideas will become apparent later on when we look at critiques of global ethics. But it is worth dwelling on the meta-ethical point Parekh and indeed others make.

I have called a global ethic so far a set of values and norms, but this account does not bring out a distinction between a set of values and norms that does not include the background account of why a person or group accepts it and a set of values and norms together with, that is, presented as embedded in, the background account. This background account may be a philosophical theory, a theology, a cultural narrative or other 'source story'. A Kantian and a utilitarian might agree on certain key ethical ideas concerning global issues (though they may disagree in other areas); an enlightened anthropocentrist and a biocentrist might agree on a lot of environmental values; a Christian and a Muslim may, as Küng argues, agree on the 'golden rule'. A global ethic does not have to be expressed in a formally articulated way let alone in public declarations; it may for instance be part of the mores of a social group with its rationale deriving from its embeddedness in social traditions.

The possibility (and indeed desirability) of a global ethic as something widely shared across the world turns on which way we interpret 'global ethic'. If someone promoting a global ethic insists on her source story as part of the package that she is trying to get others to accept, then the likelihood of agreement is much less than if she is trying to find agreement for the values and norms themselves. Indeed if various groups all see their global ethics as the 'values, norms PLUS source stories', then this is a prescription for conflict (as has been evidenced in religious conflicts).

Acknowledgement that a global ethic involves convergence for people with different source stories does not of course mean that their understanding of these norms and values is completely the same – they may be slightly differently coloured by the different source stories – and may not cover all ethical areas. Furthermore the idea of shared norms and values deriving from different sources is precisely that: it accepts that each person or group will have their own source stories; these are not given up if a shared ethic is accepted. A corollary of this is that each person or group respects in some way – or even welcomes – the different reasons for beliefs that the people accepting the shared ethic have. One of the rationales for interfaith dialogue – an important dimension of global communication – is linked to this point.

I now turn back to the idea of a global ethic as an ethic with a global content. Examples of global ethics as ethical theories – that is, theories that are examples of sources stories – are now given, which all illustrate both the idea of universality and the idea of transboundary responsibility.

Kantianism

This ethical approach – often associated with cosmopolitanism, although it is only one of a number of cosmopolitan approaches – stems from the thinking of the eighteenth-century Enlightenment German philosopher Immanuel Kant. Kant's central idea is that what makes us human is our capacity for rational agency. This is manifested in our capacity to choose means appropriate to pursuing our 'ends' or goals. It is also shown in our moral agency whereby we acknowledge that other human beings are also rational agents and thus their agency needs to be respected (Kant 1785).

This core idea is both the key to what human well-being involves – the person's exercise of rational agency – and the key to ethical obligation which he called the categorical imperative. This was expressed in a number of ways including the principle 'act on that maxim that you can will to be universal law' and 'so act that you treat humanity whether in yourself or in others

always as an end not merely as a means'. Our ethical decisions should con-
form to these principles. These ideas of the core of human well-being and of
duty are seen as applicable to all human beings anywhere.

But Kant's ethical position is not merely a universalist one; he is clear
that our duties are owed to any human being across borders. If it is wrong to
deceive (because deceiving deliberately undermines the rational agency of
others), it is wrong to deceive someone anywhere. The same norms underlying communication apply everywhere, and apply wherever the communicator
is and wherever the communicatee is located. To use a modern example: it is
as wrong to sell a medicine to someone in China or Kenya as to someone in
one's own country, knowing that it is misprescribed or defective.

A modern example of a Kantian approach is given by Onora O'Neill who
seeks to show that extreme poverty undermines human well-being. This is
primarily because it undermines or restricts the exercise of rational agency
in the form of control over one's life (O'Neill 1989). So to the extent that
international companies pursue policies that undermine that, then 'material
injustice' is being done, and individuals in other parts of the world who are
involved in the modern global economy have a duty to counteract these tendencies. The ways, for instance, mining, agribusiness or modern medical and
pharmaceutical practices are conducted will have a bearing on the life conditions of very poor people.

Utilitarianism

Another major ethical approach with significant implications for global ethics is utilitarianism. Developed in the late eighteenth century and nineteenth
century by philosophers like Bentham and Mill, its central tenet is that what
makes the actions of humans right is their tendency to promote human well-
being and wrong their tendency to reduce it. More precisely it is a maximiz-
ing principle: what we ought to do is maximize good outcomes by promoting
the best balance of good over bad outcomes. In its classical formulation the
good was seen as pleasure or happiness and the bad as pain/suffering and
unhappiness (and Bentham recognized that higher animals' pleasures and
pains were relevant too) – hence the label 'the greatest happiness principle'.
Later utilitarians have tended to broaden the conception of what the good is
in terms of, for instance, preference satisfaction (since it is not obvious that
pleasure is the only thing which is good in itself).

So what is central to utilitarianism are two key ideas – that human well-
being is understood in terms of pleasure, happiness or preference satisfaction,
and that one's duty at bottom is to promote it in any way as much as possible.
As Bentham said: 'Everyone is to count for one and no one more than one.'
This is a universal principle applying to everyone. Thus the theory is global

in the sense that our duty is to promote the best balance of good over bad for *all* people affected by one's action, near and far.

A good example of this 'consequentialist' way of thinking was Peter Singer's approach. He argued in response to famine and extreme poverty, that 'if it is in our power to prevent something very bad from happening without thereby sacrificing anything of comparable moral importance we ought to do it' (Singer 1972: 231). Singer also applied this approach later to other issues such as climate change and global governance (Singer 2002).

Take, for instance, the pharmaceutical industry and agribusiness. If rules controlling the distribution of drugs or the sale of seeds protected by intellectual property rights do not really conduce to the maximum betterment of human beings, then questions can be asked about the way the global economy runs that enables companies to exercise this kind of control that leads to what many would see as disproportionate profit-taking.

Libertarianism

Another very influential ethical approach is that of libertarianism. (Libertarianism is not often *presented* as a global ethic, certainly not as cosmopolitan, but it has in fact both the key features of a global ethic, namely universality and transboundary responsibility.)

The central value for the libertarian is liberty – the freedom of individuals from interference both from fellow human beings and from the state or other institutions that exercise coercive limitations on what individuals may do. Of course some degree of law and order is required to check the exercise of liberty that invades another's liberty (Nozick 1974). Many liberties are acknowledged, some central to global communication, such as free speech and censorship and, on the other side of the coin, the right to privacy, which appears to be massively compromised by the data held by companies that run search engines or social media platforms. But a key liberty is economic liberty – to freely enter into transactions of employment and transfer of goods – and generally this is seen as including the liberty to form economic associations – small and big – and to be subject to as little taxation as possible, since taxation is a restriction on economic liberty.

The core universal value is liberty and the duty in others is not to interfere in that liberty. The transboundary corollary of this (not always emphasized or explicitly acknowledged) is to promote libertarian ideas in other parts of the world where they are not currently (enough) in place. Hence the agendas of many powerful countries in the world is to promote liberalization – whether through IMF (International Monetary Fund) policies of structural adjustment, 'liberal peace-building', investment agreements in poorer countries and so on.

Libertarianism as outlined has to be contrasted with liberalism, which is a rather broader idea and covers other positions such as social liberalism, which is quite different from libertarianism. Social liberalism stresses a key point denied or downplayed by libertarianism: that liberty is only valuable if certain background conditions are satisfied, such as sufficient income, access to health care without the capacity to pay for it and proper education. This idea, advanced by writers like L.T. Hobhouse and T.H. Green but made prominent in recent years in John Rawls's *A Theory of Justice* (1971) is a feature of some theories discussed below.

Comparison of These Three Approaches

It will be apparent that the libertarian approach to global ethics is rather different from the previous approaches, both because it does not make much of the idea that we have positive duties to promote the well-being of others, and because it is often invoked to confer a legitimacy on the moral rights of associations in the modern form of large capitalist institutions. It is not in line with the cosmopolitan intent of the other two, if cosmopolitanism is centrally about not merely the equal moral status of the individual, but the idea of generality or of everyone being of concern to everyone, as reflected in Pogge's definition of cosmopolitanism:

> Three elements are shared by all cosmopolitan positions. First, individualism: the ultimate units of concern are human beings, or persons – rather than, say, family lines, tribes, ethnic, cultural or religious communities, nations, or states. … Second, universality: the status of ultimate unit of concern attaches to every living human being equally – not merely to some sub-set, such as men, aristocrats, Aryans, whites, or Muslims. Third, generality: this special status has global force. Persons are ultimate units of concern for everyone – not only for their compatriots, fellow religionists, or suchlike. (Pogge 2003: 169)

All three of the above theories have one thing in common: they are all rather formal/abstract both in terms of their accounts of what human well-being consists in and of their accounts of the central principle of ethics underlying the more specific rules of moral life. This contrasts with the approaches discussed later. This formality or thinness may be seen as either a weakness or strength. It may be seen as a weakness if one thinks that well-being and moral duty have a richness and complexity to them that are not recognized. This unease may come from the theories mentioned below, but it may also come from various religious conceptions of global ethics which see ethics as derived from specific theoretical sources and traditions, or from an ecological perspective that stresses the need for non-human values as well. However there is no necessary conflict between these broad philosophical theories (or indeed the ones discussed later) and specific religious sources or ecological perspectives. Indeed there may be none, if we accept the point mentioned above, namely Parekh' idea of an ethic both consented to and assented to. This thinness may precisely be a strength in addressing the challenge of relativism, as discussed below, since this thinness may allow for a way of accounting for diversity of values, which is different from the relativist account.

The following accounts of global ethics provide in varying degree a richer account of the content of a global ethic: theory of human rights, the capabilities approach and global justice. The first gives an account of the elements of human well-being we have a right to and a global normative framework for their realization, the second develops a particular conception of what human well-being consists in, and the third gives a particular interpretation of the global ethical framework necessary for the advancement of human well-being.

Human Rights

Human rights are by their very definition rights that all human beings possess by virtue of their humanity, not rights that happen to be accorded to some group of people by law or convention. Alongside their universality, a corollary obligation is usually assumed to include a transboundary obligation in others anywhere not to undermine them and to some extent to promote them. Such rights are fundamentally moral rights possessed by all human beings. Of course human rights also refer to legal human rights in international human rights law and various national and regional conventions that promote them. It is an important part of the normative framework for the protection and promotion of moral human rights that they are juridified in international law (though someone can support an international human rights framework as furthering human well-being without necessarily believing in human rights as an ethical theory, as indeed Bentham did). However the legal side is not considered here.

Human rights theory is not a single theory. It covers a variety of approaches, in terms of the theoretical justification given, the range of things which human beings have a right to, and the kinds of correlative obligations others have and who have them. In effect what we have a right to constitutes, according to the theory, the most important elements of human well-being – things like, at a very basic level, following Shue, subsistence, security and basic liberty (Shue 1996). Most theories will spell rights out in much more detail, as UN documents illustrate. There is no space here to elaborate on these.

Two key points need mentioning here. Historically, in the second half of the twentieth century up to the end of the Cold War in 1989, there were two camps: the Western one that stressed the importance of liberty rights and the correlative duty not to interfere, and the soviet camp that stressed socio-economic rights and the duty to promote them by positive intervention. After the end of the Cold War, it came generally to be recognized that this was an oversimplification and that human rights is an immensely complicated field. It remains true that for some there is an emphasis upon developing appropriate regulatory frameworks for human rights observance, and for others the main emphasis should be on positive promotion of human rights through active interventions (like development assistance) and by providing positive enabling conditions for human rights to be realized. This is not so much a conflict between those who value liberties and those who do not as about different views about what it is to value liberty. As noted before, the social liberal is far more concerned than the libertarian with providing the enabling conditions in which human beings can develop and exercise their liberty in meaningful ways through developing infrastructures including education and health care provision.

The Capabilities Approach

This approach is worth a brief separate mention because it has become a very influential way of understanding what human well-being is all about – that is, of understanding just what the elements of human well-being are that we have right to. Most notably, amongst others, Amartya Sen the Indian economist-philosopher (Sen 1999) and Martha Nussbaum, a philosopher interested in applying certain elements of Aristotelianism to modern development issues (Nussbaum 2000), have presented this approach. A human being needs to develop a range of capabilities essential to a fully rounded human life that he or she as an agent has reason to value. For this, people need both proper nurture and education to develop their capabilities and then a social and economic structure including an appropriate rights-conferring legal framework in which they are able to exercise their acquired capabilities. An important aspect of this approach is that it counterbalances an undue emphasis on economic well-being and on development as simply economic development.

Its message is certainly interpreted to be global in the sense that its account of human well-being is seen as universally applicable. The assumption, though not the explicit emphasis, is that, given this concept of human good, we all through the international community have a duty not to impede and also, where appropriate, to promote the conditions necessary for people to realize their capabilities to lead a full human life.

Global Justice

Much interest recently in global ethics or cosmopolitanism has been focused on questions of global justice and injustice. There is no single theory of global justice any more than there is for justice within ordinary social morality.

What makes claims about justice global is simply that it is seen appropriate that claims of justice can be made across borders in regard to worldwide relations. Claims about global justice are not alternatives to the above theories of global ethics which we have considered, rather particular ways of interpreting or unpacking them. O'Neill for instance sees Kantianism as providing a theory of global justice by which we can condemn what is often done by business companies as unjust; Thomas Pogge likewise develops a particular account of human rights as the basis for claiming that the undermining of rights is a matter of global injustice (Pogge 2003).

Some approaches to global justice focus on the idea of injustice involving violating or undermining human rights, or, where failure to do so is a culpable omission, failing to promote the realization of human rights, whatever rights are taken to be central. Others may put more emphasis on the general idea of distribution – that, where distribution becomes so unequal that some people have very little and others an awful lot, there is something unjust about such a distribution. This may be about the distribution of wealth or income, or more generally of the conditions which enable people to exercise their rights or capabilities effectively, or more specifically the distribution of access to things like food, health care or a healthy environment. The latter includes an environment not made worse by others' unfairly high usage of carbon dioxide by exceeding their entitlement to a share of the atmospheric commons – climate justice being a big specific aspect of global justice.

Theories of Global Ethics Compared

Before turning to some general challenges to the whole idea of global ethic, some further points about the above theories of global ethics should be noted. It should be clear that what all these theories do is to put an emphasis on the individual wherever he or she is located and accord in some sense equal moral status to all individuals. As such what these theories prescribe in terms of actions, policies and the design and development of institutions, political, legal, economic and so on, are things that may well not be what are, in fact, generally done or promoted. Why is there such a difference between the way the world is and what these global ethics prescribe? Individual and collective self-interest are part of the answer. But it is at least partly because what informs the actions, programmes etc. of both individuals and institutions, including business companies, are in fact *other* ethical theories which justify paying much more attention to the interests of more limited groups. Notable amongst these are internationalism as a theory of international relations and communitarianism as a theory about the kinds of obligations individuals have in relation to their communities. These and other theories in opposition to global ethics will be discussed shortly.

That said, there are significant differences in what all the above global ethics theories actually prescribe. Quite apart from the tensions between the libertarian approach and Kantianism/utilitarianism noted earlier, there are other tensions that are sometimes because of different values and norms that the theories put forward, and sometimes in terms of different empirical assessments of what the likely consequences are of different policies. For instance a utilitarian might favour vigorous family planning policies or even forced family limitations, whereas a Catholic might object to the first as unnatural and someone who believes in the human right of parents to have as many children as they want may object to the second. Here different global norms are at stake. By contrast, two people might both believe in the right to life as the right to conditions for a satisfactory life but one may promote radical cutbacks in carbon emissions because she believes that high carbon emissions will damage life conditions, whereas the other might question this because he thinks the risks are less and because he thinks that vigorous economic growth, which would be impeded by reducing carbon emissions, contributes to improving life conditions. Here the difference is in the main about different readings of the facts. But they are both global ethics positions.

Opposition to Theories of Global Ethics

Opposition to global ethics comes from a number of quarters. Five kinds of opposition are considered. The first two are in opposition to the general idea of a global ethic as applied to individuals. These are relativism that claims that there are no universal values, and communitarianism that says that obligations are primarily to fellow members of a community including political communities like one's state, and that transboundary obligations are non-existent or minimal. The second two are opposed to cosmopolitanism (as a global ethic is seen in this contrast) as rival theories of international relations, namely sceptical realism that claims there are no ethical relations between states, and internationalism that claims that although there are ethical relations between states, these are much more limited than any global ethics approach suggests. Finally, a typical defence of business ethics focuses on the right of companies to maximize profits, where corporate social responsibility is seen as no more than a public relations exercise.

Ethical Relativism

Basically the thesis is that there are no universal values (Wong 1984). The theory comes in various forms. Descriptive or cultural relativism simply asserts that as a matter of fact different societies have different values and norms. This is usually backed by two more complex theses: meta-ethical relativism as the claim that right just means what is approved by society and normative relativism as the claim that what is right in a society *is* what that society says it is (so when in Rome do as the Romans do). A consequence of this is that to judge the behaviour of others in other societies as wrong is intellectually wrong-headed, and to promote one's values elsewhere and, especially to impose them are wrong. Relativists often see their theory as underlining what is wrong with colonialism and modern equivalents, for example, of promoting 'modern' Western liberal values such as Western democracy or the equal status of women or homosexuals in other countries.

Relativists may acknowledge that there are some values that are common to different societies, whereas others are not. Is this in effect a 'global ethic'? If some reason accessible to all humans is given for why this is the case, then indeed we could have in effect a global ethic along the lines indicated later in this section. But if this commonality is just an accident, something that happens to be shared, then it is not really a global ethic. This leads to the second difficulty.

It also throws out more than it might seem. Often what motivate relativism are a rejection of the Western imposition of its values on the rest of the world and a rejection of colonialism as unjust; but in so doing and in not providing an alternative *universal* framework, it cannot criticize colonialism from a *global* point of view. Of course it could be part of the particular morality of a society that it criticizes colonialism, but it cannot expect as *universally reasonable* the same attitude from other societies if these societies' internal moral outlooks are not like this and are for instance hostile or indifferent to what happens elsewhere.

Another way then of seeing the diversity of values alongside a core of widely, if not universally, accepted values is to say that there is a set of core values that are the same but the ways they are expressed are different in different settings. Ways of caring for loved ones such as children, the sick or the old, may be quite different in different cultures but express the same basic attitude of care.

So the response to relativism from a global ethics or cosmopolitan point of view is to acknowledge diversity but to put forward global responsibility to promote the conditions of human flourishing where the latter is defined in a culturally sensitive universalism (see solidarist pluralism in Dower 1998, 2007). That is, the distinction needs to be recognized between some core values (the basic preconditions of human flourishing and the core moral values that are prerequisites of society) and other values (conceptions of well-being and social customs), which may vary considerably from society to society, and this distinction is a distinction between an *essentially* universal core and other variable values and variable expression of core values.

Communitarianism

Communitarianism is the second major challenge to global ethics or cosmopolitanism, and the challenge is in respect to the claim about significant transboundary obligation. It is inspired by the idea that morality is derived or primarily derived from actual community (Sandel 1982). It is in communities that there are shared traditions and shared common acceptances of certain moral norms and understandings of well-being and moral obligations derived from reciprocity. Such communities may be quite small or local but also much larger in political communities held together not merely by shared moral norms but legal norms as well. The general thrust of much communitarian thinking is to emphasize that our obligations are to members of our community, not to humanity as a whole. As such it comes into tension with the approach of global ethics or cosmopolitanism insofar as the latter emphasizes our transboundary obligations to everyone. Of course some communitarians may make something of the fact that there is also a global community – or various communities with members all over the world, such as churches and other voluntary associations – but the obligations we owe to the global community as a whole are generally seen as much less.

Such an approach of course questions a lot of the things that advocates of global ethics or cosmopolitanism would commend – significant personal generosity in aid giving to help people in distant countries, engaging in Fairtrade to help poor farmers elsewhere, or cutting one's carbon emissions. Of course all these actions, particularly the third, may seem to be sensible things to do because of the benefits that will be bestowed on the people in one's own community – less poverty elsewhere means more trading possibilities in the future, reducing climate change requires coordinated efforts by everyone etc. Measures to control an outbreak of disease in one country may stem from a desire to prevent its spread to one's own country. But the point is that the reason for doing this is the interests of those from one's own community, not the interests of humanity.

What is partly at issue between communitarianism and global ethics is the communitarian's not recognizing that obligation does not primarily or only arise from established reciprocity, but also from the capacity to affect others for good or ill – a capacity we clearly have extensively in our modern interdependent world. (Much more needs to be said about the relationship of cosmopolitanism and communitarianism and, linked to this, just how extensive transboundary obligations are claimed to be: see Dower 1998, 2007.)

International Scepticism

International scepticism or sceptical realism challenges the whole idea of a global ethic from a point of view focused on relations between nation states.

Although it derives some of its rationale from ethical theories like relativism and communitarianism, it is a specific view that there are no ethical relations between states. Because states are sovereign and do not have a higher power or political authority like a world government above them, states exist in a moral vacuum in which the pursuit of power and national interests is legitimate. Hobbes argued that because genuine moral norms require enforceability, there are no moral norms in international relations (Hobbes 1651: Ch. XIII). This does not mean that an international sceptic will be against cooperation or indeed against developing common rules or even international law. But for him these are to be favoured as and when they further the interests of one's state and disregarded (maybe secretly) when they do not, for example, by disregarding the rules or by going to war. For instance, supporting international disease control is a good idea if that helps to protect one's own state.

Supporters of global ethics will, while conceding that much of international relations is as a matter of fact conducted in this way, argue that, ethically, moral obligation does not depend on enforceability, but also that the extent of international cooperation through international institutions and law and other consequences of globalization make this an unrealistic way of reading the world.

Internationalism

Internationalism or the 'society of states' theory of international relations has been the dominant theory in the last four and a half centuries. The system of nation states was established in Europe after the Thirty Years War through the Treaty of Westphalia of 1648. This system of nation states has spread to cover the whole world, and the United Nations is itself a late expression of the model, since it is an organization whose members are nation states.

Unlike the realist position, states were seen as constituting some kind of society and as such were subject to the norms of that society. Historically these norms were seen to be the right to sovereignty with a corresponding duty of non-interference; the duty to preserve the society of states; the acceptance of the rules of war (*ius add bellum* and *ius in bello*); and the acceptance of the principle *pacta sunt servanda*, meaning that agreements such as treaties or internationally agreed laws should be observed (Bull 1977). The rationale for this tended to be either the agreement of states themselves to create and maintain the norm-governed system for mutual advantage, or some theory about the natural rights of states. Historically, the morality of states could be seen as a limited one: states as such did not have significant duties to promote the interests of other states or those of the nationals of those other states.

As such, this approach stands in contrast to cosmopolitanism since the latter grounds an ethic in the well-being of all human beings, and as such may critique what is done by states in the name of the morality of states. If a state says that it has a right to exploit its natural resources – such as by extracting fossils fuels or cutting down rain forests – this may come into conflict with a cosmopolitan view that we should restrain such activities for the global common good.

Whether or not the morality of states approach is a form of global ethic, it is clearly an 'inter-national ethic', and its emphasis is different from what is typically advanced in a global ethic, namely a focus on actions that further human well-being generally, whether they are state actions, the actions of individuals or the actions of other bodies.

An example that is significant comes from the areas of food production and medicines. The World Trade Organisation, whose representatives are states, determines many of the rules governing patents on seeds, particularly genetically modified seeds, and drugs. Although it is companies that get these patents (see next section), it is countries that determine the rules, with often the powerful countries in such negotiations also benefitting from the companies involved. Often the costs of seeds and drugs for poor people are such that their interests are not served and indeed thwarted and, from the point of view of many with a global ethic, this is deeply unsatisfactory.

That said, in the modern world, there is no clear opposition between the morality of states approach and cosmopolitanism. The historical 'limited' morality of states has gradually become transformed into a much more extended morality. This is due to a number of factors: first, the increased need for international cooperation because of common global threats, such as cyberterrorism, the spread of diseases, various environmental problems such as species loss and climate change, global food and water security; second, linked to this, the sheer proliferation of internationally agreed laws that juridify positive obligations to help others; third, the fact that due to globalization far more of countries' citizens have global moral concerns which can influence foreign policy; and fourth, increasing interest in the idea of states themselves being 'good international citizens' (i.e. citizens of the society of states) with a serious commitment to furthering, for instance, human rights (Linklater 1992). It remains true however that the morality of states approach is somewhat different from typical global ethics approaches, both in terms of justification and in terms of what it advocates.

Business Ethics

Finally, there is the issue of how to understand the ethics of business, whether that of small or transnational corporations. According to the global ethics perspective, businesses like any other body capable of agency are subject to this ethic, and if business practices clearly go against the interests of those affected overall, ethical questions can be raised. This comes up against the standard view of businesses, namely that they exist – it is their rationale – to maximize profit for shareholders (subject to the requirement of relevant laws). While there is a common view that free enterprise, small and large, contributes in the long run to human well-being, it is increasingly recognized that the way businesses operate should be subject to more ethical constraints than had often been recognized. This is expressed in ideas of corporate social responsibility, whether within a country or globally, or 'corporate global citizenship'.

Businesses are, and from an ethics point of view should be, increasingly subject to regulatory frameworks in respect to protection of the environment, workers' rights, health and safety standards and provision of health care. From a global ethics point of view this applies globally. From an ethical point of view, businesses should not merely be subject to such regulations but should accept that they ought to be subject to them. The reality is of course often rather different. Apart from the idea of patents and intellectual property rights already referred to, there is also the big issue of tax havens through which much profit is not subject to tax. From the point of view of cosmopolitanism, far more of the value of the goods or resources taken from poor countries ought to be made available to poor countries to improve the life conditions of the very poor of the world.

CONCLUSION

In this chapter various approaches to global ethics and also a number of fairly common views opposed to this approach have been mapped out, and some of a wide range of issues have been given as illustrations. It is for the reader to apply the framework to more detailed issues that arise within the field of global communication.

Chapter 3

Treacherous Tropes

How Ethicists Communicate

Maren Behrensen

In this chapter, rather than discussing the specific area of communication ethics, I want to look at how ethicists communicate. I will limit myself to the Anglophone and European context of professional ethics and professional philosophy; and my leading question will be whether there is something about the way moral questions tend to get framed in these fields – especially towards students and laypersons – that correlates with their relative lack of diversity and in turn, their relative irrelevance to many ongoing public discourses. The working hypothesis for this chapter is that the demography of philosophical ethics influences its methodology, and that – given the lack of diversity in the discipline – this methodology risks becoming a vessel of ideology.

I will begin with a brief account of the lack of diversity in philosophy and ethics (section 1), then discuss different understandings of pluralism – as a problem and as an aspiration (section 2), and then proceed to discuss three 'tropes' of contemporary analytical ethics that I regard as particularly detrimental to the goal of communicating moral concerns successfully (section 3). In the final section, I will briefly consider the positive impact a more judicious and balanced use of these tropes could have in terms of making ethics a more diverse and pluralistic discipline.

THE HOMOGENEITY OF PROFESSIONAL PHILOSOPHY

In recent years, philosophy and ethics as academic disciplines have begun to pay attention to their striking lack of diversity. This lack of diversity is pervasive in at least three ways:

a. in terms of who is regarded as an influential scholar. Ethics seems to fare slightly better in its representation of women among the most-cited and best-known scholars than other core areas of philosophy – although women are still underrepresented, especially at the very top of the discipline.[1] And 'ethnic minorities are virtually absent … at the highest levels of visibility in contemporary mainstream Anglophone analytic philosophy' (Schwitzgebel 2014b).

b. in terms of who actually studies the discipline and goes on to try to make a profession of it. A survey conducted by the American Philosophical Association (APA 2013) showed that while the percentage of bachelor's and master's degrees in philosophy awarded to members of racial and ethnic minorities at US colleges and universities had increased slightly between 1995 and 2009 – to 12% and 8%, respectively – the percentage of doctorates awarded to members of these minorities had actually dipped below 5% in the same time span. Along similar lines, Paxton, Figdor and Tiberius's empirical research suggests that 'there is an overall decline in the proportion of women in philosophy as one travels up the academic hierarchy' (2012: 953).

c. and lastly, in terms of what constitutes an appropriate scholarly interest in these disciplines. As Eugene Sun Park pointed out in his public farewell to academia: '[In] order to be taken seriously in the discipline, and to have any hope of landing a tenure-track job, one must write a dissertation in one of the "core areas" of philosophy' (Park 2014). And philosophies in non-European traditions as well as feminist and queer philosophies ostensibly belong to the margins, not the core.

The extreme underrepresentation of scholars of colour and of women in professional philosophy is by now fairly well documented, but its causes remain under debate.[2] It is also far from universally accepted that the extreme overrepresentation of white men – dead or alive – in philosophy constitutes a problem. Some might say that it can be explained – and explained away – as a mere matter of academic taste.[3] Others like Kristie Dotson – one of the few black women philosophy professors in the United States – wonder in turn not 'whether [they] are good enough to do philosophy, [but rather] whether the environment provided by professional philosophy is good enough for [them]' (Dotson 2012: 4).

The extreme overrepresentation of white men among active philosophers is mirrored in debates about what is considered canonical or even just worthwhile in professional philosophy. Scholarly interests in non-European and non-male-dominated traditions and topic areas of philosophy are often dismissed as marginal or even inimical to 'doing serious philosophy'.[4] In line with this attitude, the selection of representative texts for philosophy courses and textbooks often ignores 'non-canonical' sources and perspectives.[5] And where these sources and perspectives occur, they are frequently introduced by a special heading and presented as a singular issue – such as the one short chapter on 'feminist ethics' in a textbook or entire panels and workshops on 'philosophy of race' or 'Asian philosophy' when similar texts and events in the so-called core areas are labelled for their focus on rather specific philosophical questions and theories.

As I mentioned above, this rather sorry state of affairs has been put under scholarly and administrative scrutiny; and one thing I do not want to do here is to come up with grand solutions for how the lack of diversity in ethics and philosophy could be remedied, or to offer any new, sweeping explanations as to how we got here. Rather, I want to outline the relevance of these debates for global communication ethics, and specifically for the task of communicating ethics – across traditions, across disciplines, and across the divide between 'experts' and 'beginners'.

My main contention is rather simple, and might seem trivial: I suggest that the undertaking of communicating ethics requires attention to one's own context and presuppositions. If, however, one's own context is as demographically homogeneous as in philosophy and ethics – especially in their 'analytic' varieties – then there is a serious risk that this context and all it entails – a specific methodology, a specific canon – is seen as universal. And where such universality is trumpeted without further self-awareness, the task of communicating ethics fails, and ethics becomes a mere vehicle for ideology.

Of particular interest to me here is the buzzword 'pluralism', in some ways the complement to 'diversity', but in other ways diametrically opposed to it. Where pluralism is taken as a mere fact and a challenge – for instance, the observation that people sometimes disagree rather sharply about ethical questions – diversity is unlikely to be the outcome. However, pluralism can also be seen as an aspiration, and in this regard, it might foster diversity.

The problem is that the mainstream in professional ethics seems to regard pluralism merely as a fact, as yet another interesting philosophical puzzle to be solved. And this in turn contributes to the dismissal of traditions and topics that fall outside the mainstream – but if that is so, the answers given by professional ethicists can hardly claim universal relevance, especially if it is topics and traditions that fall under the heading of 'pluralism' which are under discussion. The case could be framed as a choice: professional ethics may be content with remaining a 'white man's game' or it can seek to develop 'a healthy appreciation for the differing issues that will emerge as pertinent among different populations' (Dotson 2012: 17).

PLURALISM AS STRANGER DANGER AND
PLURALISM AS ASPIRATION

Ethicists – and especially ethicists who promote their ideas outside the academic realm – are often pressured for clear answers. Politicians and business
leaders hope for unambiguous advice, engineers need lists with 'dos' and
'don'ts', students want to know what the one correct answer to a moral question is. This pressure can translate into an actual dilemma, especially in the
field of applied ethics: In order to stay relevant, ethicists need to provide clear
and quick answers to the questions of the day. But at the same time, their
philosophical responsibility urges them to engage in circumspect and careful
reasoning for the sake of doing justice to the messy reality of ethical questions.

In these sorts of contexts, pluralism can seem like nothing but an obstacle
to the goal of ethics – a kind of 'stranger danger'. It is a problem to be solved.
Rights and interests need to be weighed against each other, moral claims are
staked and adjudged, and a compromise is announced. The pluralism – the
disagreement – that created the conflict in the first place is relegated to being a
brute fact, tamed by ethical analysis. It is no surprise that – as Philip Ivanhoe
points out – the 'vast majority of contemporary Western philosophers who
accept the fact of ethical pluralism and take this as a cause for concern tend
to argue for tolerance in the face of such differences' (Ivanhoe 2009: 312).
On such a view, disagreements and differing value judgements are grudgingly
tolerated.

But such grudging toleration might still lend itself to the invocation of a
repressive force to quell value conflicts that are left unresolved and unat-
tended, to paraphrase Charles Ess (2006: 216). Even grudging toleration
can ensure that the voices of those who are thusly tolerated are ignored and
silenced. And where the response to pluralism is toleration, the philosopher
and the ethicist still take on the role of an external observer and a judge. Their
own perspective is allowed to remain unexamined.

To be sure, the supposed objectivity of the philosophical observer has
itself been treated as a philosophical problem throughout the discipline's
history; from ancient and early modern sceptics to post-structuralist thinkers
who understand the notion of 'objectivity' itself as a vessel for nothing but
discursive power.[6] Inspired in various ways by this long history of philosophical self-criticism, we now have an array of philosophers working in the
philosophies of race, gender and sexuality for whom the whiteness and the
heteronormativity of the discipline itself has become a central issue (see for
instance Haslanger 2008 and Coleman 2014).

Yet it seems to me that this tradition of philosophical scepticism and
humility has failed to impact large areas of philosophical ethics and applied
ethics. Things are no doubt changing: new topics are being picked up, and

many departments and publications are actively striving for diversity. It seems to me, though, that ethics has remained fairly static in terms of its style and its 'toolbox' – despite the various revivals of virtue ethics after the Second World War, and despite the rapid expansion of the field of applied ethics. This is nowhere more obvious than in the way in which ethical expertise is produced and presented for non-experts – something which Mulligan, Simons and Smith (2015: 3) in their take on 'What's Wrong with Contemporary Philosophy?' wittily and scathingly described as wavering between the horror mundi of trained metaphysicians and ontologians and letting 'philosophically naïve exponents of other disciplines … wreak ontological havoc'.

It could perhaps be said that analytic ethics is due for a change similar to that of analytic political philosophy in the wake and the aftermath of Rawls's *A Theory of Justice*. Rawls's monumental work revolutionized its field by reviving the early modern and modern traditions of contract theory for a contemporary context.[7] But Rawls was also – and in my view, rightly – accused of ignoring a vast part of human experience, especially experiences of marginalization and oppression, and of unconscionably idealizing the relations between human beings. As Pateman and Mills put it (2007: 5; see also Yancy and Mills 2014), 'Rawls's methodological decision to focus on "ideal theory" and a "well-ordered society" has been of little help in addressing the problems of our non-ideal, ill-ordered, patriarchal and racist societies'.

Uneasiness about Rawls's – and historical contract theorists' – tendency towards idealization and abstraction has generated attempts to build political philosophies that are sensitive to:

a. communal identities – as in the works of philosophers generally grouped under the label communitarians (see Sandel 1981 and Taylor 1994)
b. the history of racism and racial oppression – as in the work of Charles Mills on the 'racial contract' (Mills 1997)
c. and to the role of women and the family in the polity – as in the work of Carol Pateman (1988) and other feminist philosophers.[8]

Some features of what made Rawls's Theory seem unattractive or incomplete to these critics can be found in ethics today: unnecessary or unhelpful abstraction from the concrete, an obliviousness to historical precedent, and a reduction of political and moral issues to empty, but seemingly profound dichotomies. In Rawls's own case, one of his own dichotomies – that between the public sphere and questions of justice on the one hand, and private conceptions of the good on the other (Rawls 1971: 446–52) – helps illustrate the point. What Rawls did not consider was the extent to which liberal ideals of justice and the liberal state are themselves products of a particular conception of the good. The messy political reality of liberal states – in which political and legal processes are rarely ever unaffected by rather specific ideologies – should make us ask how helpful Rawls' dichotomy is in understanding the normative concepts that guide their assessment.

Rawls's principles sought to tame pluralism, to remove it from the sphere of the political and from the sphere of justice. But in doing so, they might have made political philosophy poorer and less inclusive. Similar things can be said about contemporary ethics: That in its urge to provide clear answers, and a clear map of our moral landscape, it ignores the messiness of reality. Accepting this messiness – with a corresponding circumspection in judgement – does not need to complicate or taint ethical analysis, it can enrich it; and it might lead to a pluralism that does not merely grudgingly tolerate difference and disagreement, but accepts them as a possible source of new insights. In the words of Elizabeth Barnes (from her autobiographical interview; 2015): 'I think that part of making philosophy more inclusive is … allowing people from a wider range of backgrounds to shape what we care about in philosophy, rather than only allowing people from a wider range of backgrounds to succeed in philosophy if they show they can advance the debates we already decided we cared about'.

I do think that the tropes that I will focus on in the next section are indicative of a failure to do what Barnes recommends: They contribute to a socially and intellectually contingent kind of discourse, while framing this discourse as universal; and they do not do justice to the messiness of reality, instead relegating this messiness to the realm of the abstract and the merely thought-provoking.

TREACHEROUS TROPES

These 'treacherous tropes' run like recurrent themes through much of applied ethics: articles, conference talks, extramural documents and teaching documents, as well as teaching styles. What I find most worrisome about these tropes is that they seem to encourage selective ignorance about the complexity of ethical issues, and towards the complexity of moral responsibility. The three tropes that I will be looking at here could be called 'just a thought experiment', 'listicle ethics', and 'empty dichotomies'. The so-called 'trolley cases', one of the most famous tropes of contemporary ethics, actually unite all these qualities, and I will discuss them here first.

Let the Trolley Go

The trolley problem was first introduced in Philippa Foot's seminal paper 'Abortion and the Doctrine of Double Effect' (1978, originally published in

1967) and then famously adapted by Judith Jarvis Thomson (1986, originally published in 1976). In its simplest form, it asks the reader to ponder the case of saving several lives at the expense of letting one perish: A runaway trolley threatens to kill five persons working on the train track, unless a bystander intervenes in some way – by pulling a switch and directing the trolley to a track where one poor soul is tied to the rails, by pushing a *very large* man onto the track, and so on, in countless variations and permutations.

Since their inception as a tool of ethical reasoning, trolleys have had an amazing 'career' in moral philosophy: books and papers are written just on particular aspects of particular trolley cases (see for instance Kamm 2007; Otsuka 2008; Liao 2008); such cases form the stock for neurological and psychological research on moral reasoning and moral intuitions (see for instance Greene et al. 2001; Cushman et al. 2006; and for a defence of the philosophical relevance of such research, Kahane 2013); and there is at least one introductory textbook in ethics that I am aware of which returns to the trolley problem in each one of its chapters (Tännsjö 2013).

It is not particularly difficult to appreciate why trolley cases have had this kind of sway over the philosophical community. Their basic setup is simple and easy to follow for philosophical laypersons, they present a limited range of choices in each case, and they can be modified in a seemingly endless number of ways.

But trolley cases can foster the illusion that ethical reflection can be reduced to picking one of a narrow range of well-defined options, and that such reflection thus stops at the level of 'intuition pumping'.[9] As Tännsjö himself notes, ethical theories that do not build on principles of right action – like virtue-ethical theories – cannot straightforwardly be applied to the trolley problem (2013: 112). Trolley cases thus foster simplistic binary thinking in the sense that the available options are fairly clearly marked as consequence oriented and duty oriented, or respectively, as partial and impartial.

But to me the strangest aspect of the trolley cases is their appeal and their success despite the fact that they are both so formulaic and so wildly cartoon-ish (Luban 2008: 36). James O'Connor, in his critique of the 'trolley method', illustrates this point with a simple summary (2012: 243):

Trolley problems very often don't involve trolleys at all, but, for instance, groups of non-swimmers being trapped on rapidly submerging islands, over-weight people on bridges being unwittingly used as makeshift brakes to stop runaway trams, exploding cave explorers, people being shot out of cannons for no sensible reason, healthy people being commandeered for organ harvesting, *very* long arms that can reach across whole continents to pluck drowning chil-dren out of ponds …; and a seemingly unlimited variety of other, more or less psychedelic scenarios.

Few people could ever be expected to end up in an actual trolley situation, that is, a situation in which they literally had to choose which person(s) die(s) at a given time – and those who do end up in them may be pitied rather than be taken as tokens of how 'we' do moral reasoning.[10] Most situations that demand moral reflection are far from the psychedelic, yet rigidly dichotomous trolley cases; normally, we are forced to decide and act under uncertainty, without being aware of all the options and without being able – in terms of available time and available information – to reduce them down to clearly defined decision-paths.

It could be argued, of course, that trolley cases are so attractive and such a helpful tool for both normative ethicists and moral psychologists, precisely because they abstract from the messiness of reality – and that this is why they are used as an 'ethical laboratory'.[11] We might wonder whether the abstraction and the reduction of complex variables is not actually a strength of this mode of ethical reasoning, just as it is in the physicist's or the biologist's laboratory. I cannot provide a full answer to this objection in this limited space, but I will at least indicate how such an answer could proceed.

Theory-driven laboratory work in the natural sciences clearly has yielded and does yield interesting insights, and these insights often have practical implications. But depending on its setup and its aims, such work might just as well never lead anywhere. 'Ethical laboratories' yield intuitions and insights that may be interesting in themselves, but where they become the standard form of ethical analysis and ethics teaching – and are no longer connected to any recognizable reality – we need to wonder what they can actually tell us about real people in the real world.

This is not to suggest that all thought experiments are useless as academic or empirical exercises. What I object to in particular is an overreliance on these figures of thinking, and a disinterest in connecting the intuitions and insights generated by them back to immediate practical concerns.[12]

Just a Thought Experiment

Trolley cases are just one among many famous thought experiments in analytic ethics. Many of these thought experiments have found their way into the 'lore' of philosophical literature that is regularly taught to introductory classes and forms a common frame of reference for many professional philosophers. Learning about these thought experiments, and how to reference them could even be regarded as an induction ritual for aspiring philosophers, at least in the Anglophone and the 'analytical' mode of doing philosophy. Beside the trolley cases, there are thought experiments like the 'experience machine' (Nozick 1974: 42–44), the 'survival lottery' (Harris 1975) and the 'ticking bomb' (Dershowitz 2002), all well and widely known, and all of them thought to be particularly effective at teasing out basic moral intuitions.[13]

The thought experiment I want to put in focus here is perhaps not as well known, but it seems to me particularly effective in showing what is troubling about excessive reliance on this kind of hypothetical reasoning – even if the thought experiment manages to draw out the intuition that the practice discussed in it is deeply wrong, as for instance the 'survival lottery' seems to do.

Some weeks ago, I was in the audience for a conference talk on the 'baby lottery'. The talk itself was a partial defence of the practice. The 'baby lottery' is a thought experiment where the reader or listener is asked to imagine a society in which babies are taken from their birth parents and allocated in accordance with whichever set of parents would give them the best care, support and education (Fishkin 1983: 57; Barry 1988: 31–32). The 'baby lottery' is meant to tease out assumptions about the relation between equal opportunities and the moral weight of familial relationships – and most commenters would presumably argue that parental rights override a presumptive interest in equalizing opportunities, or that violating these rights does not actually do a service to equal opportunities.

But if that is the desired conclusion, then we should wonder why we need a thought experiment in order to reassure us. Would we not be able to reach the same conclusion simply by reasoning about parental rights and state intervention in the actual world? What is more, we do have striking historical examples of governments and their agents engaging in horrific violations of parental and cultural rights in real-life 'baby lotteries' – because they supposedly know better than the birth parents.

Two examples of this that have been or at the very least should be called a form of cultural genocide are the Indian Residential Schools in Canada and the 'stolen generations' of Aboriginal and Torres Strait Islander children in Australia. In the Australian case, these children were forcibly removed from their birth families under 'child protection' policies in effect from the early twentieth century until the 1960s and sometimes the 1970s (Commonwealth of Australia 1997). In the Indian Residential Schools, children from Canadian First Nations were taken from their communities during school years, forbidden to speak their native languages and often kept in atrocious living conditions. In these schools, which were often run by religious institutions, physical and sexual abuse of children was ubiquitous, and an unknown but arguably sizeable number of children died from neglect, violence or disease (Truth and Reconciliation Commission of Canada 2015).

What the residential schools and Australia's policies have in common is the assumption on part of the policymakers that these children came from an 'inferior' background and would be better off separated from it and inducted into an allegedly 'superior' white culture. Familial and community attachments and the significance of language and culture played no part in this reasoning. Both policies provide real-life examples of the damages done by racist policies that aim to sever familial ties rather than foster them, policies that were given an air of 'rationality' by appealing to white supremacist notions of child welfare.

Few people outside Canada and Australia know about these criminal policies, and philosophers rarely pay attention to it. But we should ask why philosophers would rather engage in thought experiments than to address history – even more so since this history is very much alive in the sense that Canada is currently engaged in a public reconciliation process, with the report of the Truth and Reconciliation Commission on the residential schools having been published just a few months ago; and Australia still grappling with the aftermath of its 'White Australia' policies.

In the conference talk I mentioned, there was no historical context and yet the graduate student giving the talk was discussing the 'baby lottery' as a potential means to undermine racism. This is not simply ironic; it is actually deeply frightening to see aspiring scholars engaged in this kind of historical forgetfulness.[14]

Similar things could be said about the 'ticking bomb'. In this fantasy – for it is nothing more than a fantasy – we are asked to imagine that police have caught a terrorist and they know that he has hidden a bomb somewhere in the city, but will not give up its location. Time is of the essence and police decide to use torture in order to get the terrorist to talk.

Several philosophers have thoughtfully yet acerbically debunked the 'ticking bomb' as a thought experiment that is both uninformative as a philosophical exercise and politically dangerous (Shue 2006; Brecher 2007; Luban 2008). Nevertheless, it is not only still discussed in ethics textbooks (see for instance Shafer-Landau 2012) and regarded as an obvious example of the difference between consequentialist and deontological reasoning; the mode in which 'ticking bomb' examples are constructed is also invoked in political propaganda – often on behalf of governments that imprison suspect persons for years without trial and torture them, and curtail civil rights and rights of due process; all, as it were, in the name of 'national security'.

Here, as in the case of the 'baby lottery', we have ample historical evidence that shows how ticking-bomb cases are misleading: There are scores of governments that torture their political enemies, not to gain information, but to consolidate and prove their power. The United States, so fond of invoking ticking-bomb cases in its own political discourse, has itself contributed to that history with the systematic torture of prisoners with the tacit or explicit blessing of the government in Iraq, in Guantanamo and in other locations. What scandals like the revelation of the orchestrated cruelties in the Abu Ghraib prison show is that torture hardly ever seems to be used for the purpose of gaining information. The main purpose of torture is the humiliation and dehumanization of other human beings and the exercise of raw political and military power (Klein 2005).

In this light, it is deeply troubling that ethicists continue to see the neat and clean and entirely illusory world of the 'ticking bomb' and similar cases as a helpful tool in teaching and communicating their concerns. As effective as such cases might be in teasing out this or that intuition, they are also dangerous in that they encourage a disregard for reality, and in that they make things seem simple that are patently not so.

Listicle Ethics

A trend that is similar to overreliance on thought experiments in terms of its potentially oversimplifying and alienating effects is a trend towards 'listicle ethics', by which I mean a mode of doing ethics that reduces ethical analysis to a set of principles that can be heuristically applied to a given issue. To be sure, the entire point of applied ethics is to apply principles to problems – and this area of ethics can certainly be conceived as more complex than the term 'listicle ethics' may suggest (for bioethics, see for instance Gillon 1994 and Kovacs 2010). And yet there is a sense in which the pressure to make ethical reasoning straightforwardly applicable can foster an unproductive and vacuous adherence to principle.

Bioethics is sometimes ridiculed for its treatment of the 'four principles', formulated by Beauchamp and Childress (2013), as a kind of catechism. But bioethics has come a long way from the sole reliance on doctors' authority that shaped medical practice everywhere just 50 or 60 years ago (and still does in many places; see Kovacs 2010 for a concise take on this history) – not least due to the formulation and propagation of the 'four principles'. To take patient autonomy seriously is an especially valuable contribution of this development. But even so, there is a risk that the rote application of the four principles – something which is taught to students of medicine and bioethics, and factors prominently in the relevant textbooks – does not foster independent ethical thinking, but instead just leads to mimicry.

One aspect of the overreliance on a fixed set of principles is that we lose sight of the necessity for flexibility and adaptation to new contexts and new problems in ethical thinking. With the notion that all established principles have been paid attention easily comes the notion that no further questions could be raised. And thus the attachment to a particular set of principles may well breed a spirit whereby ethics is reduced to a checklist, the 'listicle ethics' mentioned above.

Given my own experience with ethics in technological projects, I suspect that this spirit is not rare, nor is its appeal incomprehensible. 'Listicle ethics' allows philosophical laypersons working in an ethically sensitive field to apply ethics on their own. A set of principles can thus fruitfully function as a heuristic that makes ethics more democratic and less reliant on special expertise. But this benefit of 'listicle ethics' needs to be weighed against its risks. Where the application of a heuristic becomes an end in itself – for instance, because it signifies 'compliance' with ethics guidelines in an R&D project – there is a danger that the heuristic tool becomes static, a set of meaningless buzzwords; and that it will eventually lag far behind the technologies and the policies it is supposed to help evaluate.

The success of 'privacy by default' (PBD) and 'privacy impact assessments' (PIA) in the surveillance and information industry can be read – pessimistically – as an example of just such a trend. Both can be translated into relatively straightforward decision-frameworks which project leaders and policymakers can apply even without the help of a philosopher or an ethicist; but both can also be criticized for focusing on a relatively circumscribed aspect of new technologies (see Wright and De Hert 2012 for an overview of various PIA approaches). And both PIA and PBD can be accused of actually missing the most concerning aspect of the proliferation of new information, communication and surveillance technologies: not their impact on privacy rights, but their contribution to the unregulated and unchecked use of power (Coady 2012: 184–185). In other words, 'listicle ethics', like overreliance on thought experiments, might encourage a selective attention that obscures a large chunk of the emerging realities ethicists are trying to capture.

Again, this is not to say that PBD and PIA – or the use of the four principles in bioethics – are useless. These and similar approaches have certainly sensitized many professionals and politicians to ethical concerns and made ethics relevant for them. Yet such achievements need to be regarded in light of a potential loss of complexity, and in light of the moral risk of obfuscating residual or emerging issues by appeals to supposedly exhaustive 'assessments'.

Empty Dichotomies

Philosophical ethics encourages dichotomous thinking in many trivial and non-trivial ways – the most trivial perhaps being that the goal of ethical reasoning is to determine the difference between right and wrong. In my above discussion of 'trolleyology',[15] I have already mentioned some ways in which dichotomous thinking obfuscates the complexity of ethical questions. In what follows, I want to explore an aspect of dichotomous thinking that relates directly to the issue of pluralism and diversity in ethics.

Above, I suggested that Rawls's distinction between the public sphere of political justice and private conceptions of the good may be an unhelpful theoretical tool. What this theoretical tool does is to remove an entire host of questions from the purview of political philosophy – for instance, questions about justice within the family, questions about the enduring prevalence of racist aggressions and discrimination in a supposedly 'colourblind' society, or questions about the enduring interest of policymakers in matters of sexual autonomy. And what remains if such questions are removed might well be an 'empty dichotomy' – a distinction that seems theoretically appealing and elegant, but does not actually provide satisfying answers to the most pressing questions. And such empty dichotomies might well reinforce implicit value judgements about different traditions and styles of political and moral debate – here the enlightened, neutral liberal; there the as of now still unenlightened religious figure, 'ethnic' activist or 'identity politician'.

The use of empty dichotomous thinking in moral philosophy can have similar effects. Overreliance on trolley problems can make us insensitive to what it actually means to face life-or-death decisions. Overreliance on purportedly ahistorical thought experiments can make us reluctant to learn from history. Overreliance on specific heuristics can distract us from the much bigger problem that looms behind the next technological or medical step forward.

What is more, by trying to distil out *supposedly* general features of ethical analysis with the help of such tropes, we might as well be 'distilling away' *supposedly* particular perspectives that could enrich the debate. The ongoing obsession with privacy as the central value in technology ethics can be read as an example of this – historically, privacy has been the kind of right that fostered oppression by protecting the abuses of landowners and homeowners against those subjected to their rule from the reach of the state. Still today, it might be a right primarily for the economically, socially and culturally privileged (Coady 2012: 177). And if the dominant dichotomy in technology ethics today is that of privacy versus security, then we should wonder about those who might be excluded from even having a stake in this dichotomy, because they live in conditions where privacy is an unattainable luxury.

Another such example – particularly interesting with regard to the issue of pluralism – are questions of toleration, autonomy and coercion; typically raised when considering 'cultural practices' that are widely regarded as strange, inimical to liberal values or plainly barbaric. Examples of such debates are, for instance, controversies regarding religious homeschooling, about banning niqabs and burqas in public spaces or about what is to be done against practices of female genital cutting. At least in the public realm, these debates are often characterized by a simplistic 'us and them' approach and come down to the question how much 'we' need to tolerate (for a treatment of female genital cutting in this spirit, see the Rachels's ethics textbook; 2012: 14–15). Potentially enlightening parallels between foreign 'cultural practices' and our own thus disappear from view (for the particularly interesting example of parallels between female genital cutting and intersex surgery, see Ehrenreich and Barr 2005 and Feder 2014: 125–128).

By selectively condemning *particular* practices, and by selectively holding up *specific* values, we run the risk of 'disconnect[ing] criticism of [others'] practices from criticism of our own, and turn reflection on other cultures into yet another occasion for celebrating our special virtues' (Tamir 2006). And this can hardly be in the interest of ethicists – regardless of whether and on what level they are committed to pluralism.

COMMUNICATING ETHICS

So far in this chapter, I have tried to map the lack of diversity in philosophy, and suggested that particular stylistic aspects of analytic moral philosophy – the 'treacherous tropes' of the title – might be seen as a result of this lack. These tropes are inimical to a truly pluralistic approach and to the goal of successfully communicating ethics. In this concluding section, I want to encourage a more judicious use of these tropes.

I think that the problems I see in these tropes are interrelated and frequently occur in conjunction – as the trolley cases show. Even the trolley cases embody a certain 'us and them' mentality, in that they ask their audience to put themselves not just in the position of an external observer, but in the position of someone who – for the most whimsical reasons – suddenly gets to decide over a matter of life and death. In that sense, they belittle the historical record of tyrants and torturers who simply take the right to put themselves in that position; and they also belittle the psychological burden on those who have to make such decisions as part of their profession. So what would drive ethicists to cleanse their 'laboratory' of such historical and practical references?

Bernard Williams, arguably more sensitive to the dangers of abstraction than most moral philosophers of his era, also has one such thought experiment of horrific proportions: 'Jim and the Indians' (also to be found in various ethics textbooks, so for instance Singer 1994: 339–345). In this story, a lone traveller by the name of Jim happens upon a scene in a 'native' village where a soldier is about to execute twenty of the 'natives' – unless Jim agrees to kill one of them. Williams intended this story to shed light on issues with utilitarianism, for he believed that the utilitarian answer that Jim should commit murder was too quick. Williams's example is clearly written in a way that encourages the reader to identify with Jim, 'the Indians' appear merely as statistical lives, as nameless accessories. Throughout, there is no awareness of and no mention of historical contexts in which native lives were treated as expendable; and for those who teach this story today, there may well be no consideration of how such an example might affect an audience that does not identify with 'Jim', precisely because the example is meant to tease out a general point. There is a harrowing account of how this particular thought experiment – and the fact that neither her teacher nor her peers seemed to question its setup – 'solidified' a young native student's feeling that she 'did not belong in this classroom, maybe not even in philosophy' (Moontime Warrior 2014). And the proper response to this is not to insist that we might as well talk about any other group of people – for Williams chose to talk about 'Indians', and this is something which, it seems to me, should be made a topic of discussion, rather than be explained away as irrelevant.

None of this is to say that philosophy should avoid the gruesome and the disgusting – after all, many topics in ethics deal with just that. But the gruesome and the disgusting needs to be contextualized, it needs to be more than an interesting theoretical plaything. What bothers me then is a certain kind of flippancy – a certain attitude that seems to say: 'I don't have any stake in it, but it seems so very interesting'. And this flippancy expresses itself in a particular kind of thought experiment, in particular forms of uninspired listicle ethics, and in the kind of selective forgetfulness that informs much of the thinking about cultural differences and ethics.

And it is this flippancy which is one reason why ethics so often fails in its quest for pluralism and diversity, and why ethicists so often have a hard time convincing people outside their academic bubble that what they are doing is relevant. Now I do not think that less of this flippancy in professional ethics will automatically lead to more diversity and to better communication. Nor do I believe that more nominal diversity – which might in the end just boost the status and social capital of those who already control the discourse – should be taken as an end in itself. But I do believe that the issue can and should be framed as a decision-point: ethicists can of course continue doing what they are doing, but then they need to accept that they may not be able to communicate successfully with those who do not already share their specific mode of thinking and arguing.

While the aim of this paper has been, for the most part, negative – an attempt to explain when and why communication fails – I should perhaps end with some concrete suggestions for how to improve the situation. Three of these shall be mentioned by way of a conclusion: In order to reduce the demographic impact on their methodology and their communication, ethicists should:

a. strive to present abstract examples and thought experiments alongside their historical context
b. explicitly acknowledge the historical and cultural context of the mainstream principles and theories in ethics

c. and in this way push back against a tendency to present minority views as merely 'cultural', 'ethnic', or in other ways informed by their proponent's marginalization – they may well be, but that is not in itself any good reason to doubt their epistemic validity and to deny them a place in moral debate.

NOTES

1. In his list of the authors most cited in the Stanford Encyclopedia of Philosophy, Eric Schwitzgebel (2014a) counted just eight women among the top 100, and only one – Martha Nussbaum – ranked in both the top 50 and the top 10. Sally Haslanger (2008: 220) found that the representation of women authors in top anglophone philosophy and ethics journals between 2002 and 2007 consistently ranked well below 20%; and that the representation of topics in feminist philosophy and the philosophy of race in these journals consistently ranked well below 5%.

2. For instance, in the debate about the underrepresentation of women in philosophy, Baron, Dougherty and Miller (2015) have suggested that it can be ascribed to pre-university attitudes, while Paxton, Figdor and Tiberius (2012) have suggested that the reason lies in the content and structure of undergraduate courses in philosophy.

3. In which case we should at least ask how philosophy and ethics can possibly continue to claim universal significance. If the implication here is that it is fine if philosophy is just a scholarly playground for academics with specific background, it would be deeply hypocritical to argue – as many philosophers and ethicists have done – that philosophy should matter to everyone.

4. This attitude is usually displayed by philosophers who want to keep the 'timeless' questions of philosophy separate from their historically contingent instantiations in, for instance, political science or sociology. With this attitude, it is indeed easy to dismiss philosophers who work in 'topical' fields, such as the philosophy of race of feminist epistemology. Elizabeth Barnes has summed up the problem rather nicely in her biographical interview (2015):

> It's pretty bizarre, when you think about it, that someone who spends their time wondering whether tables are real is considered to be working on a foundational area of philosophy, but someone who wonders whether races are real is doing something we consider a niche, 'applied' topic. Likewise, someone who tries to figure out how words like 'might' work is doing something core, and someone who tries to figure out how hate speech works is doing something peripheral.

If I am right with my suspicions here, then applied ethics is caught up in a particularly insidious version of this double bind: It must give clear answers to current issues, but in order to do so, it needs to build upon a universalizable methodology that cannot itself become the focus of analysis; and this need for a universalizable methodology could very well make the discipline insensitive to how its demography affects its methodology.

5. I have done this many times in my own courses, and I still frequently struggle to put together and find materials that challenge the currently dominant ideas about what the canon of the discipline is and which texts count as properly philosophical sources.

6. One should keep in mind that those who so humbly profess to their scepticism may still claim to wield the knowledge that they, at least, know more than anyone else – Socrates is one example, David Hume is another. Hume's famous passage about his sceptical despair in the conclusion of Book 1 of the *Treatise* begins as a verbose complaint about how he has 'expos'd [him]self to the enmity of all metaphysicians, logicians, mathematicians and even theologians [by declaring his] disapprobation of their systems' (Hume 2000: 172).

7. I thank one of the reviewers of this chapter for urging me to stress this point more. The same reviewer also expressed some disappointment that I do not discuss Rawls's construction of the 'original position' here. It is Rawls's best-known 'thought experiment' and much of what I have to say about thought experiments in ethics below also applies to the original position. I will not draw out these parallels here, however – for the sake of brevity, and because I am more interested here in the 'sanitizing effects' of the public–private distinction that pervades Rawls's work.

8. It should be noted that while all of these can be read as direct reactions to Rawls, they differ in whether and to what extent the theorists actually accept the basic tenets of contract theory as worthwhile – Carol Pateman, for instance, does not; Charles Mills does.

9. The term 'intuition pump' was coined by Daniel Dennett; he called it an 'ideal tool in the philosopher's kit' (1984: 18). As my remark here indicates, I am sceptical about this sentiment. While investigating moral intuitions certainly has its use both in the empirical sciences (psychology, sociology) and in moral philosophy, it should not be mistaken for the primary activity of moral and philosophical reflection.

10. And as for persons who do end up in such situations – paramedics, for instance, or soldiers – we may follow David Luban's suggestion (2008: 35) that such decisions are not 'a fact about rationality, or justifiability, or, ultimately, about morality. [They] are a fact about [the persons who make them]'. And perhaps, I might add, a fact about a system that forces them into making these decisions.

11. I thank the other reviewer of my chapter for pointing this out to me and for pushing me to elaborate on this point.

12. This claim, too, would need to be qualified in a longer paper. There is, of course, research in moral psychology and neuroethics that attempts to make its results relevant to questions of teaching, communication and the proper structuring of ethical discourse.

13. All of them appear, for instance, in Russ Shafer-Landau's selection of texts for his companion reader *The Ethical Life* (2012), the complement to his ethics textbook *The Fundamentals of Ethics*.

14. I debated with myself whether I should reference the talk by its title and author here and eventually decided against it – not because I want to deny credit to

an argument just because I happened to find it distasteful, but because this talk, in my mind, is just one symptom of a much larger problem; and this problem – if it indeed is one – should not be pinned on what an individual graduate student chose to do their research on.

15. The term 'trolleyology' was apparently coined by Peter Singer and at least for him did not signify a rejection of this style of doing moral philosophy (O'Connor 2012: 243).

Part II

ETHICS ACROSS RELIGIOUS
AND CULTURAL BORDERS

Chapter 4

'Western' versus 'Islamic' Human Rights Conceptions? A Critique of Cultural Essentialism in the Discussion on Human Rights[1]

Heiner Bielefeldt

A 'WESTERN' CONCEPT?

'Human rights: a Western construct with limited applicability' – this is the polemical title of an article by Adamantia Pollis and Peter Schwab, two representatives of cultural relativism and most outspoken critics of universal human rights (Pollis and Schwab 1979). Pollis and Schwab argue that since human rights originated historically in Western Europe and North America, they are essentially connected – and indeed confined – to the cultural and philosophical concepts of the Occidental tradition. Scholars from various disciplines have expressed similar opinions. The German philosopher Georg Picht, for instance, derives the idea of human rights from ancient Stoicism which, in his opinion, has provided the metaphysical basis for the concepts of human dignity and human rights. Assuming that the particular ideas of Stoic philosophy – ideas that even in Europe are currently losing ground – will hardly ever be endorsed on a global scale, Picht comes to the sceptical conclusion that 'the utopia of a global order of human rights is but an empty illusion' (Picht 1980: 127). Wolfgang Fikentscher, a German lawyer and historian, locates the historic origin of human rights in the sixteenth-century Netherlands, that is, in the context of the Dutch-Protestant liberation movement against the Spanish-Catholic occupation. With regard to the originally Christian motives underneath the Dutch struggle for rights and liberties, Fikentscher asserts ironically that 'the mainly secular-minded "Western" reformers' in third world countries unconsciously propagate Christian values: 'Not knowing what they are doing they actually continue Christian missionary work' (Fikentscher 1987: 64). The most prominent contemporary representative of an essentialistic 'Western' understanding of human rights, however, is Samuel Huntington, the prophet of the danger of a 'clash of civilizations'.

In his global political map, human rights – as well as democracy, liberalism and political secularism – belong exclusively to Western civilization (Huntington 1969). Huntington is convinced that universalism of human rights is bound to fail. For people from other civilizations, he says, the only way to have full access to human rights is to adopt essentially 'Western' values and hence to implicitly convert to Western civilization.

The assumption that human rights are essentially a 'Western' concept can lead to different practical consequences. Cultural relativists, like Pollis and Schwab on the left and Huntington on the right, reject universal human rights as a manifestation of Eurocentric arrogance or as an illusion doomed to collapse. Other scholars, like Fikentscher, seem to defend the idea that the West has a global mission to fulfil. Bassam Tibi even invokes Hegel's metaphor of a 'cunning of reason' to argue that European colonialism, for all its injustice, might also have yielded some positive results. Tibi writes: 'It was, as it were, a byproduct of the European conquest of the world, a byproduct in the sense of the Hegelian "cunning of reason," that the European cultural heritage has been disseminated; and human rights constitute a crucial component of that heritage' (Tibi 1994).

In opposition to essentialistic 'Western' claims of human rights, alternative conceptions have meanwhile been brought forward, conceptions that explicitly claim a non-Western cultural or religious origin. For instance, Muslim authors or organizations have recently published a number of Islamic declarations of human rights which, in their own way, reflect the culturalism inherent in Western essentialistic interpretations, because these Islamic declarations, too, often claim an exclusive cultural and religious heritage of human rights. One of the earliest advocates of this new tendency is Abul A'la Mawdudi, an Islamist author from Pakistan, who vehemently attacks Western arrogance in the context of human rights. Alluding to the history of Western colonialism and imperialism, Mawdudi writes: 'The people in the West have the habit of attributing every good thing to themselves and try to prove that it is because of them that the world got this blessing' (Mawdudi 1976: 13). Against human rights standards of the United Nations, which in Mawdudi's opinion were one-sidedly shaped by 'Western' philosophy, Mawdudi drafts a specifically 'Islamic' conception of human rights based primarily on the Qur'an and the tradition (Sunna) of the prophet Muhammad.

To divide the idea of human rights into 'Western', 'Islamic' and other culturally defined conceptions, however, would be the end of universal human rights. The language of human rights would thus simply be turned into a rhetorical weapon for intercultural competition. In this article I try to find a way out of the predicament of cultural relativism versus cultural imperialism. What is needed, in my opinion, is a critical defence of universal human rights in a way that gives room for different cultural and religious interpretations, and at the same time, avoids the pitfalls of cultural essentialism. In the first (sections 2–5) I investigate the relationship between human rights and what is usually called the 'Western' tradition. I then turn to a discussion of different 'Islamic' interpretations of human rights (sections 6–10). The article concludes with some remarks on human rights as the centre of a cross-cultural 'overlapping consensus' (section 11).

HUMANITARIAN MOTIFS IN EUROPEAN CULTURAL HISTORY

Human rights did certainly not develop in a cultural vacuum. Given that their historic breakthrough took place in North America and Western Europe, there are good reasons to assume that the genesis of the idea of human rights can – in one way or another – be linked to the religious, philosophical and cultural sources of the Occidental tradition. This tradition provides indeed a number of humanitarian, emancipatory, egalitarian and universalistic motifs which might have helped to shape the modern principles of human rights (Oestreich 1978). The fact that a *multiplicity* of such motifs can be identified should, at the same time, remind us that 'the' Occidental tradition is merely an abstract conception covering different, and often antagonistic, currents and movements.

A religious and ethical motif that often has been called a main source of human rights in general is the Biblical idea that all human beings have equally been 'created in the image of God' (Genesis 1:27) and thus been endowed with an unalienable dignity. Referring to the special rank of the human person as an 'image of God', the Bible states that the shedding of human blood must be considered one of the gravest crimes (Genesis 9:6). In Psalm 8 the singer, overwhelmed and struck down by the magnificence of creation, turns to God wondering: 'What is man, that thou art mindful of him? and the son of man, that thou visitest him? For thou hast made him little lower than the angels, and hast crowned him with glory and honour. Thou madest him to have dominion over the works of thy hands; thou hast put all things under his feet' (Psalm 8:4-6). In the New Testament the principle of equality before God supersedes social and ethnic difference. Thus St. Paul emphasizes: 'There is neither Jew nor Greek, there is neither bond nor free, there is neither male nor female: for ye are all one in Christ Jesus' (Galatians 3:28). Comparable ideas of a spiritual unity of all of humanity also occur outside the Jewish-Christian Holy Scriptures, for instance, in the writings of Stoic philosophers. The Roman emperor Marcus Aurelius, one of the most prominent Stoic authors, teaches that the human spirit emerges from divinity. He further points out that all human beings intimately belong together. They constitute one family united not by physical bonds of blood and seed but, primarily, by their common participation in the divine *logos*.[2]

Jewish-Christian as well as Stoic and other motifs have jointly formed the European natural law tradition that stretches from antiquity to modernity. The concept of natural law has different connotations. On the one hand, the natural law tradition claims an unconditional authority of some basic normative principles which are supposed to be prior to human legislation and in this sense 'natural' as opposed to merely artificial. Sophocles's *Antigone* provides an early example of such a conviction by invoking 'unwritten laws' of eternal validity. On the other hand, the concept of natural law also connotes independence from an exclusively theocratic foundation of society and law. In this context, normative principles are thought to be 'natural' in the sense of being understandable without explicit reference to a divine revelation and thus applicable also to people outside of the dominant (i.e. Christian) religious tradition. Under this assumption, Bartolomé de Las Casas, a member of the Dominican order, became an ardent defender of the 'natural rights' of non-Christian Indians in South America. He charged the European *conquistadores* with murder, robbery and genocide, that is, brutal crimes that violate the natural law (Höffner 1975). The natural law tradition has, therefore, often been listed as one of the most important sources of human rights in Western tradition.

Other scholars have located the historic origin of human rights in the Protestant Reformation, an event which Hegel praises as the very birth of modernity and modern freedom. In his philosophy of history he writes that the Reformation is the banner of the free spirit around which the modern nations assemble (Hegel 1986). Three generations after Hegel, Georg Jellinek (in 1895) and Ernst Troeltsch (in 1911) argue that the Protestant emphasis on the individual free conscience as a precondition of authentic faith paved the way historically for the recognition of individual human rights (Jellinke 1974; Troeltsch 1911). Important steps towards human rights can also be seen in the 'Petition of Right' from 1628 and the 'Habeas Corpus Act' from 1679. One of the contributions of the British common law tradition, it has been argued, is the insight that rights require remedies in order to be effective, because 'where there is no remedy, there is no right' (Stourzh 1994: 81).

HUMAN RIGHTS – NO 'NATURAL' RESULT
OF THE OCCIDENTAL TRADITION

It would be easy to add more examples of traditional humanitarian motifs which have been linked to the development of human rights. It would be problematic, however, to claim that these and similar motifs of the Occidental tradition represent immediate historic precursors of the modern idea of human rights. Strictly speaking, these motifs are not 'sources' or 'roots' from which human rights developed more or less naturally. The use of teleological metaphors like 'source' or 'root' harbours the danger of cultural essentialism. The problem is that, from a cultural-essentialist perspective, human rights seem to be rooted in the 'cultural genes' of a particular culture or religion which itself thus seems to be entitled to claim the achievement of human rights as an exclusive legacy. The Indian philosopher Sudipta Kaviraj criticizes such an essentialist attitude towards human rights with the following words:

> While the idea of subjects as bearers of rights existed in a sketchy fashion in premodern history of Europe, these ideas were developed by a specific historical trajectory to produce the modern conception of a civil society and civic rights. Indeed, one danger of reading this too deep into the European past is that this encourages essentialist thinking. Achievement of a civil society then gets associated with a mysterious and indefinable feature of European culture or 'Western spirit', which proves before the debate has begun that it is beyond the cultural means of other societies to create similar institutions. (Kaviraj 1993: 81)

On closer investigation, it becomes in fact evident that the humanitarian motifs mentioned above cannot be identified as premodern equivalents of modern human rights. It is well known, for instance, that the Biblical idea of every person representing an 'image of God' did not go along with demands of equality before the law. Although St. Paul emphasizes spiritual equality between freeman and slave, he never criticizes slavery in social reality but, instead, advises: 'Let every man abide in the same calling wherein he was called' (1 Corinthians 7:20). Paul even sends back the runaway slave Onesimus to his master Philemon.[3] Similarly, Marcus Aurelius, for all his stress on ethical unity of all men within the human family, does not challenge slavery as such. He praises the modesty of his father by saying that he never paid attention to 'the comeliness of his slaves' (Aurelius 1987: 19).

Thomas Aquinas vindicates slavery as a consequence of Adam's and Eve's original sin. Even in paradise, however, Aquinas thinks human beings would have lived in relationships of political domination and subordination. Legal inequality, in his opinion, is not only a feature of the 'postlapsarian' natural law, that is, the situation after the fall of man, but belongs also to the 'prelapsarian' immaculate divine order (Engelhardt 1993). In medieval cosmology inequality – including inequality among human beings in their social and legal status – constitutes the very beauty of the hierarchical order of things. It is clear that in the framework of such a hierarchical worldview, human rights, in the modern sense of rights of equal freedom and participation, are from the outset inconceivable. This hierarchical understanding of creation even affects the medieval meaning of human dignity. It is indeed noteworthy that in medieval philosophy the term 'dignity' is mostly used in the plural, thus indicating the *different dignities* of people, in accordance with their different ranks, order and estates in a feudal society.

One should also avoid overstating the impact of the Protestant Reformation on the historical development of human rights. To be sure, the Reformation marks a turning point in theological reasoning by challenging the clerical hierarchy of the middle ages. Luther's emphasis on the spiritual freedom of every Christian and the spiritual equality of all believers, however, was not meant to call into question the given social and political order. On the contrary, Luther was anxious not to conflate spiritual liberation with political and legal demands, because such a conflation, he feared, would amount to a new legalism which would undermine the liberating theological message of the gospel. Hence, if there is any connection between the Reformation and modern human rights, then it must be an *indirect* one. Ernst Troeltsch indeed emphasizes that it was not mainstream Protestantism but rather the 'step-children of the Reformation', that is, individual dissenters and marginalized Protestant denominations, who paved the way for the adoption of religious liberty in the Anglo-Saxon countries (Troeltsch 1911: 62).

Finally, the English common law tradition does not immediately lead to human rights either. The principal witness in this regard is Edmund Burke who plays off traditional rights of the Englishman against the purportedly abstract universal rights as they were propagated by the French Revolution. Referring to the 1628 'Petition of Right', Burke points out that in the English tradition rights were considered a particular heritage to be passed on from generation to generation: 'In the famous law of the 3rd [year] of Charles I., called the *Petition of Right* the parliament says to the king, 'Your sub-jects have *inherited* this freedom,' claiming their franchises not on abstract principles "as the rights of men," but as the rights of Englishmen, and as a patrimony derived from their forefathers' (Burke 1910: 30). Burke's argu-ment is that rights of freedom can never be created artificially on the basis of universal equality but must be cherished as a particular historic legacy within a particular nation, as a partnership 'between those who are living, those who are dead, and those who are to be born' (Ibid: 93).

Edmund Burke's polemic against the French Revolution is an early exam-ple of the critique of human rights. Not less than the idea of human rights itself, such critique is also part of Western history. In the wake of Burke, Joseph de Maistre ironically professes that he has never seen the subject of human rights, namely, man as such (Valadier 1994). Similarly, Hegel in his critique of the French Revolution vehemently attacks the 'abstractness of lib-eralism' (Hegel 1986: 535). From a left-wing Hegelian point of view, Marx argues that the 1789 French declaration propagates merely the rights of an isolated and selfish individual: 'The human right of freedom is not based on the community of man with man, it is based on the separation of man from man. It is the right of separation, that is, the right of an individual completely confined to himself' (Marx 1970: 364).

Carl Schmitt, a right-wing Hegelian lawyer, also perceives human rights as a manifestation of a bourgeois ideology which undermines communitarian solidarity. Historically linked to a merely private individual morality and to a liberal economy, individual human rights, he says, are an element of disintegration. 'All these elements of disintegration clearly aim at subordinating state and politics either to an individualistic and private morality or to the primacy of economic calculation' (Schmitt 1996: 379). At times, even Hannah Arendt seems to join the critics of human rights. Referring to the situation in refugee camps after the two world wars, she points out that people want to be recognized as members of their particular cultural and political community rather than as abstract human beings (Arendt 1974: 466).

Conservative criticism of human rights used to be a widespread attitude among the Christian churches in Western and Central Europe. Traumatized by anti-clerical radicalism in the Jacobine phase of the French Revolution, the Catholic Church played, for more than a century, the role of the most influential opponent to human rights in general and religious liberty in particular (Hilpert 1999). Starting with Pope Pius' VI letter of protest against the Civil Constitution of the French clergy (1791), a number of anti-liberal Papal documents were published climaxing with the 'Syllabus Errorum' in 1864. In this document Pope Pius IX harshly condemned religious liberty and freedom of the press as examples of the grave errors of the modern era. After a period of a careful rapprochement that started at the end of the nineteenth century, the Catholic Church finally endorsed human rights and religious liberty during the Second Vatican Council, that is, as late as in the 1960s.

The fact that the Catholic Church – as well as other Christian churches – rejected human rights over a considerable period of time indicates that human rights cannot appropriately be described as an 'organic' result of the Occidental history and culture as a whole. Human rights did not develop as a 'natural unfolding' of humanitarian ideas deeply rooted in the cultural and religious traditions of Europe. On the contrary, people in the West, too, had (and still have) to *fight* to have their rights respected. In fighting for their human rights, they faced resistance not only from traditionally privileged groups like the aristocracy or from advocates of an authoritarian state. Anti-liberal currents were also strong among representatives of the churches who feared that the emancipatory spirit of human rights would undermine the moral fabric of Christian society and the hierarchical structure of the clergy. Dieter Senghaas is thus right in rejecting cultural essentialistic interpretation of human rights. These rights he emphasizes are 'achievements brought about in long-lasting political conflicts during the process of modernization in Europe. They are by no means the eternal heritage of an original cultural endowment of Europe' (Senghaas 1994: 112).

RETROSPECTIVE CRITICAL CONNECTION BETWEEN HUMAN RIGHTS AND WESTERN TRADITION

Human rights involve far-reaching normative changes in the understanding of politics and law. Unlike in premodern times, people living in modern societies can no longer resort to more or less unquestioned authoritarian traditions to gain normative orientation. Instead, norms have become an object of active efforts; they are enacted by human legislation and remain open to challenges and critical debates. Habermas, therefore, suggests that human rights belong to a 'posttraditional' normative reasoning which, he says, has replaced traditional forms of ethics rooted in religion or metaphysics (Habermas 1992: 129).

The term 'posttraditional' rightly indicates that normative justification under the circumstances of modernity cannot be achieved simply by conjuring up traditional authorities. And yet the term is misleading, because it can nourish the idea that 'posttraditional' human rights require a rupture from all tradition. This, however, would be a problematic assumption. If human rights were to imply an abstract dichotomy between tradition and modernity, then those who continue to cherish their religious or cultural traditions would be conceptionally excluded from having full access to human rights. In other words, the acceptance of human rights, at least in principle, would be confined to a circle of people who implicitly or explicitly have broken away from their religious, philosophical or cultural traditions. As a result of such a dichotomized view, universal human rights would eventually get lost in an ideology of progress, an ideology perhaps not less exclusivist in its consequences than is the essentialistic equation of human rights with a particular list of exclusively 'Western' or 'Christian' values. Christian or Occidental missionary work would be replaced by a modernist *mission civilisatrice* directed against 'premodern' cultures or worldviews. There are in fact scholars who subscribe to such a dichotomized view. The German philosopher Hans Ebeling, for instance, argues that people representing 'premodern' cultures and religions, in particular Muslims, should be excluded from immigration and political participation in European societies (Ebeling 1994). Alluding to the battle between Tours and Poitiers (732) in which the Franconians repelled the Muslim invasion, Ebeling calls for a new intellectual battle of Western modernity against the influx of 'premodern' Muslim immigrants and asylum seekers who, he thinks, are currently conquering Western societies (Ibid: 75).

Against such an abstract dichotomy of tradition and 'posttraditional' human rights, I would argue that human rights can meaningfully and productively be connected with different traditions. Once again, the Catholic Church provides an illuminating example. After a long period of reluctance if not resistance, the Catholic Church finally did endorse human rights and religious liberty (Hilpert 1991). The Second Vatican Council's declaration *Dignitatis humanae* (1965) explicitly appreciates the modern understanding of human dignity based on the recognition of human freedom and responsibility. Even though the Vatican Council's declaration clearly marks a turning point within the history of the church, it is not meant to be a total rupture from the Catholic tradition. Rather, the church considers human rights to be a modern way of protecting that unconditional dignity of every human being which has always been a part of the Christian message. The church's commitment on behalf of human rights, albeit a rather recent development, thus appears to remain in keeping with the Christian tradition, more precisely: with a revised and modernized version of Christian tradition more appropriate for Christians living under the circumstances of modernity. The idea of the person being an 'image of God', Christian conceptions of the natural law, the old insight that authentic faith requires a free decision – these and other motifs allow building a bridge between tradition and modern human rights which themselves thus need not appear to be a merely external imposition.

Protestant denominations today also understand and foster human rights as a consequence of Biblical commands and Christian impulses. In 1977 the churches of the Lutheran World Federation held a conference in which they claimed that secular human rights can be appreciated from the perspective of the Christian Reformation, because 'it was the intention of the reformers that man should learn to let God be God, in order that man himself might become man, and the world remain the world'(Lutheran World Federation 1977: 41). The working papers published by The World Association of Reformed Churches in 1976 point to the right of resistance as a contribution of the Calvinistic tradition to the development of human rights (Moltmann and Lochmann 1976: 66). Connecting human rights with humanitarian elements of the Western tradition, of course, is not a privilege of Christians only. One can also refer to ancient Greek philosophy, the Renaissance, the English principle of the 'rule of law', the early modern Enlightenment, and other currents in Western history which, in one way or another, provide occasions for an 'inculturation' of human rights. Given such possibilities of inculturation, human rights are certainly not 'posttraditional' in the sense of being simply disconnected from cultural or religious tradition.

It would be problematic, however, if this inculturation were to go along with claims to an exclusive cultural heritage, claims that may follow from a teleological view of history, as criticized above by Kaviraj. When looking back into the past, we easily become 'Hegelians' who regard the chain of historic events as entailing a concealed plan of history, a plan according to which antiquity harbours the 'cultural genes' of what later ripened and finally culminated in the modern era. Modern democracy thus appears to have its 'roots' in the ancient Greek Polis. Likewise, modern standards of human rights seem to be grounded in the basic sources of Occidental culture, religion and philosophy at large. And even modern secularism is often traced back to the Bible, for instance, to the word of Jesus: 'Render unto Cesar the things which are Cesar's and unto God the things that are God's' (Matthew 22:21). Such a Hegelian way of thinking easily leads to the assumption that what is 'rooted' in the original sources of a particular culture can legitimately be claimed as an exclusive heritage of that culture. Against such an essentialistic appropriation, it is necessary to reflect on the contingency of human history, a history that does not develop in the way of a 'natural unfolding' of a pre-existing cultural potential. Recalling this contingency of human history would be a first step towards abandoning the essentialistic appropriation of human rights which themselves cannot simply and exclusively be deduced from the 'genes' of any particular culture.

One should also be aware of the hermeneutic standpoint from which we look at history. Connecting human rights to humanitarian elements within religious, philosophical or cultural tradition is possible only from the standpoint of modernity. It is *from a modern standpoint* that we can discover traditional humanitarian motifs which allow building a bridge between the present and the past. It is *in retrospective* that we see an analogy between modern ideas of human dignity and the Biblical message of the person being an image of God. *By looking back into the past*, we can trace the genesis of the rule of law to the 1215 'Magna Carta' and other medieval or ancient documents. *In retrospective* it may also make sense to compare modern principles of freedom and equality to Luther's doctrine of the free religious conscience and the spiritual equality of all believers before God. And it is even possible to connect *retrospectively* secular human rights to aspects of a desacralization of the cosmos which can be found already in the Bible. Generally speaking, hermeneutic awareness should teach us that the above-mentioned traditional ideas are not 'roots' or 'sources' which harbour the potential of modern human rights, a potential that gradually ripened in history. It is the other way around in that the modern idea of human rights characterizes the standpoint from which we can *retrospectively* discover humanitarian motives that facilitate a critical reconstruction of aspects of continuity between the present and the past.

In such a hermeneutical retrospective, not only aspects of continuity, but also experiences of discontinuity and change should be taken into consideration. Down to the present day, the Christian churches have a tendency not to pay sufficient attention to the changes they had to undergo to be able to endorse human rights and religious liberty. Rather than ignoring or harmonizing traditional conflicts, however, it would be more appropriate to acknowledge the fact that the recognition of human rights on the part of the churches is the result of a complicated and lengthy learning process (Hilpert 1991). A self-critical reflection of this learning process – including all the misunderstandings, polemics and reforms inevitably involved in such a process – would provide an excellent basis for inter-religious and intercultural dialogue on human rights.

THE EUROPEAN HISTORY OF HUMAN RIGHTS AS AN EXAMPLE

Back to the initial question: Are human rights 'a Western construct with limited applicability', to quote Pollis and Schwab? Obviously, the answer depends on what we understand by the 'Western origin' of human rights. I have argued that human rights are neither a natural result of European culture and history nor completely disconnected from the Occidental tradition. On the one hand, the idea of human rights is not 'Western' in the emphatic sense of the word as if this idea was deeply rooted in the genes of the Occidental culture at large. On the other hand, the endorsement of human rights does not require us to abandon tradition altogether and to take a 'posttraditional' standpoint, a standpoint from which 'the West' would be merely a geographical term without any cultural meaning. Rather, the 'Western origin' of human rights means the simple fact that the idea of universal rights of freedom and equality, as far as we know, was first proclaimed in Western Europe and North America. By investigating this historic fact more closely, we can discover various factors – political, economic, cultural and religious – which in one way or another might have helped to foster the development of human rights. These factors, undoubtedly, also include important currents of the philosophical and religious tradition in the West. One should bear in mind, however, that the historic breakthrough of human rights took place at a time when the traditional European society was in a deep *crisis*, a crisis triggered by the split of European Christendom in the wake of the Reformation as well as by decades of civil wars between conflicting religious and political factions. Crisis of tradition does not necessarily mean a decline or even loss of tradition. What it does imply, however, is a serious transformation of tradition. Experiences of structural injustice – civil wars, religious intolerance, arbitrary detentions and other acts of state oppression – demonstrated the urgency of far-reaching political and cultural reforms. Thus people gradually learned how to achieve peaceful coexistence and cooperation in a modern pluralist society on the basis of equal freedom and participation, that is, in the normative framework of human rights and democracy.

The modern awareness of freedom has its ethical core in the profession of human dignity. Understanding human dignity in Kantian terms as moral autonomy and connecting this autonomy to universal rights of freedom and participation is certainly a specifically modern achievement (Bielefeldt 1997). For all the novelty of universal human rights, however, the underlying profession of dignity can at the same time be meaningfully connected to the Bible, to Stoic philosophy, as well as to other founding documents of what we usually call the Western tradition. Although human rights cannot simply be derived from this tradition in a deductivistic or essentialistic way, they are certainly not 'posttraditional' in the sense that all connection between modern rights conceptions and traditional ethical principles must be severed.

Two systematic insights can be gained from looking at the European history of human rights, insights that can be helpful for a cross-cultural normative dialogue. On the one hand, European history shows that people fighting for their basic rights often faced a lot of *resistance*. This resistance was not only a political one, but also included cultural and religious opposition epitomized, for instance, by the Christian churches which over a considerable period of time were quite reluctant to support modern principles of political emancipation. On the other hand, European history also shows that a critical *reconciliation* between modernity and tradition was possible, a reconciliation which today clearly includes the churches, meanwhile often ardent advocates of human rights.

The history of human rights in the West is neither a binding 'model' which allows us to make forecasts about the prospects of human rights in other parts of the world; nor should this Western history be covered by a 'veil of ignorance' on behalf of a purportedly neutral standpoint in cross-cultural debates. Rather, the history of human rights in the West gives us an *example* – not the paradigm *per se*, but merely an example – of the various obstacles, misunderstandings, learning processes, achievements and failures in the long-lasting struggle for human rights. Such a self-critical historic perspective may enhance our sensitivity for the problems and opportunities, be they different or similar, which human rights advocates are facing in 'non-Western' cultural contexts, too.

Perhaps even more importantly, a self-critical attitude of Europeans and North Americans towards their own complex and complicated history of human rights is also a necessary precondition for overcoming the suspicion, on the part of many people, that by fighting for human rights 'Westerners' simply try to impose their own cultural values and norms in an imperialistic fashion. This suspicion is widespread in Muslim countries whose populations historically suffered from European colonialism and, in many cases, still feel threatened by Western imperialism. In the face of such widespread mistrust, it seems all the more important to make it clear that human rights do not constitute a set of essentially Western values that are to be exported on a global scale. Rather, what underlies human rights are experiences of structural injustice culminating in those 'barbarous acts' which, as the 1948 Universal Declaration of Human Rights emphasizes in its preamble, 'have outraged the conscience of mankind'. Taking seriously this fundamental experience requires us to embark on a common learning process towards establishing efficient human rights mechanisms, a learning process in which claims of cultural legacies should cease to play a dominant political role.

CONFLICTS BETWEEN *SHARIA* AND HUMAN RIGHTS

It is a trivial observation that religion constitutes merely *one* component within a whole range of political, economic, social and cultural factors which inhibit or foster the implementation of human rights. When it comes to Islamic countries, however, this truism seems worth recalling, because Islamic religion and culture are often portrayed as being the chief obstacle to an improvement of the troubling human rights situation in some of these countries. Against such a one-sided view, Sigrid Faath and Hanspeter Mattes have pointed out that most of the human rights violation that they have analysed in North Africa do not show specifically 'Islamic' features (Faath and Mattes 1992: 133).

On the other hand, one can hardly deny that the relationship between Islam and human rights is complicated and raises a number of problems. These problems do not derive from Islam *per se* but have to do with the Islamic *sharia*, more precisely: with traditional or fundamentalistic interpretations of the *sharia* by which the latter is rendered a comprehensive system of politically enforceable normative regulations. Given the fact that the basic features of the *sharia* developed in the first centuries of Islamic history (Coulson 1964) whereas the historical breakthrough of human rights was roughly a millennium later, differences and conflicts between these two normative systems can be no surprise. Concrete conflicts centre primarily around questions of gender equality and religious liberty. Although acknowledging woman's legal personality, the traditional *sharia* did not include the principle of *equality in rights* for men and women. It is especially in matters of marriage, family life, divorce and inheritance that differences in legal standing between the genders have persisted to the present day. Measured against the benchmark of modern human rights, they must be regarded as discriminating against women.[4] Further, despite the Islamic tradition of religious tolerance, some forms of discrimination against religious minorities – such as restrictions on inter-religious marriages – are still legally in force in most contemporary Islamic countries today. Another infringement on religious liberty stems from the *sharia* ban on 'apostasy'. There is a minority of Islamic countries – like Iran, Sudan and Saudi Arabia – in which apostates from Islam are threatened by capital punishment. But even in those more 'moderate' countries in which the death penalty for conversion from Islam to another religion no longer exists, other legal sanctions – including enforced dissolution of the convert's marriage – run counter to the human right to adopt a religion on the basis of a person's free decision.[5] Beside these problems of gender equality and religious liberty, a minority among Islamic states apply *sharia* criminal law, including corporal punishment like flogging or amputation of limbs, penalties which from the standpoint of human rights must be rejected as cruel and degrading (Abu-Sahlieh 1994).

Facing these conflicts the question arises as to whether and how practical solutions can be achieved. With regard to this question, different positions are currently being brought forward. Despite many overlaps, one can distinguish between four basic positions which I have labelled Islamization of human rights, pragmatic approaches, liberal reconceptualization of the *sharia* and secular positions.[6]

'ISLAMIZATION' OF HUMAN RIGHTS

One way of dealing with the relationship between Islamic *sharia* and human rights is simply to deny that there are any problems. Representatives of the traditionalist or fundamentalist currents of Islam typically claim that human rights have always been recognized in the Islamic *sharia* which, due to its divine origin, provides an absolute foundation for protecting the rights and duties of every human being. An early example of this tendency is the booklet *Human Rights in Islam* written by Abu l-A'la Mawdudi. While adopting modern rights language, Mawdudi never addresses critically the above-mentioned conflicts between *sharia* and human rights. Moreover, his section on 'equality of human beings' reveals a rather restricted understanding of equality. Whereas Mawdudi rejects 'all distinctions based on colour, race, language or nationality' (Mawdudi 1976: 13), his list of criteria of non-discrimination does not include gender and religion, the two main issues over which traditional *sharia* and modern human rights collide. Mawdudi's approach, after all, leads to a superficial and uncritical 'Islamization' of human rights, that is, an ideological conception which is certainly not less essentialistic than essentialistic 'Western' or 'Christian' readings of human rights. The widespread tendency in Western concepts of human rights to claim that these rights have their 'roots' in the Occidental tradition can thus analogously be found in essentialistic Islamic interpretations that trace human rights back to Qur'an and Sunna.

A radical example of an essentialistic Islamic occupation of the concept of human rights was given by some Iranian participants of the fourth German–Iranian conference on human rights which took place in November 1994 in Tehran. At the opening of the conference, Ayatollah Taskhiri from the holy city of Ghom presented a conservative Islamic conception of human rights from which he drew the conclusion that a full understanding of these rights must be reserved to faithful Muslims. In his exclusivistic and dogmatic approach the Ayatollah compromised even the idea of universal human dignity by distinguishing between a 'potential' and an 'actual' dignity. Assuming that all human beings are called upon to lead a virtuous life well-pleasing to God, all humans, he said, are 'potentially' equal in their human dignity. However, it was clear to Taskhiri that he who fulfils his duty faithfully can ultimately claim a higher degree of 'actual' dignity than he who fails to meet the religious standard – let alone he who refuses to accept his divine vocation altogether. This is to say that such a dogmatic type of reference to a divine foundation of human dignity leads to a concept of dignity which, in sharp contradiction to Article 1 of the Universal Declaration of Human Rights, serves as a vindication of human inequality rather than justifying universal equality of all humans in dignity and freedom.

Such a tendency of an essentialistic 'Islamization' of human rights has meanwhile found expression in a number of semi-official documents on human rights issued by various Islamic organizations.[7] For instance, the final theses of a seminar on Human Rights in Islam held in 1980 in Kuwait include the following statement: 'Islam was the first to recognise basic human rights and almost fourteen centuries ago it set up guarantees and safeguards that have only recently been incorporated in universal declarations of human rights' (Human Rights in Islam 1992: 9). Likewise, the Introduction to the Universal Islamic Declaration of Human Rights, issued in 1981 by the Islamic Council of Europe, a non-governmental organization sponsored by Saudi Arabia, starts as follows: 'Fourteen hundred years ago, Islam gave to humanity an ideal code of human rights'.[8]

A more recent example of this essentialist tendency is the declaration of Human Rights in Islam, adopted by the foreign ministers of the Organization of the Islamic Conference at the 1990 annual session of the OIC held in Cairo (Müller 1996). The central role of the Islamic *sharia* as both the frame of reference and the guideline of interpretation of the Cairo Declaration manifests itself throughout the document, especially in its two final articles which state: 'All the rights and freedoms stipulated in this Declaration are subject to the Islamic *sharia*'. 'The Islamic *sharia* is the only source of reference for the explanation or clarification of any of the articles of this Declaration'

(Cairo Declaration 1991). In article 1 the Cairo Declaration emphasizes that all human beings are 'equal in terms of basic human dignity and basic obligations and responsibilities, without any discrimination on the grounds of race, colour, language, sex, religious belief, political affiliation, social status or other considerations'. This concept of equality goes beyond Mawdudi's and Taskiri's understanding and yet remains vague, because equality in dignity is not clearly connected to claims of equal *rights*. The same problem comes to the fore in article 6 of the Cairo Declaration. While stressing equal dignity of men and women, the article concludes with a statement that seems to support the traditional role division between husband and wife: 'The husband is responsible for the support and welfare of the family'. What is striking in article 5, which also deals with family matters, is the formulation that the right to marry and build a family should not be restricted according to criteria 'stemming from race, colour or nationality'. What is missing in this formulation is a rejection of restrictions based on religious difference. Thus, traditional *sharia* obstacles to inter-religious marriages remain unchallenged. Even more troubling is article 10 which not only gives Islam a privileged status superior to all other religions, but also seems to ban missionary work among Muslims. The article reads as follows: 'Islam is the religion of unspoiled nature. It is prohibited to exercise any form of compulsion on man or to exploit his poverty or ignorance in order to convert him to another religion or to atheism'. Protection of the Islamic religion, as demanded by traditional *sharia* interpretations, thus apparently prevails over religious freedom of the individual as well as over the principle of equality of different religions. In short: the Cairo Declaration amounts to a one-sided and uncritical Islamization of human rights language, at the expense of both the universalism and the emancipatory spirit of human rights.

PRAGMATIC REFORMS IN THE FRAMEWORK
OF THE *SHARIA*

If conservative Muslims are frequently reluctant to undertake an open criticism of the traditional *sharia,* this does not mean that changes towards modern human rights are completely excluded. From early on, Islamic scholars had to face the problem that legal norms and institutions of non-Islamic origin played a role, sometimes an important one, in Muslim societies. To deal with this situation, legal elements of non-Islamic origin had to be integrated into the overarching framework of the *sharia*, for instance, by referring to some general principles such as that of common welfare (*maslaha*). Whatever seemed to be useful for society could thus be justified as being in accordance with, and indeed part of, the *sharia*. At the same time, those elements of the *sharia* whose implementation could lead to undesired consequences were suspended pragmatically. It was argued that a full and thorough implementation of the *sharia* could be enacted only under ideal circumstances as it was the case in the original Muslim community of Medina. As Joseph Schacht has observed: 'As long as the sacred Law received formal recognition as a religious ideal, it did not insist on being fully applied in practice' (Schacht 1964: 84). Thus, except for some 'puritan' *sharia* schools, flexible interpretation and pragmatic application of the normative rules have always accommodated moderate reforms. As a result, within most *sharia* schools a tradition of humanitarian pragmatism has developed which facilitates a mediation between the validity claims based on religious revelation and the practical necessities of daily life. The Qur'an itself seems to justify this attitude, because *Sura* 2:185 emphasizes: 'God intends every facility for you; he does not want to put you to difficulties'. The humanitarian pragmatism, which is typical of large currents within Islam today, also permits taking steps towards a gradual reconciliation with modern ideas of freedom and equality, even though the conceptual differences between *sharia* and human rights may yet remain unsettled.

With regard to amputation penalties, for instance, many Muslims refer to a precedent enacted by the second caliph Omar who is said to have suspended amputation for theft in times of starvation (Said 1989). From this precedent even conservative Muslims often conclude that such cruel forms of corporal punishments should not be applied in practice unless and until a perfectly just society will be achieved. That is to say that even those Muslims who do not deny the *validity* of the harsh *sharia* penalties in theory, frequently reject their *applicability* by invoking insuperable obstacles to their practical implementation. Such a way of reasoning is not thoroughly new. As Schacht emphasizes, there has always been 'a strong tendency to restrict the applicability of *hadd* punishments [i.e. the punishment based on divine guidance] as much as possible' (Schacht 1964: 176). To achieve this goal, traditional *sharia* schools introduced narrow definitions of the crimes in question, short statutes of limitation, and extremely high evidentiary requirements. The fact that the vast majority of contemporary Islamic states do not list *sharia* penalties in their criminal codes does not seem to pose a problem for the Islamic population at large. On the contrary, many Muslims, including moderate conservatives, hold the opinion that the cruel forms of corporal punishment mentioned in the Qur'an are meant to be an ethical admonition and should be no part of an applicable criminal code (Mayer 1993).

Pragmatic interpretation of the *sharia* has also helped to bring about a tradition of religious tolerance. To be sure: this traditional Islamic tolerance should not be equated with religious liberty in the modern understanding of human rights, because traditional tolerance does not imply *equality* of rights.

But still it is worth emphasizing that 'the Muslim world, when judged by the standard of the day, generally showed far greater tolerance and humanity in its treatment of religious minorities than did the Christian West', as Ann Mayer has observed (Ibid: 148). Although in theory only the 'people of the book', that is, adherents of the monotheistic religions of revelation, could count on being tolerated, in practice coexistence between Muslims and members of other religions – for instance, the Hindu religions in India – proved also possible (Mottahedeh 1993). Although in theory apostasy was considered a capital crime, there are few examples of executions of apostates in recent Islamic history. During the Ottoman Empire, the last death penalty for apostasy was reportedly carried out in 1843 (Johansen 1986). When in January 1985 Mahmoud Muhammad Taha, a Sudanese Muslim reformer, was publicly executed as a 'heretic', many Muslims in Sudan were shocked. As Ann Mayer reports: 'Outrage and disgust over the execution and televised heresy trial prevailed, even among Sudanese Muslims who had no personal sympathy for Taha's theological positions' (Mayer 1993: 186).

Pragmatic reforms are even possible in the delicate issues of *sharia* family law. In his study on 'Law Reform in the Muslim World', James Norman Anderson has presented a number of impressive examples in this field. The 1917 Ottoman Law of Family Rights, for instance, was meant to curb polygamy by officially recognizing stipulations which, on a voluntary basis, could be inserted into a marriage contract, in order to bestow the wife with the right to judicial divorce in case that her husband took a second wife.[9] Again, whereas the theoretical *validity* of polygamy remained unchallenged, the *practice* of polygamy could be restricted to a certain degree. At the same time, this reform slightly improved women's opportunities to go to court in order to get a judicial divorce. It may be worth mentioning in this context that already at the end of the nineteenth century the famous Muslim reformer Mohammed Abduh argued that the Qur'an prohibits polygamy implicitly, because the theoretical permission to marry more than one wife depends on the prerequisite that the husband can do justice to all his wives (*Sura* 4:3), a prerequisite which according to the Qur'an itself can hardly ever be met: 'Try as you may, you cannot treat all your wives impartially' (*Sura* 4:129) (Esposito 1991: 51). This is another example that new interpretations of the *sharia* can lead to gradual reforms without denying the validity claims of traditional *sharia* in theory.

CRITICAL RECONCEPTUALIZATION OF THE *SHARIA*

Although the possibilities of pragmatic reforms within the framework of the *sharia* should be taken into consideration, one should also be aware of the limits of such a pragmatic approach. As long as the superiority of the *sharia* as a divine and inalterable set of legal norms is unchallenged in theory, the legitimacy of human rights remains precarious. Either human rights suffer from the failure of not being considered legitimate in the full sense of the word, or the danger arises that conceptual differences between *sharia* law and human rights are simply harmonized with the result of an 'Islamized' version of human rights.

Liberal Muslim intellectuals therefore do not content themselves with suggesting merely pragmatic reforms. What they demand is a courageous and frank criticism of the Islamic *sharia*, a criticism which – though not necessarily calling for the dismembering of the *sharia* tradition – is meant to lead to a thoroughly revised understanding of the main sources of the *sharia*, namely, *Qur'an* and *Sunna*. Liberal reformers argue that by means of such a critical examination the *sharia* can be liberated from the bulk of medieval legal casuistry which, in the course of time, has unjustifiably overshadowed the essential normative message of *Qur'an* and *Sunna* (Mahmasani 1982).

With regard to Qur'an and Sunna, Fazlur Rahman points to the progressive tendencies embodied in the original normative guidance of Islam, tendencies that later have been lost, to a large degree. What is therefore needed, he argues, is not blind or passive submission to given legalistic rules, but instead an active and responsible type of obedience that tries to capture the deeper meaning of the Qur'anic principles and apply them to the ever changing needs and circumstances of human society. Rahman writes that

> whereas the spirit of the Qur'anic legislation exhibits an obvious direction towards the progressive embodiment of the fundamental human values of free-dom and responsibility in fresh legislation, nevertheless the actual legislation of the Qur'an had partly to accept the then existing society as a term of reference. This clearly means that the actual legislation of the Qur'an cannot have been meant to be literally eternal by the Qur'an itself. (Rahman 1966: 39)

Some reformers go a step farther by calling into question the mainly juridi-cal connotations of the *sharia*. Muhammad Said al-Ashmawy, a well-known Egyptian judge, points out that the term *sharia* etymologically does not mean 'law' or 'jurisprudence'; it originally means something like 'the path to the source in the desert', which is a metaphor for religious and ethical guidance in the broadest sense (al-Ashmawy 1989: 124–125) Ashmawy therefore insists that the *sharia* not be equated with traditional jurisprudence (*fiqh*), as often happens. He even accuses those who blur the line between revelatory guidance and historic jurisprudence of coming close to polytheism, because they dilute the uniqueness of divine revelation by mixing it with the results of human legislation and human jurisprudence (Ibid: 101). By distinguishing clearly between *sharia* and *fiqh*, the body of norms that has usually been called 'Islamic law' can be analysed as a result of human history with all its contingencies. This opens up the conceptual space for historic criticism as well as political reforms in accordance to democratic principles and modern standards of human rights.

Liberal Muslims further argue that the principles of human rights and democracy can be connected meaningfully with the spirit of the *sharia* – provided that the *sharia* is primarily understood as an ethical and religious concept rather than a legalistic one. The Qur'an, which is the main source of the *sharia*, repeatedly emphasizes the dignity of the human person. According to *Sura* 2:30, God has called upon Adam to act as his deputy (*khalifa*) on earth, thus giving him a special rank above all other creatures. God even commands that the angels bow down before man (*Sura* 2:34). Along a similar line, *Sura* 17:70 emphasizes that God has honoured the children of Adam. *Sura* 33:72 tells the story that when God, at the very beginning of time, offered a divine trust (*amana*) to the heavens, the earth and the mountains, they all shrank back from accepting it, because they were frightened by this offer. By contrast man, though being frail and vulnerable, proved courageous enough to take on the divine trust voluntarily, thus showing himself superior to the most mighty things of nature, including heaven and earth.[10] Riffat Hassan, an Islamic feminist, reads these and other verses of the Qur'an as an Islamic foundation of the dignity of every person as 'an end in itself' as she puts it using Kantian terms (Hassan 1992).

A very courageous and, at the same time, highly controversial interpretation of the Qur'an has been proposed by the Sudanese scholar Abdullahi An-Na'im. Taking up a method developed by his teacher Mahmoud Muhammad Taha, An-Na'im distinguishes systematically between suras revealed in Mecca und suras revealed in Medina. This difference has always been acknowledged in Islamic exegesis. What is new in An-Na'im's approach, however, is that he understands the two stages of revelation as entailing a theological ranking: Whereas the suras of the Mecca period contain the eternal theological message of Islam, the Medina parts of the Qur'an mostly refer to the specific needs and circumstances of the first Muslim community and cannot be immediately applied to modern society (An-Na'im 1990). Although An-Na'im does not deny the divine character of the Qur'an in its entirety, he introduces a criterion by which he can distinguish between different degrees of validity within the Qur'an itself. Whereas, in An-Na'im's opinion, some Qur'anic principles are indeed of timeless validity, others contain rules that can be appreciated as *examples* of an Islamic way of life within a particular historic context without being immediately binding for Muslims today. In such a way An-Na'im wants to develop a modern version of Islamic law that is to be in accordance with international standards of human rights.

An-Na'im is not the only contemporary Muslim scholar who calls for a new hermeneutic approach to reading the Qur'an – although there are few who share his specific methodology. Fazlur Rahman, for instance, criticizes the common exegesis of the Qur'an as 'piecemeal, ad hoc, and often quite extrinsic' (Rahman 1982: 4). Making use of modern hermeneutics to achieve a more subtle understanding of the text is therefore an urgent need. Norani Othman, a representative of the Malaysian 'Sisters in Islam', a liberal Islamic NGO committed to promoting women's rights, points to the difference between the time of revelation and the present day, a difference that must always be taken into consideration for an appropriate understanding of the Qur'anic text to be possible. She writes:

> We in the present have to read those texts in order to understand them at all; but in seeking to understand them we – like all Muslims throughout history – bring to our own reading of those past texts the frameworks of understanding of our own time and place. We hear the past voices that speak to us speaking with contemporary accents, as it were – our own. So we are always, like all the great *ulama* of the past – even if they were not aware of it – both reading the present back into the past from which we seek contemporary guidance, and also left with the problem ... of deciding *how* we are now to implement or proceed upon that understanding. (Othman 1994: 128)

The awareness of historic distance, Norani Othman argues, is a way to do justice to the Qur'anic text. At the same time, this hermeneutic awareness helps to fight the temptation to simply 'apply' purportedly timeless Qur'anic principles to the different circumstances of a society at the threshold of the twenty-first century.

The Egyptian professor Nasr Hamid Abu Zaid thinks along similar lines. The purpose of his proposal of a new hermeneutics is to recapture critically the guiding principles of the Qur'an out of those many historical details which belong to the circumstances of revelation but do not constitute the essential message of the Qur'an. In this way he wants to bring to new life the spirit of justice which, in his opinion, lies at the core of the Qur'anic ethical principles. Among other things Abu Zaid calls for reforms in the field of Islamic inheritance law, because he thinks the general tendency of Qur'anic justice is to foster equality among all human beings. What matters for Abu Zaid is that the Qur'an endows women with dignity and respect, thus giving them a legal standing that they did not enjoy in pre-Islamic times. Concrete details, such as the difference between men and women in their heritage claims, however, should be seen as a historically contextualized application of this general tendency. These historic details should therefore not prevent modern Muslims from going further in the general direction of justice and equality as demanded by the Qur'an (Abu Zaid 1996).

A decidedly feminist reading of the Qur'an has been proposed by Riffat Hassan. She refers primarily to the strict monotheistic creed that constitutes the theological centre of Islam. In the light of the Islamic warning that the transcendence of the divine creator must never be amalgamated with His creation, Riffat Hassan argues that the invocation of God as a pretext to legitimize earthly power relations must be rejected as a violation of Islam. In particular she attacks the traditional hierarchy between the genders that has often provided the husband with almost a quasi-divine authority. According to Hassan, this religious justification of social authority borders on blasphemy. She thus points out sarcastically: 'The husband, in fact, is regarded as his wife's gateway to heaven or hell and the arbiter of her final destiny. That such an idea can exist within the framework of Islam – which totally rejects the idea of redemption, of any intermediary between a believer and the Creator – represents both a profound irony and a great tragedy' (Hassan 1982: 63). Riffat Hassan's argumentation demonstrates that the Islamic doctrine of strict monotheism, a doctrine from which fundamentalist authors like Mawdudi derive authoritarian political consequences, can also be understood in an emancipatory sense in that monotheism provides a theological basis for challenging absolute power relations between human beings.

It is also with reference to the monotheistic creed that Mohamed Talbi, a Tunisian scholar and committed human rights advocate, calls for a full implementation of religious liberty, beyond the limits of traditional Islamic tolerance. He is convinced that respect for the inscrutable divine will implies respect for one's fellow humans' inner convictions; for no one can pretend to know God's plan with the individual person. Talbi comes to the conclusion that 'from a Muslim perspective ... religious liberty is fundamentally and ultimately an act of respect for God's Sovereignty and for the mystery of His plan for man, who has been given the terrible privilege of building on his own responsibility his destiny on earth and for the hereafter. Finally, to respect man's freedom is to respect God's plan' (Talbi 1991: 31).

POLITICAL SECULARISM IN ISLAM

Islamic monotheism has also been taken up as an argument for promoting a secular understanding of law and politics. Political secularism is currently not a popular position in most Islamic countries (Wielandt 1982). Even liberal Muslims mostly show reluctance to endorsing secularist concepts which they often associate with an anti-religious ideology. In general, there seems to be little awareness in the Islamic context about the fundamental difference between a political secularism based on religious liberty, on the one hand, and an ideological form of secularism that aims at banning religion from the public space, on the other hand (Bielefeldt 1996). Nevertheless, there are a number of Muslim thinkers who explicitly plea on behalf of secular political and legal reforms by referring to genuinely theological arguments.

One of the first advocates of political secularism in Islam was Ali Abdarraziq, a professor of the prestigious Al-Azhar University in Cairo, who in his famous book on 'Islam and the Bases of Power' [original: 1925] (Abdarraziq 1934) welcomed the abolishment of the caliphate, an event that had stirred emotions throughout the Islamic world. Abdarraziq points to the fact that the Qur'an does not contain any detailed guidance as to how to build and govern a state. If it is true that the Qur'an is the final and complete book of revelation, as faithful Muslims assume, then it follows that state politics cannot belong to the core message of Islam. Consequently, Abdarraziq draws a clear conceptual distinction between the prophetic and the political role of Muhammad.

Taking up Abdarraziq's line of thought, Said al-Ashmawy calls the confusion of religion and state politics a 'perversity' (al-Ashmawy 1989: 11) because it is destructive to both: it debases religion by rendering it an instrument of everyday power politics, and it results necessarily in a problematic sacralization of politics, which itself is thereby shielded against critical public discourse. Whereas theocracy, in which earthly rulers claim a quasi-divine authority, comes close to polytheism, the monotheistic dogma of Islam, according to Ashmawy, demands a clear conceptional and institutional distinction between state and religion. This distinction opens up the space for political and legal reforms on behalf of human rights whose basic normative idea, the recognition of every person's unalienable dignity, at the same time fits together with the ethical teachings of the Qur'an (Ibid).

Fouad Zakariya, another Egyptian author, unmasks the antithesis of 'divine law' versus 'human law' as an ideological construction. Those who conjure up divine law to legitimize their own political positions and interests actually are and remain finite human beings. However, they refuse to recognize their finiteness and to submit their political projects to an open democratic discourse and criticism. Zakariya writes

> The real alternative is not one between divine law ... and human law. It is the alternative between two versions of human law one of which admits frankly to be human whereas the other version pretends to speak in the name of divine revelation. This latter version of human law is dangerous because it tends to base its particular positions on divine law, thus attributing to its passions and errors a sacredness and infallibility to which is has no title. (Zakaria 1989: 115)

In contrast to such an ideological occupation of divine law, political secularism tries to do justice to the finite nature of human beings. At the same time, political secularism can be understood as an expression of respect for the transcendence of the one God whose inscrutable will must never be instrumental for the purposes of power politics.

CONCLUSION: TOWARDS A CROSS-CULTURAL 'OVERLAPPING CONSENSUS' ON HUMAN RIGHTS

Both in Western and Islamic countries, human rights have become a matter of debate and controversy. The multiplicity of positions voiced in this debate range from liberalism to conservatism, from libertarianism to socialism and from theocratic claims to outspoken secular ideas. Hence there is no such thing like *the* Western or *the* Islamic conception of human rights. Historic analysis indeed shows that human rights have always been a *political* issue, not the natural result of any 'organic' development based on the genes of a particular culture. Any cultural-essentialist occupation, such as an 'Occidentalization' or 'Islamization' of human rights, should therefore be rejected.

The rejection of cultural essentialism, however, does not imply that cultural aspects become altogether meaningless. On the contrary, culture and religion can be, and indeed often are, powerful motives of practical commitment on behalf of human rights, motives that deserve to be recognized historically and to be cherished politically. Hence the question of how we can maintain the connection between human rights and religious or cultural tradition without getting trapped in the culturalist fallacy.

What I would like to suggest is that we understand human rights as the centre of a cross-cultural 'overlapping consensus' on basic normative standards in our increasingly multicultural societies. It is well known that the term 'overlapping consensus' has been coined by John Rawls (Rawls 1993). What Rawls wants to clarify by introducing this concept is the complex relationship between the guiding idea of political justice in a modern liberal society on the one hand and the multiplicity of religious or philosophical convictions held by the members of that society on the other. Although Rawls's considerations neither refer to international issues nor cover questions of multiculturalism, some of his insights may be helpful also for an analysis of international human rights in a cross-cultural perspective. I take up three aspects from Rawls and apply them briefly to the topic of human rights: (a) the genuinely normative and critical claims of political justice, (b) the limited scope of political justice as compared to 'comprehensive' world views and (c) the possibility to appreciate political justice from different religious or philosophical perspectives.

a. Rawls repeatedly emphasizes that his concept of political justice goes beyond a mere 'modus vivendi', that is, it must be more than just a compromise between all those normative convictions that happen to exist in a given society. The liberal principles of political justice embody genuinely normative substance and thus are bound to collide, for instance, with authoritarian values or racist political programmes. In such a conflict the principles of political justice claim a practical priority over competing values and convictions. The Rawlsian 'overlapping consensus' is thus not merely a descriptive concept; it poses a critical challenge. What is at stake is not a factual but a *normative consensus* in the sense that people holding different convictions should, nevertheless, be enabled to agree on some basic principles of justice, in order to shape their coexistence and cooperation on the basis of equality and freedom. The 'overlapping consensus' is an *ideal* for a pluralistic modern society, not a description of the status quo. On the one hand, it opens up the conceptual space for a plurality of different world views, ideologies, religions, philosophical doctrines, etc. On the other hand, the 'overlapping consensus' also defines limits of political tolerance in a liberal society.[11]

Similarly, universal human rights have a critical normative force in that they are designed to lead to a political and legal order based on equal freedom and participation. Constituting a morally *demanding* conception of human rights is not from the outset compatible with all religious or philosophical doctrines or with all cultural ways of life. Rhoda Howard is right in saying: 'A culture and community based on systematic degradation must be challenged; if individual rights threaten such as society, so much the better. Human rights may sometimes require cultural rupture' (Howard 1995: 9). No society, culture or religion can claim to comply with human rights unless it is willing to undertake political and intellectual reforms. It is no coincidence, for instance, that the recognition of human rights on the part of the Catholic Church went along with far-reaching doctrinal changes, including the renunciation of the traditional concept of state religion. Similarly, it seems clear that in order to achieve a critical reconciliation between human rights and Islamic tradition, reforms towards recognizing equal rights between the genders must be put on the agenda. And there can be no doubt that universal human rights and a traditional caste society do not fit together. In short, an 'overlapping consensus' on human rights must go beyond the smallest common denominator between the existing traditional values of different cultures. Human rights are a normatively *challenging* conception in that they call for changes, self-criticism and reforms to foster the mutual recognition of humans on the basis of equality.

b. In order not to overstate the normative claims of human rights, however, it is worth noting that their normative scope is limited. This is the second aspect I would like to take up from Rawls. To put it in his language, the idea of political justice is not a 'comprehensive doctrine' but, instead, it focuses on 'the basic structure of society' (Ibid: 11). The political and legal institutions underlying society may well be basic. And yet they can hardly be called an all-encompassing *weltanschauung*.

The same holds true for human rights. While constituting political and legal standards they do not entail a comprehensive guidance as to how to lead one's life both as an individual and within one's community. Human rights do not give any answers to the existential questions of the meaning of life and death. And they do not provide rituals and symbols through which people can express their mutual respect and appreciation beyond the sphere of politics and law. In short, human rights are neither a 'comprehensive doctrine' nor a comprehensive ethical code of conduct. They cannot compete with cultural and religious traditions, although they do exercise a critical effect on the interpretation and the development of these traditions.

The focus of human rights is on political and legal justice. Although the emancipatory spirit of human rights certainly poses a challenge to authoritarian traditions, a multiplicity of religious or non-religious world-views, individual and communitarian ways of life, and an abundance of different cultural expressions are possible. Human rights do not constitute an all-encompassing 'global ethics' or a globally binding 'civil religion'. Commitment on behalf of international human rights should therefore not be perceived or propagated as a modern form of missionary work, let alone a new version of the crusades. The idea of an 'overlapping consensus' on human rights does not even require us to work for a worldwide ecumenical reconciliation between all religions and ideologies, because people are free to define their (individual and communitarian) identities *against* each other, provided they respect universal equality in human dignity and rights.

c. Rawls points out that, although his idea of political justice is not a 'comprehensive doctrine', it is, on the other hand, not simply disconnected from more comprehensive worldviews. He argues that the guiding idea of political justice can be meaningfully appreciated from the perspectives of various philosophical or religious doctrines. The same holds true for human rights. It is especially the idea of human dignity that can connect human rights with different religious, philosophical and cultural traditions, because the insight into the unalienable dignity of every human being constitutes both the basic ethical principle of human rights and a central element of the teachings of various religions and philosophies. The *Project on Religion and Human Rights* based in New York has come to the conclusion that 'there are elements in virtually all religious traditions that support peace, tolerance, freedom of conscience, dignity and equality of persons, and social justice' (Kelsay and Twiss 1994: 116).

One should be anxious, however, to make sure that the appreciation of human rights from the standpoint of different religious or cultural traditions does not lead to forms of an essentialist occupation. It would be problematic immediately to 'base' human rights on the Bible, the Qur'an, the holy scriptures of the Hindus, or the teachings of Confucius. For as a result of such deductivist and essentialist approaches, the idea of universal human rights would easily get lost in a variety of competing religious and cultural conceptions. What I have emphasized above with regard to the 'Western' tradition therefore applies to other traditions as well: One should always be aware of the hermeneutic problem that it is only *in retrospective* that we can build a bridge between modern human rights and the sources of religious or cultural tradition. Such a hermeneutical awareness is the best way to fight essentialist appropriations of human rights by which their inherent universalism would be swallowed up by competing claims of particular cultural legacies.

POSTSCRIPTUM

According to Michael Ignatieff, human rights today serve as 'the lingua franca of global moral thought'. Whereas a few generations ago, the language of human rights was a specific 'jargon' mainly spoken by a limited number of progressive intellectuals, it meanwhile has become an indispensable medium of communication in international law, international diplomacy and international advocacy work, thus indeed playing a role comparable to a lingua franca. This is an enormous historical achievement, testifying also to the persuasiveness of human rights. The process of their globalization started with the 1948 Universal Declaration of Human Rights, from which subsequently a number of legally binding international treaties emerged. Today, not only governments, but also civil society organizations, trade unions, religious communities, indigenous peoples and many others have learned to use the worldwide language of human rights when articulating their normative interests and persuasions. Unlike a century ago, when human rights still faced open political and cultural opposition, including within the West, it seems that nowadays no one can afford to openly reject their claims.

However, it would be naïve to take all rhetorical commitments to human rights at their face value. Apart from the unwillingness of many governments to deliver upon their promises, human rights semantics itself often displays a certain ambiguity, since it may be utilized for all sorts of strategic purposes. This becomes particularly obvious when notorious human rights abusers – China, Vietnam, Russia or Saudi Arabia – take the floor in human rights forums, such as the UN Human Rights Council based in Geneva.

While seemingly subscribing to universal rights to freedom of equality, these and other governments typically insert broad caveats on behalf of national security, the primacy of economic development or the need to accommodate specific cultural or religious contexts. The normative status and the context of human rights may thus become increasingly blurred, and the ubiquitous rhetoric of rights often enough may merely hide the lack of any substantive international agreements. Moreover, by amalgamating international human rights with 'Western' accomplishments or a particularly 'Western' lifestyle, European governments or civil society organizations may further add to the existing confusion and inadvertently play into the hands of those who denounce the universal validity claims underneath human rights as a manifestation of Eurocentric arrogance.

Among the various arguments typically employed to question the idea of universal rights, cultural relativism – in conjunction with its twin: cultural essentialism – continues to play a prominent role. Unmasking 'Machiavellian' interests of those using relativistic arguments, tempting though it may be, does not get us very far. It does remain troubling to realize that universal human rights have inevitably been *articulated* in *particular* languages, in (conscious or unconscious) continuity to *particular* religious and/or philosophical traditions and by invoking the *particular* narratives or metaphors familiar to *particular* nations. How then can we even distinguish between the universal and the particular? Moreover, in retrospect we clearly see that historical human rights declarations typically used to privilege the positions of certain groups rather than recognizing the rights of all human beings equally, which adds yet another dimension of particularistic bias. Hence, it looks as if the universal validity claims underneath human rights have always been tainted by various particularities, and we should better be aware of it.

Is there a way out of this predicament? In my opinion, the only promising defence of universal rights is by taking cultural relativism even more seriously than do those who resort to relativistic arguments for strategic purposes. A good starting point is the acknowledgement that cultural diversity constitutes a hallmark of modernity, at the global level as well as within most societies. This includes an abundance of different ethical traditions, often based on religious or philosophical teachings which only parts of humanity (or even parts of a society) have endorsed. Human rights are not intended to wipe out or marginalize such diversity. Instead, they call for even more diversity by demanding that everyone should have their voices heard in the articulation of cultural, religious, ethical and other diversity. Any genuine appreciation of diversity must include internal minorities, dissidents or proponents of new readings of traditional sources, such as feminist theologians or other critical voices.

From the perspective of human rights, the acknowledgement of diversity always presupposes free and broad articulation. This is an indispensable requirement. Indeed, why should respect for diversity stop once it starts challenging party monopolies or traditional cultural or religious hegemonies? How can the Chinese government expect recognition for a particularly 'Chinese' development strategy, when the same government suppresses any internal discussions on what the 'Chinese way' of development should look like? How credible is a policy that employs the language of diversity only when questioning claims of international human rights law, while not allowing any open challenges to the existing one-party system? Similar questions can be raised against regimes like Saudi Arabia or Brunei, which claim to follow their very distinct political path by promoting a tightly knit religious homogeneity, which itself does not accommodate even the slightest internal distinctiveness in religious interpretations and practices.

Universal human rights are both ambitious and modest. They are modest in that they do not provide an epistemologically privileged vantage point from which one could make a comprehensive assessment of the various cultural, religious and ethical traditions of humankind and fully see their advantages as well as shortcomings. Such an epistemologically superior standpoint does not exist. Instead, human rights acknowledge a vast diversity of perspectives, while at the same time insisting – this is their ambition – on free and broad articulation as an indispensable precondition for living together in our complicated pluralistic world. This insistence on free and broad articulation can become a plausible entry point for various rights to communicative freedom (freedom of opinion and expression, freedom of thought, conscience, religion or belief) as well as the organizational preconditions for meaningful public communication (freedom of peaceful assembly and association). For public communication to be a manifestation of free practice, people also need the possibility to withdraw from the public space into a safe haven of privacy, which requires respect for a number of rights to privacy. Moreover, human rights are not even conceivable without everyone having resort to effective judicial complaint mechanisms in cases of violations. In short, the whole range of human rights somehow comes into sight once we insist on the need for claims of diversity to be freely and broadly articulated.

Of course, the insistence on free and broad articulation does not render the content of what is articulated irrelevant. Far from paving the way to a culturally uniform world, human rights spell out normative preconditions for living together under the irreversible conditions of diversity. This requires respect for all human beings in their dignity, freedom and equality, a respect that is institutionalized in a broad range of international human rights norms.

Now, what about the undeniable fact that the language of human rights itself obviously carries a particular index of time, space and cultural environment?

This has been, and continues to be, a main objection to the universal validity of human rights. Are human rights a merely Western accomplishment? Let us assume it is true that the idea of human rights first emerged in Western countries. Still, this does not mean that these rights are essentially and eternally confined to particularly cultural heritages of the West. The specific European history of human rights merely gives an *example* illustrative of the various obstacles, misunderstandings, learning processes, achievements and failures in the unfinished struggle for finding a plausible normative consensus in our irreversibly diverse societies. More important than the cultural 'territory' on which – or the cultural 'horizon' within which – human rights were first publicly declared are the experiences of injustice to which human rights try to give a normative response.

The task remains to open human rights principles and norms to intercultural communication by de-dramatizing the cultural particularities which have first accompanied the development of human rights in the West. These particularities of the specifically Western genesis of human rights, at any rate, do not provide the binding model which people in non-Western societies are supposed to simply adopt. If it is true that human rights are the *lingua franca* of global moral thought today, it must be possible for people from most different cultural or religious backgrounds to use that language to articulate their own experiences, yearnings and aspirations without, thereby, Westernizing themselves.

NOTES

1. This chapter was previously published in *Political Theory*, Vol. 28: 1, 2000, pp. 90–121. Reprinted by permission of SAGE Publications, Inc.

2. Cf. Marcus Aurelius Antoninus, p. 335: 'And thou forgettest how strong is the kinship between man and mankind, for it is a community not of corpuscles, or seed or blood, but of intelligence. And thou forgettest this too, that each man's intelligence is God and has emanated from Him ...' (Aurelius 1987).

3. Paul calls on Philemon to receive Onesimus like a brother – 'not now as a servant, but above a servant' (Philemon 16) – and not to punish him. The idea of spiritual equality before God thus leads indeed to ethical consequences. But Paul never challenges slavery politically.

4. For a detailed analysis with reference to both the traditional *shariah* and the legal situation in contemporary Arab countries (Abu-Sahlieh 1994: 159ff.).

5. On the questions of religious liberty and equality between Muslims and non-Muslim minorities (cf. Abu-Sahlieh 1964: 87ff.).

6. A similar scheme can also be found in Stahmann (1994).

7. Cf. the collection of many of these documents (in French translation from Arabic) in Abu-Sahlieh (1994: 461ff.).

8. Quoted from the French translation from the originally Arab text, in Abu-Sahlieh (1994: 481). Note that an independent English and French version of the UIDHD was published by the Islamic Council of Europe itself. This translation, however, differs substantially from the Arab original text.

9. Cf. article 38 of the 1917 Ottoman Law of Family Rights: 'If a woman stipulates in her marriage contract that her husband shall not marry another wife and that, should he do so, then either she herself or this other wife will be divorced, the contract is valid and the stipulation recognized' (Anderson 1976: 49).

10. Commenting on this verse Fazlur Rahman points out: 'There can be hardly a more penetrating and effective characterization of the human situation and man's frail and faltering nature, yet his innate boldness and the will to transcend the actual towards the ideal constitutes his uniqueness and greatness' (Rahman 1966: 35).

11. To put in Rawlsian terms: 'unreasonable doctrines' are excluded from the 'overlapping consensus' (Rawls 1993: 58ff.).

Chapter 5

Peng Chun Chang, Intercultural Ethics and the Universal Declaration of Human Rights

Hans Ingvar Roth

In our globalized and multicultural world, the need for shared moral principles has become more and more urgent. Mankind is lucky in the sense that there is a document that expresses a global ethic that is more or less accepted as the obvious moral lingua franca in the world today namely the UN Declaration of Human Rights (the UDHR). Hence, the UDHR stands as a role model for successful intercultural communication concerning ethics. However, the wide-spread acceptance of this document stands in sharp contrast to its actual fulfilment. The world today is characterized by more or less serious human rights violations in nearly every country.[1]

The writing of the UDHR has often been associated with the name of Eleanor Roosevelt (1884–1962), the wife of the former US president Franklin D. Roosevelt. This is of course accurate in an important sense as Eleanor Roosevelt had a crucial role as chairman of the group that wrote the document – not at least on the basis of her diplomatic skills and her clear visions about the purpose of the document. However, there were also other less well-known people behind the document that had a very important role to play concerning the character and the content of the UDHR (Glendon 2002; Morsink 1999).

This chapter is a presentation and an analysis of the Chinese diplomat and philosopher Peng Chun Chang's (1882–1957) contribution to the Universal Declaration of Human Rights (UDHR). Chang was one of the key members of the committee who wrote this important declaration. Among other important participants one could mention the Lebanese philosopher Charles Malik, the French lawyer René Cassin and the Canadian law professor John Humphrey.

In spite of the great importance of Chang in the writing process of the document, not many articles or books (in comparison to the other writers of the UDHR) have been written on his contributions – especially not in the light of his overall philosophy and previous work. Chang was a scholar (university professor), a diplomat and a play writer, and he has been described as a Renaissance personality (Glendon 2002). He was also a so-called multicultural personality in the sense that he was influenced by many cultural traditions through his encounters with people around the world and through his education both in China and in the United States. He also worked as a diplomat in Turkey and Chile, as a professor in the United States and as guest researcher in the United Kingdom before he started his work for the United Nations (Cheng and Cheng 1995).

In his writings he emphasized more or less implicitly the importance of intercultural communication and he developed 'a theory of intercultural ethics' that was later on used in his contributions to the UDHR. Chang's idea of interculturalism anticipated the American philosopher John Rawls's famous conception of an overlapping consensus, something that we will touch upon below (Bell 2015). Chang made a theoretical contribution in this field with important practical impact in the sense that he presented a proposal to define the conditions for reaching a fair and legitimate ethical consensus in a situation characterized by religious, philosophical and ideological pluralism.

One of Chang's most important contributions to the UDHR was his input concerning the first article ('All persons are born free and equal') where he addressed fundamental questions concerning the philosophical bases of human rights from an intercultural perspective. Chang was, for example, against all attempts to ground human rights on a specific theology or philosophy such as theism or natural law theory, and he strived instead to justify human rights from a so-called 'neutral' perspective that could include several ethical traditions. The traditions that Chang especially focused upon were French Enlightenment philosophy and Confucian ethical traditions. For Chang the objective of universalism was pivotal. Hence, the UDHR should be a document that all members of the human family could identify themselves with. This attempt to strive for religious neutrality stood in sharp contrast with, for example, one other important writer of the UDHR, namely, the Lebanese philosopher Charles Malik who stressed a Thomist and a natural rights perspective (even though he also endorsed neutrality and universalism as objectives for the working group – especially in the end of the writing process).

The chapter will include a short presentation of the UDHR, and its historical setting, Chang's life and an analysis of his contributions to the document, including the specific form of intercultural dialogue that Chang used in his argumentations concerning the content of the UDHR. It is a so-called critical reconstruction of the statements that Chang did in the discussions on the UDHR in the UN context mainly during the years 1946–1948 (Schabas 2013).

THE UDHR

The story and the origin of the UDHR is well known for many people (Woods 2015; Klug 2015). After the creation of the United Nations and the UN charter 1945, many delegates found it necessary to create a working group that was able to explicate and expand the notion of human rights and fundamental freedoms that was mentioned in the UN charter (Klug 2015). The notion of human rights became widespread in the beginning of the 1940s, especially after President F.D. Roosevelt's famous speech in the congress in 1941 about the four freedoms (freedom from want and fear, and freedom to expression and worship). The lack of clear standards of human rights was seen as a contributory cause to all the conflicts and wars that mankind had experienced since the turn of the century. Hence, a human rights commission was set up in 1946 in charge of drafting a universal bill of human rights. But, as Eleanor Roosevelt claimed, the purpose of the UDHR was a very wide one: These rights were not just aimed at securing freedom and justice on a global scale, but were intended to affect 'small places' where every man, woman and child seeks equal justice, equal opportunity and equal dignity without discrimination (Address to the UN Commission on Human Rights 1958).

The UDHR was a product of many people's contributions and was created through many meetings during a two-year period (from January 1946 to December 1948). The main writing of the document took place both in the New York area (Sperry Gyroscope Plant in Lake Success on Long Island) and in Geneva. The key writers were an exceptional group in terms of interests, knowledge and life experiences. One could without any hesitation say that it took a very long time until the philosophical and political debate concerning human rights reached the level of the UDHR group and the UNESCO group that did a parallel more philosophical project (if it has been done at all) (Maritain 1949). The setting for the main part of the writing of the UDHR was no ordinary philosophy seminar room, no bureaucracy, no political debate in a parliament or committee or any interest group meeting. It was something else and radically new as nothing similar had happened in world history.

A drafting committee was then appointed consisting of representatives from various countries (Australia, Chile, China, France, Lebanon, Soviet Union, United Kingdom, United States). At the time of the writing of the UDHR, six of the fifty original UN members were within the Soviet bloc. In eleven states Islam was the majority culture and in four countries Buddhism was a strong religion. Thirty-seven of the UN members were from Western/ Christian countries.

The discussions on the UDHR did not reveal a simple East–West divide or a North–South Dichotomy or clashes between different religious traditions.

The working process was more complex than that also given the facts that certain personalities become more influential during the two years the UDHR was produced, and that some representatives of the various states managed to keep their own countries' religious and political traditions in brackets.

Interesting to note is that Chang came from a country that had committed many human rights abuses such as political oppression (as well as other member states of the drafting group such as the race discrimination in the United States and the colonial policies from the United Kingdom, France, Belgium and Netherlands). One could also add that it has been a debate concerning the standing of human rights thinking in Chinese traditions. Some authors have claimed that the human rights perspective has not been present in any obvious sense in China, while others claim that there exist Chinese articulations of human rights theory and practice. Confucian ethics has often been linked to social hierarchies in public imagination and has emphasized duties to one's society. But at the same time it has also included concepts that are highly relevant for human rights thinking such as benevolence and taking care of the needy (Wen and Akina 2012). However, several members of the group rose to the moment – and became first and foremost individuals with a commitment to human rights. Even the members from the Soviet Union came forward with some useful insights and support for important rights principles, such as the article on anti-discrimination, in spite of the tough political control from Moscow (Morsink 1999; 2009).

The UDHR is a remarkable text for several reasons. We should mention five of these reasons here:

1. Through the creation of the UDHR it was the first time in history when the individual person received a standing in international law.
2. The document has become a *moral lingua franca* and a new Magna Carta for mankind and has functioned as an inspiration for various declarations and conventions in the post-war period.
3. Related to the former point, one could say that the UDHR is an intercultural or multicultural document in several senses. First of all it was a multicultural or intercultural creation in the sense that people from various cultures and religions were involved in the writing of the text. Second, the UDHR was intercultural in the sense that it involved articles that voiced a concern for cultural belonging and the importance of culture for the wellbeing of the individual person. In a third sense the document was intercultural as it was a product of what one could call 'intercultural strategies and dialogues', that is, argumentations that tried to reach agreements even though the drafters had very different cultural/ethical backgrounds and views. Chang was interested in all these three senses of the term 'intercultural' with reference to the UDHR – and in particular – contributed to

the intercultural aims in the second and the third meaning of the term. He was also eager to strengthen the first meaning of the term as he was one of the most vocal critics of colonialism and wanted a more inclusive United Nations with a wider representation of peoples around the world.

4. It was also impressive that such an ambitious text could be formulated and accepted through the new organization United Nations in such a conflict-laden period (especially as the Cold War had just started). The declaration includes a broad list of human rights that has functioned as a blue print for international morality and domestic law and the UDHR has inspired succeeding attempts in the post-war period to formulate various conventions and declarations concerning vulnerable groups such as women, children, ethnic and religious minorities and disabled people.

5. The history after 1948 has also shown the remarkable significance of the UDHR as a tool for political change (e.g. the fall of the Iron Curtain in Europe and the ending of Apartheid in South Africa).

THE LIFE OF P.C. CHANG

So who was P.C. Chang? He was born 1892 in a dramatic period of Chinese history. He belonged to a special generation of people who experienced both the time of the rule of the Emperor and the Republic. Other well-known members of this generation were Mao Zedong (1893–1976) and Chiang Kai-shek (1887–1975). The generation of Chang faced dramatic events. The Boxer Rebellion occurred between 1898–1901 and the old imperial regime was crumbling at the turn of the century, and the revolution that created the new republic took place in 1911. Chang was brought up in an educated family with strong interests in the fine arts, education, philosophy and politics. His older brother Poling who became a demanding father figure for Chang after the death of their father created the Nankai school system (and the Nankai University) which had the purpose of introducing ideas from Western educational traditions in a way which also was sensitive to China's own tradition. This was also a school system in which Peng Chun Chang later on worked with both as a professor and administrator. Nankai University achieved a special standing in China through its nationalistic stance and its criticism of the politics of Japan. The fact that Zhou En Lai was a student of the university also contributed to the university's positive reputation after 1949 in mainland China, and this fact explained why it could keep its original name after the victory of Mao Zedong. (After the communist victory the universities changed their names except for Nankai.) According to Chang's son Stanley, his father claimed that Zhou En Lai never was a student of him but that he sat in on some of his lectures.

Before the creation of the Chinese republic in 1911, Chang went to the United States on a scholarship through the Boxer Rebellion Indemnity Fund and studied at Clark and Columbia Universities. At the latter university he received a Ph.D. degree with the well-known philosopher of education John Dewey as supervisor (Cheng & Cheng 1995). His PhD thesis was called 'Education for Modernization in China' and was an attempt to apply modern educational ideas from the West to the Chinese context (Chang 1923). One main statement in this thesis was that the school system in China should try to create a 'frontier mentality' in order to fulfil educational progress and a modernization of the society. This mentality had characterized the United States during several centuries and had enhanced openness, cooperation and progress. These were ideas that were also in tune with the educational philosophy of John Dewey. This philosophy encouraged the close combination of thought and action. (The so-called frontier thesis was first presented by the American historian Frederick Jackson Turner in 1893. Turner expressed the view that the various groups that had immigrated to the United States throughout history were step by step liberated from their origins through entering into the frontier areas of the West – the so-called unbroken ground (Roth 1999)).

During his time of study in the United States, Chang was involved in various theatre projects he wrote and directed plays, and he was also engaged in Chinese student- and Christian associations. It is interesting to note that after his student years at Clark and Columbia Universities it seems that Chang was not involved in any religious activities in the same way as he did as a student and in the same way as his older brother Poling who was a converted Christian in the beginning of the century and an active member in the Y.M.C.A. P.C. Chang did not write anything on Christianity in a normative sense after the beginning of the 1920s, something he had done during his student years at Clark and during the first years of his studies at Columbia University (Chang 1914). It is relevant in this context to refer to John Dewey's possible influence as he was one of the least religious philosophers among the well-known pragmatists in the United States (Bernstein 2005). During the 1920s and the 1930s Chang worked both as university lecturer and as a theatre director in China, and he was also a guest professor at the Universities of Chicago and Honolulu. In 1922 he married a very bright Chinese student from Vassar College in New York State – Miss Tsá Sieu Tsu. She was also from the Boxer scholarship programme, and they had two girls Ming-Ming and Ruth and two boys Chen and Stanley all born during the 20s. As Peng Chun Chang was often away on various missions and travels, his wife took care of the children not seldom during very difficult circumstances such as the Japanese invasion. Chang was also a demanding father and his communication with some of the children was often problematic.

After the Marco Polo Bridge (Lugou Bridge) incident on 7 July 1937, and the Japanese attacks on Nankai University, Chang went on a political mission to Europe and the United States and gave testimonies of the Japanese atrocities in China.

Among the most famous speeches Chang made during this time, was made in an national protest meeting at the Royal Albert Hall, on 5 October 1937, which the *Liberal Magazine* organized ('Japan's attack against civilians'). In connection to that meeting, a campaign was also launched for the boycott of Japanese goods. Eight thousand people attended the protest meeting to be greeted by the short film *Bombs on China* (advanced loudspeakers were used, which surprised the audience). Chang (who later met privately with Clement Atlee at the Labour Party conference) spoke about how his university in Tientsin (the Nankai University) was destroyed in 1937 by the Japanese attacks. Archbishop of Canterbury Cosmo Lang was also one of the distinguished speakers at the event (Buchanan 2012).

After this 'propaganda' work that also turned out to be successful (not at least in terms of economic sanctions against Japan), the republic gave Chang diplomatic posts in Turkey and in Chile, where he became ambassador in the beginning of the 1940s. One can speculate what these experiences contributed to Chang's interests in terms of politics and human rights. Turkey was right in the middle of a radical secularization and modernization process in the 30s and 40s after the creation of the modern republic, while several South American countries such as Chile had experienced animated political debates focused upon socio-economic issues. (Chang later on also stressed religious neutrality as a desideratum for the UDHR, and he was a strong advocate for the socio-economic rights in the UN declaration.) After his diplomatic period in Chile, Chang became representative of China in the San Francisco meetings concerning the creation of the United Nations. In 1945 he was later on appointed to become vice chairman in the Human Rights Commission that had as one of its main purposes to create a UDHR.

In other words, here we have a person whose earlier years seemed to be a preparation for an uppermost important role – to be one of the key persons in the creation of the UDHR (Kumbrien 2015; Cheng and Cheng 1992). He had a cosmopolitan and, in some ways, a privileged background. He belonged to a family with strong cultural interests and his family was rather well off comparatively speaking. He had a tight but also at many times a conflict-laden relationship with his talented older brother Chang Poling who gave Chang a very tough upbringing after the death of their father. In other words, Peng Chun Chang was a brilliant person who had many interests intellectually, artistically and professionally, and he had also the chance to express all these interests in concrete important projects. His work and personality were also very much appreciated by his closest colleagues in the Human Rights

Commission such as Eleanor Roosevelt, John Humphrey and Hernan Santa Cruz. Eleanor Roosevelt, for example, had the following remarks of him in her autobiography.

> Dr Chang was a pluralist and held faith in charming fashion on the proposition that there is more than one kind of ultimate reality. The Declaration, he said, should reflect more than simply Western ideas and Dr Humphrey (the secretary) would have to be eclectic in his approach. His remarks though addressed to Dr Humphrey was really directed at Dr Malik (the rapporteur) from whom it drew a prompt retort as he expounded at some length the philosophy of Thomas Aquinas. Dr Humphrey joined enthusiastically in the discussion and I remember that at one point Dr Chang suggested that the Secretariat might well spend a few months studying the fundamentals of Confucianism. (Roosevelt 1961)

After his work in the United Nations and his contributions to the UDHR, he 'lost' his home country when Mao Zedong's regime took over the control of mainland China and the republic moved to Formosa in 1949. I asked Chang's son Stanley how his father perceived the civil war in China in the end of the 1940s and why his father decided to stay in the United States. Stanley gave me the following answer: 'My guess is that my father felt that he could contribute in the United Nations and so he sort of kept a blind eye as to what was happening in China. I believe that he really thought in the beginning that the communists would not last too long in China. He thought that communism was like a childhood disease such as chicken pox, mumps etc". However, as time went on, it became clear for Chang that Mao were going to stay, so he took the easy way out and stayed in the United States according to Stanley. In 1952 he finally decided that he did not represent China but an offshore island, so he resigned. He had also problems with the head of the Chinese delegation at the United Nations and was not even paid a regular salary (he was paid per diem). Stanley's impression from side remarks that his father made is also that he did not have any respect for Chiang Kei Shek. Further, he was not a member of the Kuomintang party. However, he was a friend of Madame Chiang Kei Shek who he met during his university period in the United States and he helped her prepare her famous speech before the US congress in 1943.'

In connection to his resignation from the United Nations Chang's health deteriorated. His heart failed him through heart attacks (one serious one in 1952 and the last and fatal one in 1957). He was estranged in the UN community and harassed by representatives from USSR, who did not want him in the UN system after Mao's victory in China. Even though he had several friends and colleagues in the United Nations that supported him (for example Roosevelt and Humphrey), he left the United Nations in 1952. The short time until his death in 1957 he spent in the small town of Nutley in New Jersey more or less alone in a country that he had accused for selfish individualism and materialism (Glendon 2001). According to Stanley, his father was a very lonely and bitter man in the last years of his life. He spent his time with music (collecting LPs), playing the game solitaire with tiles and reading the philosophy of Tao. One of the few friends that regularly visited him in Nutley during the last years of his life was his best friend the linguist professor Y.R. Chao who was also a student from the same Boxer scholarship programme.

P.C. CHANG'S CONTRIBUTIONS TO THE UDHR

P.C. Chang's pivotal position has been recognized with reference to UDHR only during the last couple of years. One could ask why this has occurred so late and why it took such a long time for him to be acknowledged in the literature on human rights and the UDHR (Liu 2014). China and human rights issues have come to the forefront more and more in global politics today. Commentators on China have been eager to show that there were people who represented China and worked on human rights early on, such as P.C. Chang. These pioneers could also function as role models for modern China. Further, the issues that Chang was involved with, for example, a critique of European notions of civilization and culture and questions on religious tolerance and pluralism, have become the main stock of current public intellectual debates.

Why then has Chang been recognized so late as a human rights pioneer? One hypothesis is that Chang was mainly seen as a representative of the Republic of China, which has been described in many quarters as an authoritarian state, especially during the last decade of its existence in mainland China. However, this critical opinion has been challenged and commentators have stressed the independence and originality of Chang's thoughts in relation to the regime that he represented (and also to the other writers of the UDHR) (Liu 2014 and Krumbien 2015). Some writers such as the Swedish scholar Marina Svensson has, on the other hand, challenged the sincerity of the representatives of the Republic of China concerning the progressive views on human rights. Svensson claims that 'Chinese nationalists needed the help and recognition of the Western powers and may therefore have wanted to appear in a favourable light in their eyes' (Svensson 2002). Chang acted, however, quite independently from his government, which is, for example, shown by the lack of correspondence between Chang and his government during the years that the UDHR was written (Will 2007). One could also bring forward the hypothesis that Chang had the opportunity to act quite independently in the United Nations during the years 1947–1948 as his government was heavily involved in the civil war of China. According to Chang's son Stanley, his father would expound his ideas with total disregard for what the government would say. Stanley never saw him reading coded telegrams during his period in the United Nations like he did when he was a diplomat in Turkey.

For Chang, Japan's aggression against China was important as a background for his engagement in the UDHR, similar to, for example, the French representative René Cassin's, who's family was murdered by the Nazis, experiences of Nazi Germany. (Cassin who was of French Jewish origin had experienced that almost all of his family was murdered by the Nazis.) In other words, both Chang and Cassin had experienced atrocities themselves through Japan in China and Germany in France. However, the Japanese atrocities have not been recognized at the global level to the same extent as the German ones, as Japan was more seen as involved in 'local' Asian conflicts. This phenomenon is something that still creates grievances among people in several Asian countries. Maybe this could also be a partial explanation why Chang's role in the writing of the UDHR has been downgraded in the 'Eurocentric' commentaries on the UN document, who have more emphasized the destructive role of Nazi Germany.

A further reason why Chang has not been so well known in the United Nations as one of the founding fathers of the UDHR is that he died early (1957). In comparison with the other main writers René Cassin, Charles Malik and John Humphrey, he did not travel around extensively and talk about his role as a key writer of UDHR after the UDHR was finished (especially in comparison to Cassin and Humphrey who were working within the UN system for a much longer period than Chang).

Some of the other key writers of the UDHR such as Eleanor Roosevelt, John Humphrey, Charles Malik, René Cassin, Hernan Santa Cruz and Carlos Romulo had also the possibilities to write memoirs or publish their diaries which contributed to their fame with respect to the UDHR. It does not seem that any diaries from Chang exist except from some years during the 1920s.

The research concerning the UDHR and its framers was also rather late. It is not until the last two decades that we meet commentators such as Mary Ann Glendon and Johannes Morsink (Glendon 2002; Morsink 1999). However, these two writers did not highlight Chang's special importance in comparison to the other writers (Glendon's main choice was Malik and Morsink's was Humphrey) even though they granted Chang's work significance in the context of the other writers.

As the American historian Samuel Moyn has claimed in his important book 'The Last Utopia', a real interest in wider circles to refer to human rights in political rhetoric appeared as late as in the 1970s through the breakthrough of human rights organizations such as Amnesty and Human Rights Watch and through the rhetoric of the US president Jimmy Carter in his foreign policy during the 1970s (Moyn 2010).

Hence, the UDHR did not show itself to be the important document as it really was during the 1950s as the Cold War dominated world politics and questions of human rights were not at the top of the political agenda. After P.C. Chang's death in 1957, the importance of the UDHR began show itself – during the 1960s first and foremost in the form of two conventions of human rights (1966) and – as was said before – during the 1970s in the form of human rights activism among various NGOs and as a central concept in the public debates around the world (Nickel 2014).

Chang's Importance for the UDHR Project

What kind of questions were Chang most interested in with reference to the UDHR? Similar to the Lebanese delegate the philosopher Charles Malik, Peng Chun Chang was interested in matters of principle and 'the overarching ethics' of the UDHR, and he was involved with some key articles such as article 1 (Malik 2000). He was further concerned with questions of implementation, formulation and logical structure and the 'overall philosophy' or purpose with the document.

Being important as a writer of a document such as the UDHR could mean different things. A common interpretation is that one has been responsible for the bulk of the UDHR articles and the overall structure of the document. If that interpretation cannot be applied – given the collectivity of the work – one has to focus upon other interpretations of the concept of importance. An interesting interpretation of the concept of importance (with respect to the writing of the UDHR) is the role which the author played concerning the key characteristics of the document. In other words, is the document as a whole *congruent* with the writer's overall philosophy in crucial ways? In the case of Chang one could answer yes. Chang emphasized that the UDHR should be universal and religiously neutral. Further, it should be clearly structured, logical and written for the layman in order to fulfil its main purpose of being a moral educational project. Chang's philosophy was a kind of non-metaphysical, pragmatic philosophy that stood in sharp contrast with, for example, Charles Malik's Thomism and natural law theory as well as with the Marxism of the Eastern delegates and the theism of certain Christian delegates such as the one from Brazil and the representative from Netherlands who wanted a religious underpinning of the document.

Chang also managed to solve conflicts through compromises and through his personal style and manner. Through humour and quotations from Confucius, he often succeeded in overcoming stalemates in the debates. He had also a vision of intercultural contacts that was grounded and crafted before his time in the United Nations, a vision that we will address and discuss below (Chang 1936b). Even though he was excellent in solving stalemates and reaching fruitful compromises among the delegates, he was also forceful and strategic in defending some of his own central thoughts – for example, that the UDHR should be a religiously neutral document. One could also say that the UDHR became a document that was in tune with the Chinese philosophical traditions that stress the importance of 'art of living' in comparison to metaphysical speculation. Chang was eager to emphasize that the main purpose of the UDHR was the humanization of man.

As was mentioned before, he also made important contributions to ideas about 'strategy for implementation'. The strategy was first a declaration, then a convention, when the time was ripe. For Chang it was important to act now when the world opinion (in spite of the Cold War) was eager to formulate a human rights document in the light of the atrocities that had affected mankind. To focus instead upon a binding convention (with all kinds of qualifications) would instead slow down the working process (see also below).

In a summary record from the United Nations it was stated that Chang recalled the development of human rights thinking and practice during the last one hundred and fifty years, and felt that there existed now a new humanism as otherwise there would be no incentive for the efforts that were made (concerning human rights). The fact that rights of men were included in 35 or 40 of the world's constitutions indicated that large measure of agreement was possible in spite of differences of philosophy or ideology according to Chang (Schabas 2013). The incentives for the efforts made were the ideals of human freedom and human dignity, according to Chang. It is interesting to note that Chang wanted the preamble of the UDHR to express the philosophy of the UDHR even though he was sceptical of including substantial philosophical views in the different articles (such as natural law theory). In the philosophy of the preamble the concept of elevating human dignity was crucial for Chang (especially with reference to the differences between human beings and animals). Chang also linked dignity to equality. Respect for equality (and human dignity) in this context means that one should take into account the responsibility and the self-reliance of individual human beings, but also the unchosen unlucky circumstances that human beings can face in life. These kinds of thoughts are very similar to the ideas that the American legal philosopher Ronald Dworkin expressed in his writings (Dworkin 2011).

Chang was also engaged with answering some of the most common criticism of the human rights project in the United Nations – especially the cultural relativist criticism from the American Anthropological Association (Roth 2012). After the creation of the UDHR, there was paradoxically a cultural relativist criticism not only raised from social anthropologists but also stated from colonial powers such as France and Belgium when they claimed that non-self-governing territories (or colonies) were not 'mature' enough for the declaration or that the principles did not fit their specific conditions. These colonial powers were using a so-called 'civilization argument', according to Chang. The West had obtained a civilization that was needed for the implementation of the human rights. However, P.C. Chang was very sceptical of these statements. He thought that the whole idea about human rights was that they should be *universal* and should apply to all people irrespectively if they lived under a jurisdiction in an independent nation state or in a non-sovereign territory. (Apart from this meaning of the term 'universal', Chang also endorsed that the UDHR should be universal in the sense that it should be accessible to all [easy to understand] and acceptable for all according to their own ethical traditions). Chang also thought that holding (European) civilization in high esteem overall was an unreasonable stance with respect to what Europe had gone through with two bloody world wars and Nazi Germany's politics of racial inequality.

As Professor Lydia Liu claims, Chang perceived the classical standard of civilization as the principle obstacle (for universal human rights application) and noted its imperial logic and ethnocentrism (Liu 2014). Chang said: 'The point was ... that there could surely be no reason to suppose that the people of the territories involved did not desire human rights.' Chang also emphasized that if human rights are inherent in human nature (as the French delegate René Cassin has said), how can the degree of evolution of the society prevent a country from having them? (Schabas 2013).

Chang claimed that it was true that there were different technological and other forms of advancement (and different conditions for fulfilling their human rights, that is, the establishment of education and court institution), but, as the charter clearly showed, that did not mean that less developed areas were to be exploited by outsiders and should not have human rights as standards. In a sense, colonial administration was both a burden and a blessing, according to Chang. Apart from the suffering of the peoples of non-self-governing territories (or the colonies) and from the benefits accruing to the colonial powers, the latter also suffered because power corrupted them.

It is important to note in this context that Chang generally seemed to have had a very complicated relationship with the French representative Réne Cassin. However, in the literature on Chang and the work on the Universal Declaration Chang's relationship to Charles Malik has been seen as especially problematic given their different philosophies. (Glendon 2002) (According to Malik's son Habib Malik may also have been angry that Malik's version of the preamble was accepted, a version that included a metaphysical concept such as inalienable that Chang wanted to get rid of). But, according to Chang's son Stanley, who was the only witness during the writing session in the summer of 1947 at Sperry Gyroscope Plant on Long Island, his father had no serious problems with Charles Malik who he often described as the good Malik (in comparison to the Russian representative

Josef Malik). The only delegate that Chang really disliked among the drafters was the French representative Cassin. According to Stanley, René Cassin was always belittling Confucius, saying how Peng Chun Chang was out to make that the most important aspect. Cassin often stressed the importance of French ideas instead.

Stanley remembers that his father was always very tense in his relationship with Cassin and that they often had heated arguments. In comparison, Chang could relate to all the other drafters in a pleasant way with humor. Chang who was the vice chairman in the Human Rights Commission dominated the sessions according to Stanley in comparison to Eleanor Roosevelt who was almost invisible during the meetings. Chang had, according to Stanley, a so-called middle country attitude towards the world, (i.e. China as the centre of the world), and this stance could also explain the clashes with Cassin and his strong French nationalism and his identification with European traditions.

Chang was also negative *vis-à-vis* human rights thinking that could be seen as expressions of selfish individualism with no clear connections to the duties that individual persons owe to their society. (Here we can trace a Confucian characteristic in Chang's thinking on human rights as Confucian ethics often include responsibilities to one's society and its social culture.) Also, as was said before, Chang rather seldom talked about the concept of human rights in the specific discussions concerning the content of the UDHR. He emphasized instead 'the art of living'. The rights talk that he referred to was more or less assumed when he talked in terms of duties (as human rights are correlated to duties). For example, he stressed that the writing group or the drafters should start off from Enlightenment philosophers and their talk about rights and their concepts of freedom, equality and brotherhood. In other words, he talked more about values and virtues that could be seen as 'overarching' or complementary to the rights scheme, for example, sympathy for others (against egoism) and duties/responsibilities (against individualism). Chang explicitly paid attention to the *human* part of human rights and the *duty* part – as rights for the most times correspond to duties.

One should add in this context that there was no clear definition or characterization of the concept of human rights in the UDHR. Those who worked with the document more or less assumed that they knew what the concept meant (Alfredsson and Eide 1999). This common starting point was that human rights are rights that persons have in virtue of their humanity (and not because of other group identities) and that human rights are of international concern and obligation. The closest one can get to a partial characterization of human rights in Chang's writings is a statement in a speech in October 1950 (in addition to his reference to the French Enlightenment philosophers and their deliberations on rights). In this speech Chang emphasized the fundamental nature of the rights involved, and their legitimacy across cultures:

'The draft covenant did not deal with such matters as road traffic, customs duties or narcotic drugs: it dealt with human rights and no one could assert such rights should be qualified'. Hence, Chang emphasized that human rights should be phrased to such large extent as possible in abstract terms and should not be mixed up with the concrete methods for fulfilling them or with 'local' policies (Third Committee 295th Meeting, Friday 27 October 1950).

With regard to implementation, Chang had constantly urged (not at least after the work with the UDHR) that the UN declaration/convention 'should not be visualized as an essentially negative concept referring almost exclusively to complaints concerning violations of human rights, but that due attention should also be paid to its positive aspects, that is – education and promotion and protection of human rights'. Much of the current debate did not actually centre on implementation so much as on complaints (a comment from Chang concerning the extension of the declaration to become a convention). He feared the development of a tendency to look for complaints as experienced in other fields and argued that complaints and stern discipline were neither the only nor the best methods of promoting the achievements of positive goals.

Citing the Chinese proverb 'Good intentions alone are not sufficient for political order and laws alone are not sufficient to bring about results by themselves', Chang said that the declaration's main goal was to build better human beings, and not merely to punish those who violate human rights. Chang wanted positive cooperation among the nations rather than legalistic corrections (Malik 2000). Hence, the most efficacious way of correcting the wrongs (of the world) was to set a common standard such as the draft declaration sought to establish.

Chang proposed to enact a declaration instead of a binding convention as the first step for the following reasons:

1. a convention imposing legal obligation may provide excuses for great powers to intervene in other countries,
2. the most urgent need of the international community was to make a document to protect human rights after the two world wars, while a binding convention would lead to a very time-consuming process,
3. the imposing of legal obligations would limit the universality of the document, since some countries might be put off by the compulsory contents.

Based on these considerations, Chang suggested enacting a bill of human rights in the following order: a declaration, a convention and an enforcement measures text. This also became the decision the commission (Morsink 1999; Schabas 2013).

How Has the Project of the UDHR Been Characterized from Different Perspectives?

Could the reading of the UDHR through a study of Chang's ideas bring a new perspective upon the document? For several writers such as Cassin, the German Nazi atrocities were in the foreground, while for Chang in addition to Germany and Italy, Japan was also in the foreground even though he did not mention Japan and its colonialism so frequently in the discussions concerning the UDHR. As was said above, Chang was involved in campaigns against Japan's war against China during the 1930s, and he travelled to Europe and the United States to persuade politicians to introduce economic sanctions against Japan (Chang 1939b; Cheng and Cheng 1995). Often when one talks about the creation of the United Nations and the UDHR, it is Nazi Germany and the Holocaust that have been seen as the main explanations for creating a new moral world order in the vein of the UDHR (Morsink 1999; Orend 2002).

In comparison, Chang's perspectives on atrocities also included Japan's actions and its colonialism through the specific experiences of China and the Asian world (Cheng & Cheng 1995). We mentioned above that a Eurocentric perspective often neglects Japan's role concerning the atrocities of the Second World War (it becomes 'just' one of the Axis powers). Germany is then always more highlighted as it is placed in the centre of Europe among several reasons. For Chang the atrocities that Japan committed to the world were similarly essential for his engagement in human rights (and how technological development can be used for evil, destructive purposes) – and – how cultural imports and exchange can go wrong. The quick superficial absorption of modern science and technology by Japan could be characterized as a case of nightmare due to 'indigestion', according to Chang. Chang was here referring how modern science and technology were used in Japan for destructive military purposes.

On the other hand, Roosevelt who represented the United States was very much involved in the war with Japan, but through the atomic bomb and Hiroshima and Nagasaki the conflicts and the atrocities made by Japan may have been somewhat 'downgraded' in the political debates because of the catastrophes that Japan experienced in the end of the Second World War. The atomic bombs presented a kind of atrocities that mankind never before had experienced in world history.

Two Challenges for Chang

The different drafters of the UDHR perceived, formulated and highlighted the challenges of writing a human rights document in various ways. In Chang's statements one could trace at least two main challenges.

One challenge was the following crucial one:

1. How should one explain the effort to write a document with the purpose for protecting man from cruelties that were solely created by man?

The phrase 'man's inhumanity against man' was often used by Chang in the initial discussions in the Human Rights Commission concerning the content of the UDHR, according to his son Stanley who was a witness. For Chang man had a dual nature – one good human part and one evil or bad animal part. The purpose of the document should primarily be to protect the good human part from the animal part and 'raise the moral stature of man' through an increasing awareness of men's duties towards one another with the overriding objective to respect the individual human being's dignity (which in Chang's terminology was his/her ability to show sympathy towards one another).

The phrase 'man's inhumanity against man' used by Chang could be traced to Burn's poem in 1785 'Man was made to mourn: A Dirge'. For Burns the brutality of man against man far extended any other brutalities that mankind had suffered ('Man's inhumanity to man makes countless thousands mourn'). Similar sentences had been expressed by Samuel V Pufendorf in 1673, 'More inhumanity has been done by himself than any other of nature's causes' and Primo Levi, 'If this is a man/Truce' 'I am constantly amazed by man's inhumanity to man.' It is interesting to note that Chang who otherwise was less inclined than some of his fellow writers (such as Charles Malik) to talk in terms of philosophical anthropology on man's nature did this in this specific context (Malik 2000).

Chang also said that it was disregard and contempt for human rights and not ignorance of them that was the real problem during the Second World War. According to Chang the perpetrators knew that they were violating human rights when they committed their crimes, so ignorance was not the real problem. One could of course make use of a broad concept of knowledge and mean that human rights knowledge implies awareness of (a) what are human rights and (b) that they are morally reasonable – and in conjunction with that – (c) that one has internalized them and (d) acted upon them. In this case Chang is assuming a narrower notion of 'human rights knowledge' that only includes the first two elements.

If one should take Chang's distinction between the animal and the *human* part of a person more literally, one could ask how well the notions of disregard and contempt fit with the idea that it is the *animal* part of the human being that is the main cause of conflicts and atrocities in the world. If one stresses on the animal part of the human being, a notion of ignorance of human rights may be more proper to cite as an explanation for the committed atrocities. However, often the atrocities were committed on the basis of careful deliberation and investigations what the victims identified themselves with, something which made the crimes so horrifying. Hence, in these latter cases the brutalities were really 'human' in the sense that they presupposed human rationality. One could then maybe use the word 'animal' (in Chang's expressions of man's animal part) in a more metaphorical sense.

Other writers of the UDHR such as Charles Malik and René Cassin talked in this context less in terms of human nature than Chang, and talked instead of characteristics of various nationalisms and the state. Cassin described Nazi Germany as a Leviathan state that needed to be combatted. These kind of states were based upon a perverted romanticized nationalism. The purpose of the UDHR was to present human rights that were necessary for the protection of the individual *vis-à-vis* such states (and nationalisms). Charles Malik talked in the same vein about collectivist ideologies that downgraded the standing of the individual person and he expressed aptly the words that 'The human person had not been created for the state, but that the state existed rather for the sake of the human being' (Malik 2000). However, both Malik and Cassin also talked about the importance of changing the mentalities of people so that they should not fall victim of totalitarian tendencies.

Given the different diagnoses and the explanations of the atrocities that mankind had faced during the Nazi period and the Second World War, the remedies or methods of change became different. As Chang's main focus was the individual human being (and his or her propensity for both good and evil), the main strategies became educational for Chang in a broad sense of the term. One of the main purposes of the UDHR was 'the humanization of man' and – as was said above – to raise the moral stature of man. With reference to the moral educational function of the UDHR, it became important for Chang to stress the characteristics that he assumed when he talked about the capacities and incapacities of man given these moral educational objectives. Chang did not hesitate to talk about the *innate* goodness of man (the capacity of sympathy for others) in this context.

However, notions such as innateness, inalienable, inherent were avoided by Chang when he talked about other characteristics of man than goodness (and in other contexts). One could ask why Chang was so eager to use the terms 'innate' and 'natural' in the case of the so-called human (or good) part of the human being and not words like 'inherent', 'inalienable' etc. more generally in his characterization of man. Maybe this fact was connected to Chang's conception of the function of the UDHR – the moral educational project of 'the humanization of man'. Words like 'innate' and 'natural' had then relevance as they pointed towards the preconditions for this moral educational purpose – a so-called "thin" metaphysics. (One could assume that if something is natural or innate it was also inalienable for Chang.)

For Cassin and Malik the focus was more on the state institutions and how to prevent them from threatening basic rights and fundamental freedoms than on educational/psychological methods focused upon the individual persons. The measures taken were in other words more political-structural and legal in character. As also Malik and Cassin claimed (and many other commentators of the UDHR stressed) national sovereignty should be curtailed by an international order, where the UDHR and an international bill of rights should have a prominent role. It is also striking that a notion of a so-called sacredness of the individual human being (or similar notions) could not be found among Chang's comments in the UN setting – a fact that could be traced to Chang's more dualist view of 'human nature'.

Another challenge was the following:

2. How should we, that is, the commission and the drafting group, be able to reach agreement on the content of the UDHR, given the religious diversity and the cultural, philosophical and ideological pluralism that characterize the world population?

Chang expressed certain optimism in terms of overcoming this problem of religious and ideological pluralism. In a statement on 10 December 1948, the day the General Assembly should vote on the UDHR, Chang expressed the following words:

> Our gratifying and historic agreements have occurred when the real subject of Human Rights is held unconfusedly before our minds and hearts. Our clanging and wrangling disagreements have come from tangental excursions prompted by what is often narrowly conceived as 'political' preoccupations. (Chang 1948)

It is not perfectly clear what Chang here means with political preoccupations, but given his statements in other contexts, one could interpret him to mean national self-interest and parochial ideological inclinations, where the notion of human rights was not clearly in the foreground. One could also – on the basis of Chang's conceptions of the purpose of a human rights document such as this – see that certain discussions were irrelevant, futile or unreasonable when it came to the topic of human rights in the UDHR discussions. At this stage we could also refer to the project of coming to terms with man's inhumanity to man as a basis for ethical agreement in spite of various ethical divergencies. (Here Chang's thoughts are similar to the political philosopher Judith N. Shklar's ideas that it is often easier to reach agreements concerning what is an injustice than reaching agreement about what is a just condition (Shklar 1992)). Chang also endorsed various intercultural strategies to reach an ethical consensus, something we will discuss more thoroughly below.

CREATIVE ADJUSTMENTS AND
INTERCULTURAL COMMUNICATION

If we study Chang's earlier work we will find ideas that were highly relevant for his later work with ethics and human rights in the UDHR project. In previous writings Chang stressed that one should be careful about emphasizing cultural differences among so-called Western and Eastern nations and exaggerate the conflicts between them. There are many 'Wests' and 'Easts', not just one monolithic West that stands in conflict with one monolithic East, according to Chang. There could be compatibility with one West and one East while incompatibility may occur between other Easts and other Wests (Chang 1937b; Cheng and Cheng 1995). As the terms 'East' and 'West' are good hiding places for all sorts of prejudices, Chang wanted instead to use more concrete sociological terms such as 'socialized habits' and 'group behaviour' in characterizing the nature of various intercultural contacts.

Chang expressed interesting ideas about cultural interaction with reference to China's history and actual circumstances in his early writings that also could be generalized to other settings (Chang 1923, 1933, 1936a, 1937).

First, China faced a period of *self-sufficiency* when the country was not eager to change its traditions. A revealing illustration of this phenomenon is the traditional education system in China (Chang 1933; 1937). This education had for centuries emphasized the readings of Chinese classics (in a more or less mechanic manner) and had not included other important subjects such as technology and natural science which were highly relevant with reference to the urgent needs of society. Then about a generation or so – a period of *hurried borrowing* from the Western world occurred, which was more or less a superficial imitation with no deep knowledge of the contexts, where and how the borrowing should be applied. For example, Chang claimed that 'the important thing for China is not how to teach science from textbooks already written by Western scientists, but to find the best way to teach science to the Chinese' (Chang 1936b). With reference to Chang's idea that communism was like a childhood disease such as chicken pox, one could add to this idea that communism and marxism also could be interpreted as a too hurried borrowing from the Western world according to Chang's perspective on cultural exchange.

The third stage was an attitude of *creative adjustment* which consisted of: (1) a sensitive recognition of the 'fringe of dissatisfaction' (with different forms of intensity, wideness and durability) and a necessity to get to know one's tradition, (2) an extensive survey for suggestion and stimulation, (3) a liberated inventiveness (a notion that will be explained in more detail below). The extensive survey is for suggestion and stimulation but not for the kind of hurried borrowing or imitation which Chinese have made the mistake of doing, according to Chang.

According to Chang, it was necessary to attain a *liberated inventiveness,* for example, liberation from formulated inertia, being liberated from looking at cultural forms as if they could not be broken up, looking at cultural forms as if they had dropped from heaven as a whole or as if they were glasses that could be moved around on a table. Chang meant that only by questioning into the conditioning circumstances of each cultural form that comes under our extensive survey can we become liberated. After one has gone through this process of getting hold of certain formulated things in past experiences for suggestion and stimulation, one ought to go through the process of finding out the *conditioning circumstances* out of which these things evolved. The project was to split formulations into bits, not for the sake of destruction but for the sake of understanding.

One cannot assimilate/force people to one culture according to Chang. He endorsed the right to freedom of religion and what he called *pluralistic tolerance* in contrast to an uncompromised dogmatism in his work with the UDHR. Trying to implement a uniform ideology on the world population (as the colonial powers had tried to do) was not a stable solution as it is often forced, according to Chang – and – it could not capture the whole truth. When it came to human rights it seems, however, that Chang endorsed a position that human rights should be implemented as quickly as possible, irrespectively of the culture and the organization of society. In other words, certain ideas such as ideas of fundamental freedoms were clear-cut and obvious and ready for implementation, while others were more difficult to apply automatically such as the ones that concern the more specific political and economic organization of society.

APPLYING THE INTERCULTURAL APPROACH TO THE UDHR

One could ask how this earlier notion of creative adjustment from Chang could be applied to the human rights discourse and the institutional frameworks that had been created at an international level before the United Nations and the UDHR. The remarks below express some possible applications of the former concepts introduced above:

1. A *fringe of dissatisfaction* concerning the lack of a common global ethics and successful international institutions. Previously there were only limited examples, that is, national or regional codes. The League of Nations was also seen as a failure in many respects, and it did not stress the importance of individual human rights generally (even though it endorsed rights for ethnic/national minorities to some extent). Mankind had also experienced serious atrocities such as war and genocide and a disrespect of

human dignity more generally. Hence, the recognition of the urgent need to create a new international organization and to formulate international strategies and rights schemes that could hinder that history should repeat itself in these respects.

2. An *extensive and comparative survey* for suggestion and stimulation (a broad working group within the United Nations and several surveys of previous rights documents). This was done mainly by the drafting group of the UDHR, where especially the Canadian law professor John Humphrey had an important role to play.

3. A *liberated inventiveness* concerning the function and the content of the UDHR – 'raising the standard of man' or the humanization of man. The educational project of creating a standard for raising the moral stature of man was in other words the overarching moral ideal for Chang with reference to the UDHR. Then comes the stage of creating an awareness of certain duties and obligations – the very important ones. Among these are the duties to respect human rights and human dignity. In these statements from Chang, the human rights come as 'the last part' in the moral educational project.

Chang claimed that certain issues – such as metaphysical ones – were not suitable to be discussed in a setting like this (the Human Rights Commission and the drafting group) and that they were intractable, unsolvable issues. More generally, one could see that Chang thought that certain topics were not suitable for inclusion in the UDHR discussions for different reasons. Certain statements were not apt for voting in committee meetings such as theological and metaphysical issues and they could create sharp disagreement and conflicts. Further, they could reflect standpoints that were too parochial from a cultural point of view – and – they may also be irrelevant for 'the UDHR project' in Chang's terms. For Chang this was a moral educational project with the main purpose of making human beings more aware of their moral duties – duties that were correlated to human rights.

In other words, there was no need for the Human Rights Commission to take any stand on ultimate principles/causes and metaphysics. These remarks of Chang presented 'the space' for cultural negotiation or communication with reference to the ethics of human rights in the UDHR. One could also say, as was claimed before, that the main challenge 1) above (concerning 'man's brutality against man') pointed to a common denominator among the delegates as one of the main purposes of the UDHR project was to prevent atrocities of the same kind that had occurred during the Second World War.

On the other hand, Chang did not want to exclude people with strong views on metaphysics and theology from accepting a document like this. One had to find compromises that all main parties could accept. A good example of this strategy concerns the formulation of article 1 in the UDHR ('All human beings are born free and equal in dignity and rights. They are endowed with reason and conscience and should act towards another in a spirit of brotherhood.') We will discuss why this is a good example below.

Chang's reasoning was crucial to the decision of the Third committee of the United Nations to remove the phrase 'by nature' from the so-called Geneva draft. He argued that the deletion of that phrase would 'obviate any theological question, which could not and should not be raised in a declaration designed to be universally applicable'. From the summary of the discussions: 'The Chinese representative would refrain from proposing that mention of them (ideals and traditions in China) should be made in the declaration. He hoped that his colleagues would show equal consideration and withdraw some of the amendments to article 1 which raised metaphysical problems.'

Chang claimed: 'For Western civilization, too, the time for religious intolerance was over.' The first line of article 1, Chang suggested, should refer neither to nature nor to God. Those who believed in God could still find the idea of God in the strong assertions that all human beings are born free and equal and endowed with reason and conscience, but others should be allowed to interpret the language differently. Chang declared that 1869, the year of the publications of Darwin's treaties, really marked the beginning of the so-called conflict of religion and science. The effects, already eighty years old, of that manifestation of the human spirit, could not be sufficiently deplored, and its influence could be felt in the committee itself. For that reason he stressed the necessity of studying the problem of religious expression in its true perspective. In order to throw more light on the question, he wished first of all to explain to the committee how the Chinese approached the religious problem. According to Chang, 'Chinese philosophy was based essentially on a firm belief in a Unitarian cause', expressed on the human plane by what Chang called a *pluralistic tolerance*.

That philosophy considered that man's actions were more important than metaphysics, that the art of living should be placed above knowledge of the causes of life, and that the best way for man to testify to the greatness of the Divinity was to give proof of an exemplary attitude in this world. In the eyes of Chinese philosophers it was pluralistic tolerance manifesting itself in every sphere of thought, conscience and religion, which should inspire men if they wished to base their relations on benevolence and justice.

These statements from Chang about prioritizing action and 'the art of living' in comparison to speculative metaphysics were also in tune with his teacher John Dewey's philosophical thoughts and other pragmatist philosophers' ideas (Twiss 2009).

It is interesting to note that Chang referred to 'the greatness of the Divinity' in the statements above. As was said before, Chang expressed that the best way to honour the divinity is to engage in an 'art of living'. Chang claimed that: 'In other words, it is again that humanistic attitude. It is to respect the spirit *as if* it were there – emphasizing the influence of that respect on humanity, and not so much the nature of the spirit itself, which we human beings should be humble enough to acknowledge we do not know.' When Chang explicitly discussed Confucius's attitude towards spiritual things and 'concerning the attitude to worship' he cited *Analects 6:22*. The original statement expresses 'To give one's self earnestly to the duties due to men, and, while respecting spiritual beings, to keep aloof from them, may be called wisdom'. As was claimed before Chang often expressed the statement 'respect the spirit *as if* the spirit were there' in the context of this statement from Confucius.

However, Chang did not show any interest in any church or religious activity after his student years in the United States and it is difficult to recognize any religious beliefs that he clinged on to in later years. Not any of his writings during the 1930s and the 1940s expresses any religious inclinations even though he showed respect for religious beliefs and believers. The 'agnostic' statement that one should act 'as if God exists' also fits that picture. According to Chang's son Stanley, his father was never involved in any religious activities during the time that Stanley lived with him during the 1930s, 1940s and the 1950s. However, his father often expressed the words 'Ru Tsai' in daily life which means 'as if present'. One should always behave with that in mind. God is ever present.

Chang – more than anyone else among the drafters of the UDHR – stressed the importance of getting rid of notions of God, natural law and controversial metaphysics in the UDHR as the document should be a document for all, irrespectively of their religions and substantial philosophies (i.e. it should be *universal*). When Chang was endorsing the UDHR, he was in other words challenging any form of cultural parochialism that downgraded the universalist ambitions of the drafters. According to Chang's agnostic perspective, religious and metaphysical issues were also unsolvable and their relevance for 'the humanization purpose' of the UDHR could be seen as questionable. They were also not questions that were apt for voting.

RESEARCH ON CHANG'S CONTRIBUTIONS TO THE UDHR

So, how should we understand Chang's contribution to the UDHR? Did he represent a specific world view, for example Confucianism? In recent years some authors have published articles on Peng Chun Chang and his contributions to the UDHR. A common opinion has been that Chang's main contribution to the UDHR was a Confucian perspective (Twiss 2009). A representative statement from this group of writers is the following: 'Peng Chun

Chang was widely regarded as one of the most philosophically astute among the delegates. He was a noted Confucian humanist, philosopher, diplomat and playwright who had held diplomatic posts in Turkey, Chile, had emanated a zeal for promoting Chinese culture and had been fond of drawing connections between Islam and Confucianism' (Kao 2011).

However, this view about the presence of Confucian thinking in Chang's statements has also been challenged recently (Kumbrien 2015). According to this latter view, Chang did not mention Confucius and other Chinese philosophers in his speeches to any larger extent, and we could also trace elements in Chang's thinking from other sources and ideas that stood in sharp contrast with the so-called Confucian thinking. For example, Chang often emphasized the importance of liberal freedom and rights from the Enlightenment period in Europe, but he had never argued that human beings could flourish only within their own original cultural communities.

Other scholars have had a much broader perspective than the ones mentioned above and have not primarily discussed if Chang was a Confucian or not. Mary Ann Glendon has been more eager to stress Chang's multifaceted thinking even though Confucianism also played an important part in his thinking according to her (Glendon 2002). In a private conversation (2015) Glendon made the following remarks to me concerning Chang (and his relationship to the other philosopher in the drafting group, Charles Malik):

> Charles Malik's strands of thoughts were very varied (and so was also Chang's). They also worked with a project that was highly complex and it was room for political compromises and improvisations. This was not a project where one could apply a definite theory, the problems had to speak for themselves and a more piecemeal, gradual approach was needed.

An interesting analysis of Chang's thoughts that brings forward the multifaceted character of his ideas is done by Pierre Etienne Will (2007). Will has claimed that Chang was too smart, and too much of a cosmopolitan, to act as an ambassador of Confucianism. According to Will, Chang used three approaches at the same time when he was engaged in the writing of the UDHR.

First of all, Chang wanted to prevent the UDHR from being a document which the citizens of non-Western nations would not be familiar with. Chang would in other words use formulations that should be seen as general, inclusive, neutral or all encompassing. He was, for example, against all references to natural law theory and theism in various forms.

Second, Chang also used a more positive approach that made references to various traditions in order to enhance the universal value or validity of the UDHR. He made references to, for example, the Confucian notion of '*ren*' (benevolence or sympathy for others), which he regarded as the *natural* goodness of man, an innate capacity for empathy towards one's fellow human being that should be included as a characteristic of man in addition to reason in article 1 of the UDHR. He also referred to the French Enlightenment philosophers such as Voltaire and Diderot when it came to the formulation of fundamental freedom. Hence, he claimed that different traditions had something valuable to contribute to the more general validity of the UDHR.

In this context we could use the concept of *bricolage* borrowed from the American philosopher Jeffrey Stout (2001). Stout used this concept to characterize Martin Luther King's genius for borrowing from multiple moral traditions in order to organize a broad coalition of democratic reform. We could here draw an analogy with Chang who borrowed from several moral traditions in order to create a consensus around the content of the UDHR.

Chang also claimed that various countries had relevant experiences and ideas that could enhance the realism and the plausibility of the UDHR. For China, religious pluralism had never been a problem to the same extent as in Europe, as religion in China had not been politicized in the same manner as in Europe. However, one could qualify these statements from Chang with references to religious rebellions in the Chinese history such as the Turban Rebellion during the Han dynasty, the Red Turban Rebellion during the Yuan dynasty and the Taiping Rebellion during the Qing dynasty in the middle of the nineteenth century. In recent times certain religious minorities have also faced serious discrimination, for example, the Falun Gong. Some commentators also mean that communism in China developed traits that have been almost 'religious' in character. Even though these qualifications are valid, we could still say that China and Europe have been different in terms of religious wars and conflicts. In China, the rulers have never been using religion as a way of distinguishing an 'us' from a 'them' in the same manner as the rulers in European countries, which could explain the different conflict patterns.

Third, Chang used some Confucian and Chinese notions to convey a point or reach a compromise. As the secretary of the drafting group the Canadian law professor John Humphrey claimed, 'Chang was a master in the arts of compromise, and under the pretext of some quotations from Confucius, he often succeeded in providing the Commission with a formula that would help it get out of a deadlock' (Glendon 2002).

Here are some examples of proverbs from Chang: 'Sweep the snow in front of one's own door. Overlook the frost on other's roof tiles.' That made for good neighbours.

He also wished to lay great stress upon the need for careful consideration of the amendments before the committee. Another Chinese proverb suitable in this context ran: 'Matters allowed to mature slowly are free from sharp corners.' Concerning confrontation and the use of tougher or softer methods, he wrote : 'A matter of fighting with a fist on one side, and a soft glue on the other.' 'A belief that the softer way always conquers the stronger way which is also stiffer and more brittle' (Chang 1939b).

Will's analysis is very illuminating and it seems to be adequate with reference to Chang's statements in the UN context. However, one could make some additions and qualifications. The first point about formulating an inclusive intercultural language could be exemplified in two different ways.

Concerning article 1 in the UDHR ('All men are born ...'), Chang said that the idea of man as an autonomous, rational being was a concept that was compatible with the concept of God (and hence theistic traditions) and there was no reason to refer to man as created in the image of God, as for example, the Brazilian delegate to the commission had wanted. Chang also assumed that this notion of man was compatible with secular, humanistic world views. Here one could claim that Chang used an argumentative strategy that was similar to John Rawls's idea of overlapping consensus – the idea that one could reach the same kind of moral conclusions on the basis of different life views or philosophies (Bell 2015). The social liberal thoughts of Rawls that expressed the idea of catering for all needy in the distributional schemes of society also fitted well with Chang's socio-economic thoughts (that were influenced by Confucian traditions) (Cheng and Cheng 1995).

Chang also wanted the UDHR to be open in terms of overall metaphysics. When he stated that it was enough to claim that man is endowed with reason and conscience (in Chang's concepts 'the sympathy for others' – *lianqxin*) and that one should not express one's idea about the specific origin of the endowment, he left the door open for various metaphysics such as 'by God', 'by Nature', 'by Chance'.

One could add a fourth point to Will's three-point list of Chang's intercultural strategies. Chang made references to what he meant to be the primary function of the UDHR – the moral educational project of 'raising the moral stature of man' or the humanization of man. This purpose of the document implied that certain issues (such as 'explanatory' metaphysical concepts) were not really relevant in the writing process. Connected to this function of the UDHR was the problem of how to handle 'man's inhumanity against man'. For Chang this was one of the most important ethical and political challenges, and one could assume that he meant that this was a clear common denominator among the delegates, irrespective of where they came from and which religious and political traditions they adhered to.

How then did Chang distinguish between cultural parochialism that ran the risk of estranging people from the UDHR and the cultural contributions from various countries that he meant had a more universal value for the UDHR? My answer is that the latter in contrast to the former did not concern overall philosophical issues that influenced the whole character of the document. Instead, they highlighted or clarified something that also found its 'echo' among several of the representatives in the drafting group. They concerned problems that many of the representatives had more or less recognized and the new contributions presented here reasonable solutions to the problems. In the case of Chang's contribution of the concept of *'ren'* (benevolence or sympathy for others) from the Confucian tradition, other delegates such as Eleanor Roosevelt had already felt the need of finding a more social, emotional complement to the characteristic of reason or rationality in the characterization of man in article 1, and Chang's contribution filled this gap in a reasonable way.

If one uses a common conception of a compromise strategy with reference to the UDHR as a whole, Chang gave clear expressions of that kind of strategy in his work (Gutmann and Thompson 2012). That conception implies that both parties have to give up something in order to gain something new and valuable (in order for the UDHR to fulfil the objectives universality, inclusiveness, religious neutrality, being easy to grasp for the layman and being practically useful for the moral educational project of the humanization of man). The delegates in the Human Rights Commission had to 'give up' certain of their cherished philosophical and theological ideas and issues – at least in an explicit sense with reference to the UDHR. Hence, the demand for non-parochialism and concepts that were non-metaphysical. In other words, Chang argued that the delegates and the drafters should show constraint in their attempts to influence the UDHR with their own metaphysical ideas and customs.

In his argumentative strategy, Chang also emphasized the importance of all nations to downgrade their urge to influence the UDHR in a way that could be seen as unjust and unreasonable from the perspective of other nations. It was not relevant how large the country was in terms of population and size. China which is one of the largest nations of the world had showed constraint in this project, and it would be reasonable if the other countries did the same, Chang argued. He also focused upon relevant concepts such as equality and dignity and the right to non-discrimination, as well as pluralistic tolerance with reference to freedom of religion. All these ideas pointed towards an ideal of universality and inclusiveness.

Did all parties then perceive the compromises as just or fair to the same extent? Some parties may have to sacrifice more than the others and the compromise may not be on equal terms. In the case of article 1 and the phrase 'endowed with reason and conscience', one could say that the detachment of words such as 'by God' and 'by Nature' was a fair proposal as both theists and materialists had to suppress their specific metaphysics to the same extent. (Chang assumed here that 'by Nature' was a materialistic notion rather than a humanistic notion and that it stood in conflict with a theistic notion of creation.)

The introduction of the concepts free, rational, conscious being in article 1 must also have to resonate strongly among advocates of different philosophies and compensate for the loss of more explicit theological or metaphysical notions (such as created in the image of God). Here one could say that even though the concepts are compatible with the concept of God, as Chang claims, the characterization could be seen as more sufficient for a humanistic view that may not strive for any metaphysical underpinning in the same way as the theist. (The theist may on the other hand claim that it is the reference to God that explains the moral importance of the article.) The detachment of these different philosophies from the content of the UDHR must in other words be compensated by the objective to create a universal document that most people could identify themselves with – and hence – be a part of a peace-building project.

CHANG'S LEGACY

In this chapter I have given a presentation and analysis of Peng Chun Chang's intercultural contributions to the UDHR. Chang's ideas about intercultural communication and dialogue were formulated long before he started to work with the UDHR, and these earlier ideas proved to be fruitful in order to avoid stalemates in the discussion concerning the content of the UDHR. It is interesting to note that Chang at an early stage also expressed views very similar to the American philosophers John Rawls and Ronald Dworkin concerning fairness and social equality. He also expressed views similar to the Indian philosopher Amartya Sen's views concerning the implementation of the UDHR. Legislation was not enough. Educational methods were also essential for the fulfilment of human rights.

Chang's exposure to liberal thoughts and human rights thinking during his time as a student and scholar in the United States could be one partial explanation why he later on became such a prominent advocate of human rights in the UN system. And he was also eager to distil human rights thoughts from other ethical traditions – not at least from traditions in his own country China. The characteristics that we mainly associate with the UDHR today – its universalism, its religious neutrality and its aim of fostering pluralistic tolerance and raising the moral stature of man (or the humanization of man) – had as one of their strongest defenders in Peng Chun Chang. No one was as eager as him to formulate sentences that could be accepted by most people around the world. Here lies Chang's main legacy with reference to the UDHR – a legacy that has proved to be more and more important during the time that has passed since 1948.

Chapter 6

Critical Thinking and Culture

Shared Values, Different Guises

Soraj Hongladarom

This book addresses two very important questions, namely how one can communicate ethics in the era of globalization, and whether it is possible to overcome cultural differences and agree across cultural borders on some common values and principles. It goes without much saying that these are among the most important questions in today's world; however, they are notoriously difficult to find a satisfactory answer. Nonetheless, this is what I set out to do. My short answer to the first question is that ethics can certainly be communicated across cultures. The answer does not presuppose any kind of cultural universalism; in fact I will argue that cultural universalism is not a tenable idea.

'Universalism' here is used in the sense of one's believing that one's own particular set of viewpoints and values is the only true one. This is a logical consequence of the belief that one's version of value system and description of reality is the real truth, which implies that others' versions are only fabrications. That would indeed be detrimental to the project that this book tries to accomplish from the beginning. The task, then, is left to find a condition of possibility for cross-cultural communication of ethical ideas, which I propose can be found in human's *practical* nature as evidenced in how they use reasons and engage in critical thinking. Thus my answer to the first question implies directly a positive reply to the second: It is certainly possible to overcome cultural differences and come to a kind of cosmopolitan mutual understanding. It is my view that people can indeed come to agreement on values and principles because deep down they are practical creatures in the sense that they always search for ways and means of achieving their goals; thus when the goals of different people coincide, then, people being practical, they communicate with one another and attempt to achieve their common goals together. It is this common practicality that leads people to adopt more or less common ways of engaging themselves in critical thinking and reasoning. Since logic is universal, this universality is expressed in some common human traits that transcend the different ways one and the same truth is presented and embedded in different contexts. This does not mean that those different ways are not important. In fact many wars have been fought just about these different ways of portraying the same truth, so a way has to be found to accommodate both the common core and the different representations at the same time.

I will lay out a basis for my argument through a historical analysis of how different cultures view logic, reasoning and critical thinking. I argued in a previous paper (Hongladarom 2006) that the culture of critical thinking, which consists of not accepting any belief unless it is thoroughly supported by sound evidence or argument and the trust in the efficacy of rational argumentation as a means towards agreement, could actually be found in the two main traditions of Asian philosophy, namely the Chinese and the Indian. Critical thinking here means the kind of thinking that serves as the goal of study in a course on informal logic in a typical undergraduate curriculum: a kind of study that fosters healthy scepticism, rational argumentation, evaluation of reasons, all of which are essential for functioning effectively in contemporary society. In this way, then, critical thinking is a very important component in a discussion of ethics and communication across cultures. This is because critical thinking is a set of skills that have as its foundation logic and rationality. As logic and rationality are the basis on which communication and comprehension are possible, in a situation where there is a lack of critical thinking, then there would be no way in which common language or successful translation can be constructed, which obviously results in breakdown of communication.

However, there have been a number of arguments purporting to show that logic and critical thinking were the prerogatives of the West (See, e.g. Lun et al. 2010 and Chan et al. 2011). This implies that if one wants to achieve whatever result that the West has achieved, namely achieving scientific, technological and thus economic progresses, one has, in effect, to become a Westerner in the sense that one has to immerse oneself in the tradition leading back to Thales and Aristotle. I argued that this argument is not tenable because there were strong traditions of logic and critical thinking both in India and in China, so it is false to claim that logic and critical thinking belong to the West only (Hongladarom 2006). I also argue that the reason why critical thinking as a value in education seems in Asia to lag behind Europe is because it is actively promoted by the cultures themselves, who give priorities to other competing values.

I would like to argue, then, that critical thinking can indeed be found in any culture because it is necessary for survival of the members of that culture themselves – hence the practicality of human beings I alluded to above.

One might object to this by pointing out that in many cultures, especially non-Western ones, critical thinking does not seem to be its strongest aspect. This is attested by a number of studies showing that in Thai culture at least, critical thinking is only paid lip service to but not actively encouraged.

An anonymous author writes in the *Kyoto Review* that critical and independent thinking is not listed as one of the missions of higher education in Thailand (Anonymous 2015). Jonathan Richmond also presents an analysis of the lack of critical thinking culture in Thailand and proposes a programme for remedy (Richmond 2007). These writers, in short, offer an analysis as to why critical thinking has not taken root in Thailand. I argue further in this paper that the reason why in some cultures it does not seem to be as visible is that the opinion leaders within these cultures enact policies that inhibit the growth of critical thinking, such as not promoting critical thinking in schools and encouraging rote learning and unthinking loyalty to the main institutions of the culture, all of which are clearly detrimental to the growth of a critical thinking culture. The elites in those cultures, which actually include such people as high-ranking civil servants, monks, leading professionals and so on, believe that the set of belief handed down to them by the previous generations is more valuable in itself and thus it is more efficient to impose or instil the set onto the next generation rather than letting the next generation try things out for themselves.

A close look at critical thinking and its relation to culture, I argue, is necessary for an ethics of communication, especially in the context of globalization, because the values presupposed by critical thinking are ones that enable effective communication across cultures to take place. In an attempt to communicate ethical values across cultures, those values not only have to be translated into the vocabulary that is pertinent to the receiving culture, but it has to be pointed out that these values are there in the receiving culture from the beginning, from within the indigenous source of the values and traditions of that culture themselves. The core is common to all cultures – practical and resourceful nature of human beings, their ability to solve problems facing them, but the ways the core is presented can be very different. Thus my argument is a way to offset the charge that the values of critical thinking are merely Western values imposed on those of the receiving culture.

In order to accomplish this I will offer some cast studies drawn from Thai history and educational policy. It is well known that Thai education is based on an attempt to restrict critical thinking, much as it has been advertised otherwise (See, e.g. Lao 2015). Lao shows the historical source of the lack of emphasis on critical thinking as a goal of education in Thailand. However, I will supplement these studies by providing an ethical analysis as to why this has been the case and what can be done in the future. This will have strong implications in the discussion on ethics of communication and globalization as a whole. The Thai case presented here is also relevant to other similar countries in that Lao's study shows some common themes which could be readily applicable, such as the culture of borrowing which happens when leaders in a culture have to 'pick and choose' elements from the external, more powerful cultures while finding ways to maintain their identity (See also Lao 2015).

CRITICAL THINKING AND LOGIC IN INDIA AND CHINA

It is well known that modern logic has its origin in the philosophy of Aristotle. The structure of logic itself has not changed since the time of Aristotle until the advent of modern symbolic logic in the late nineteenth century (Kneale and Kneale 1962). This may have given an impression that logic is a unique product of Western civilization.

However, there are no less sophisticated logical traditions in the two major Asian civilizations, namely that of India and China. These civilizations developed their own logical tradition independently of the Greek. It might be possible that there could be contacts between Indian and Greek civilizations through the channel opened up by Alexander the Great around the fourth century BC (Beckwith 2015). However, those contacts, even if they were really there, were too little to justify the sophistication of the Indian logical and mathematical tradition. After all, it was the Indians who came up with the numeral zero, which greatly revolutionized mathematics the world over. Furthermore, the Indians also had a strong tradition of debating and using reason to investigate phenomena. In Buddhist philosophy, for example, reasoning and logic are the main instruments by which one comes to understand its tenets. One is reminded of the pictures of monks in Tibetan monasteries debating with one another vigorously, a tradition which they carry over from India. Buddhist logic is also a well-developed discipline that many generations of monks and scholars have studied. I gave an example of what could be called an Indian syllogism, which shows that there was a systematization of logical thoughts in the same way as in Aristotle. The Indian syllogism looks like this:

1. There is fire on this mountain.
2. For, there is smoke there.
3. Smoke goes with fire always (or, in all cases, or in all places): witness, kitchen.
4. This is also a case of smoke.
5. Therefore, there is fire there (on the mountain). (Matilal 1990: 5, quoted in Hongladarom 2006: 164).

The structure may sound rather unfamiliar, but the argument purports to show as its conclusion that there is fire there. The premise of the argument is that there is smoke, which is seen, and that smoke is always accompanied by fire, such as in the kitchen. So, since smoke is always accompanied by fire and since there is smoke on the mountain, there is fire on the mountain. The argument is valid, and this example shows that Indian culture knew something about logic, and many scholarly works on the topic attest that Indian logic is at least as advanced as its Aristotelian counterpart (See, e.g. Vidyabhusana 2006). As logic is the basis of critical thinking, critical thinking and its theorization were certainly known in medieval India.

In China there is also a tradition of logic and critical thinking whose most outstanding representative was the philosopher Mo Di, who lived roughly around the same time as did Confucius and Socrates, that is, the sixth century BC. Mo Di was the first philosopher about whom we have evidence that he promoted logic and argumentation in Chinese philosophy, a kind of utilitarian ethics, and a belief in universalism of values. What is interesting for our purpose in this chapter is his view on logic. The article on Mohism (doctrine of Mo Di) by Chris Fraser in the Stanford Encyclopaedia of Philosophy captures the gist of the matter very well:

> Their basic model of reasoning can be thought of as comprising three parts. (1) One or more fa (standards, models, or examples) are cited by which to distinguish 'this' from 'not' or to guide the use of some term, such as *ren* (humane) or *yi* (morally right). (2) Then it is indicated how some object, event, or practice does or does not 'match' or 'coincide' (*zhong*) with the fa. (3) Accordingly, the thing in question is distinguished as 'this' or 'not', as humane and right or not-humane and not-right. So what we think of as the major premise in a syllogistic piece of reasoning, the Mohists probably see as citing a fa. What we call a minor premise, they see as a claim that something 'coincides' with the fa. What we think of as drawing a conclusion, they see as distinguishing whether or not something is the same kind of thing as the fa. Later Mohist texts make it clear that this reasoning process is regarded as a form of analogical inference or projection, which they call 'extending kinds' (*tui lei*) – that is, 'extending' our judgment of what counts as 'of the same kind' to include new cases. In practice, 'extending kinds' amounts to taking the judgment that things are 'of a kind' (*lei*) in one or more respects as a basis for treating them as 'of a kind' in another. (Fraser 2014)

Thus in Mohism we also have a form of reasoning that is comparable to the standard Aristotelian syllogism. At least there was an attempt at systematization of logical thought in China, something that has not been appreciated much in the study of Chinese philosophy, which tends to focus almost exclusively on Confucianism. Nonetheless, the logical tradition in China is there. Unfortunately Mohism has not been given much attention at all either by the Chinese philosophical tradition, the traditional state apparatus or by contemporary scholars.

The seed that was first sown by Mo Di could have been developed and consequently propelled China to become a leader in logic, mathematics and the sciences. This would have satisfied Joseph Needham, a pioneer who studied scientific civilization in China and who wrote a monumental set of volumes on the topic, who wondered what actually prevented China from becoming such a centre, as China had been much more advanced that Europe in terms of commerce and technological innovation until Europe surpassed it with the scientific and the industrial revolutions in the seventeenth and eighteenth centuries (Needham 1978). The question of what prevented China from having its own scientific and industrial revolutions then became known as 'Needham's Question'.

Furthermore, Needham's Question can also be asked about India, which also had a comparable level of advancement in science (though less in technology than China). In any case, the evidence I have put forward here shows that India and China had their own traditions of science, mathematics and logic which were as advanced as any in the Greco-Roman world, if not more. Thus the argument for the view that logic and critical thinking are culture bound and are only the prerogatives of the West is not supported by evidence.

CASE STUDY: CRITICAL THINKING IN THAILAND

Educational policy in Thailand, I argue, can illustrate the point of communicating ethics across culture through critical thinking. Education in Thailand has been a subject of substantial research, as many are perplexed by the persistent lack of quality in education despite huge amount of budget allocated by the central government each year. The symptoms of the lack of quality are clear: Students are not encouraged to think for themselves; there is much emphasis on rote learning; teachers are not motivated to focus their work on the students, but on countless other distractions and the list goes on. This has resulted in Thailand being ranked consistently near the bottom of any ranking of quality of education, such as the one done by the Programme for International Student Assessment (PISA). The problem is why it is that Thailand is always ranked so low despite the very intense attention paid by the government and the public on education and huge amount of budget, much more in terms of budget per student than in other countries.

It is tempting to draw a conclusion from this Thai phenomenon that logic and critical thinking actually belong exclusively to the West. This is because the PISA tests obviously require skills in logic and critical thinking, but the poor Thai results show that these subjects are not *natural* to Thai students, so to speak. The culture of educational system in Thailand, where students are not encouraged to ask critical questions but made to follow their teachers blindly, also gives support to the idea. However, the surge of countries such as China, Hong Kong, Taiwan and Singapore in the PISA tests shows that the contrary is more likely to be true. Thus the problem must lie within Thailand itself.

In a recent study, Rattana Lao (2015) shows that the policy of adopting practices originated from the West is tinged with indigenous cultural values, which distort how the adopted policy is expressed and implemented. Thus, when the system of Quality Assurance (QA) (a programme developed in the West of making quality in education objective through a set of measurable indexes) was adopted by the Thai policy makers, what resulted was not a focus on improvement of quality of Thai education, but more on consolidation of the powers of the elites and the continuation of the status quo in the new appearance obtained through QA (Lao 2015). In this case, Lao's observation is not different from my own earlier observation that the blame should lie with the overarching policy of the Thai elites, consisting of high-ranking nobility and members of the royal family who controlled every aspect of public policy in Thailand since the mid-nineteenth century. When the European powers arrived in Siam with their gunships, a crisis took place in Siam that prompted these leaders to find a way to accommodate the ideas and knowledge coming from the West, such as the modern scientific knowledge within the cultural universe of the Siamese people. What resulted was that the leaders adopted only those Western ideas that were related to material technologies and they tried to keep the religious worldviews intact. In their case, the religious worldviews are derived from Buddhism and these form the basis of their system of moral values. In other words, the elites sought to allow in technical expertise from the West which was useful in, for example, building canons and ships, but they kept out those ideas, such as the scientific attitude towards nature and critical thinking, which they saw to be disruptive to the moral order. The emphasis on rote learning can then be explained by this policy as rote learning is the fastest way to modernize the country so as to respond to the European threats. Another result of the same policy is that the elites can then maintain the status quo, where they retain their hegemony over the population, which hegemony is based strongly on the value system that puts them at the top of the social hierarchy, and it is this value system that has been kept intact (Hongladarom 2002). For the elites the philosophical ideas underpinning modern science, such as the belief that nature is ruled by objective law which can be known by everybody, were not seen to be important because Thailand already has Buddhist philosophy. On the contrary they need the more recent technical expertise which would make the country materially stronger. However, the philosophical ideas also include the understanding of the basic science that make technology possible, and this basic understanding of science in the West comes hand in hand with the tradition of logic and critical thinking which allows for a spirit of free inquiry and persistent questioning. In their haste to modernize the country, however, the Thai traditional elites selected only what worked in the short term and neglected to import the tradition of free inquiry from the West. I would like to argue that this is the root cause of the malady affecting Thai education to the present day (Hongladarom 2002).

The complaints that many are voicing regarding the lack of the ability to think critically and to engage in the atmosphere of free inquiry among Thai students is a direct consequence of the policy to modernize the country through exclusive focus on the short term only, namely on the technical skills and knowledge that make Thailand *appear* to be modern. What is lacking is then the atmosphere of free inquiry and critical thinking. Thus Thailand is very good at manufacturing according to given specifications, but very lacking in original scientific research. This emphasis on appearance rather than substance is also bolstered by the typical Thai attitude towards epistemic values such as truth. To put it simply, traditional Thai culture regards other values such as continuity or harmony as even more important than truth (Hongladarom 2002a).

All these make it seem that critical thinking and the spirit of free inquiry are only Western imports, but then the logical traditions in India and China discussed in the previous section seem to belie this assessment, and Thai culture is an heir to both Indian and Chinese cultures. However, the traditions of reason that flourished in India and China actually had its heyday many centuries ago. In India the tradition coincided with the golden age of Buddhist philosophy, which is roughly between eighth and twelfth centuries AD, and Mohism in China flourished during the Warring States period, around fifth century BC. Some might argue that if it were indeed the case that there were traditions of logic and critical thinking in India and China, it happened and died away so long ago that it hardly has any impact today. Mohism, for example, was not given any support by the state establishment in imperial China, so the tradition was almost entirely forgotten. Indian logic and philosophy did not fully die away, but it did not function as an impetus towards propelling India to become an industrial powerhouse at the time when Europe became ascendant. This shows, so the objection goes, that the logical traditions that existed in the past are actually irrelevant today; furthermore, the logic and critical thinking that are being studied both in India and China have their roots in Aristotle, not in Dignaga (one of the most well-known Indian logicians) or in Mo Di. Thus, according to the objection, critical thinking is a Western product after all.

I am not denying that logic and critical thinking that are being studied in India, China and indeed all countries in the world today are part of the European tradition. But that does not mean that traditions such as Indian or Buddhist logic, and Mohism are completely irrelevant. On the contrary, it clearly shows that it is possible for a culture, if they are advanced enough, to develop its own, home-grown logical tradition. Greek also developed its own logical tradition, as is well known, so there is nothing in principle that could prevent other civilizations from doing the same. The fact that these traditions died down and did not receive state support are actually historically contingent factors which would require a whole book to explain satisfactorily, something that obviously cannot be achieved in this chapter. That there existed traditions such as Indian logic and Mohism implies that a culture can develop its own indigenous logical culture, complete with all the qualities that are associated with freedom of inquiry, relentless questioning, healthy scepticism and so on. This shows that the values that are associated with critical thinking are not essentially Western ones.

The Thai example shows the point that I am making here very well. Since Thailand is a small country, its culture depends on that of the two Asian giants for resources. An almost exclusive intellectual resource for Thai culture is Buddhism, which was received from India. The clash between values that I mentioned earlier in the section was between the traditional ones and the ones coming with the Western powers and their gunboats. The élites, namely the king and his circle, tried to preserve what they saw to be valuable in their traditions while at the same time they modernized the country so that it became strong enough to resist the Europeans, or more often to make the country appear 'civilized', thus offsetting the argument often made by Europeans that they were on a civilizing mission. If Siam (as the country was called then) was civilized enough, so reasoned the Thai élites, then there would be no excuse for the Western powers to colonize the country. And chief among the internal civilizing missions for the élites was to make the country appear modern. Thus there were attempts to make the country look like a typical Western country; there were reforms of law codes; railways were laid down; roads were paved; modern hospitals were set up and so on. However, deep down Siam remained resolutely Siamese at the core, and the élites defined the core as a Buddhist polity where they themselves held on to hegemonic power.

The élites divided European thoughts and ideas into two kinds, those that they were eager to import and those they wanted to keep away. As previously mentioned the former were those which were necessarily for material power, and the latter were those that were seen to threaten the core values of the élites themselves. Critical thinking unsurprisingly belonged to the latter group, as the practices of asking questions, not believing anything without investigation, and so on, were seen to threaten the continuity of the hegemony of the élites directly. It is only when critical thinking, as part of the modern educational system, became a part of the teaching programme that students had a chance to study it. The lively tradition in Buddhism of debating and using reason to find out the truth for oneself was not encouraged at all when Siam adopted the religion, which became the state religion. Instead much emphasis was put, and still is, on memorizing the canonical texts without investigating on one's own what they mean. This goes very much towards destroying the spirit of free inquiry and critical thought. All this policy implementation flows out of the belief of the elites as they issued decrees, edicts and so on based on the idea. This can be seen from the frequent phrases that are found throughout documents issued by the Thai government, 'preserving Thai identity'. The Thai identity that is going to be preserved is precisely the view that the elites in the mid-nineteenth century sought to preserve against the onslaught of the Western powers – supremacy of Buddhist moral order based on the hierarchy that puts the king at the top. Thus students who ask too many questions or who dare to disrupt the order will be regarded as social outcasts. This includes adults too. Bureaucrats who question the order will also be seen as outcasts and 'unThai'.

Critical thinking then remains only at the surface, something that is only there just to show the outside world that Thailand is modernized. In other words, there are teaching programmes that include critical thinking in the curricula, such as in high schools and in universities, but deep down at the level of real, daily life it is not encouraged at all. This results in many cases where critical thinking is mentioned in the school curricula, but seldom acted out in the classroom.

All these show that whether critical thinking flourishes in a culture or not actually depends on more conscious decisions rather than on whether the culture in question is essentially receptive to it or not. We have seen that the latter option is untenable because the logical traditions actually flourished in Asian cultures as we have seen. It is then the conscious decision of the Thai elites that has kept critical thinking only at the surface. Studies by Lao and others show clearly that critical thinking is virtually kept out of the reach of students, especially in primary and secondary schools where critical thinking is non-existent (Lao 2015; Hongladarom 2002). The focus of Thai education is more on producing farmers or low-skilled workers, together with very few members of the elites who get very good education, than on middle-class workers who will become a backbone of an industrial nation.

The political decision here does not mean that at a particular instance there is a conscious order from the authorities forbidding the teaching of critical thinking. The order does not have to come in such a direct form, which would disturb the facade of modernity that Thailand is presenting to the outside world. On the contrary there are subtle ways of fencing Thai people in, so to speak, so that they do not see that what is going on outside of their country can be applied inside. The subtle ways include repeated discourse on the uniqueness of Thai identity. This is told to the students over and over since the time they enter kindergarten, so much so that vast majority of students grow up believing that norms that are valid in other countries do not have to be valid inside Thailand. Thus critical thinking is not actively encouraged in Thailand because it is seen to create disruptions, disharmonies and even lack of national security. When people really believe that critical thinking and its associated values are foreign to Thai culture, it is only a short step from that to a hegemony by the elites because an important part of the policy of not encouraging critical thinking is that the elites are believed to always act in the best interest of the Thai nation, and this belief provides the elites with legitimacy to continue their hegemony.

HUMAN'S PRACTICAL NATURE AND CRITICAL THINKING

In the last section I argued that whether a culture embraces critical thinking and its associated values depends more on conscious decisions by the leaders of that culture rather than on whether that culture is essentially receptive to critical thinking or not. In this regard, Thai culture is not much different from other cultures, though it may seem otherwise. I have shown that whether a culture is receptive to critical thinking and its values depends on active decision by the elites, which is then adopted by the other members of the culture. It is not the case that Thai culture is *essentially* alien to critical thinking; otherwise positive change would not have been possible. We have also seen how Thai culture has been beset by the problem of lack of critical thinking, which hampers the nation in many ways. There is a linkage between lack of critical thinking on the one hand and the hegemony of the elites on the other. However, an advantage of this situation is that, instead of critical thinking being an essential aspect of a culture, it has been shown in the previous section to be more its *contingent* aspect. That is, it is possible for a culture to have, or not to have, critical thinking and its associated values as parts of it without that culture, thereby losing its identity. Here I disagree with theorists who claim that human rights essentially belong to a particular culture, such as the European one, such that if other cultures are to adopt human rights practices, they have to change themselves and become European (See, e.g. Pollis and Schwab 1979, quoted in Bielefeldt 2000).

The values associated with human rights overlap a good deal with those coming with critical thinking. As the latter depends crucially on rationality as well as values such as impartiality in judging evidence and not believing anything too hastily, these values are already associated with human rights and how they are justified. For example, lack of the ability to judge the reliability of evidence on one's own would lead to the subject being controllable by the authorities as they have to depend on the authorities for information. The two concepts then belong together as indelible aspects of contemporary liberal democracy. Such a liberal democracy has to install an effective system of guaranteeing and enforcing rights, including human rights, and it also has to have an equally effective system of education where critical thinking is emphasized so that its citizens are capable to participate in the democracy fully. Thus if critical thinking and its values such as healthy scepticism mentioned above are contingent, so are human rights. That is to say, human rights are not an essential aspect of any culture and to claim that human rights are essentially European is thus untenable. What is more interesting is to find out what historical contingencies took place during the course of European history so that the systems and theories both of human rights and of critical thinking first took root there and not in India or China. When we know about these contingencies, then we can devise what can and should be done in order that these other cultures could develop their own systems of human rights and critical thinking as a matter of policy. Certainly we cannot replicate history; thus to turn back the clock and to reset these other cultures so that they follow the same trajectory as did the European one is certainly hugely impractical and indeed impossible. Nonetheless, as human rights and critical thinking have become very important in today's world, the other cultures where these concepts have not been actively encouraged since their remote past can also find a way to bring back these concepts and make them integral parts of their own identity again.

The contingency of critical thinking in culture points to the fact that it is human practicality that is at work when critical thinking and its associated values are going to be promoted in the culture or not. The Thai case I have discussed above shows that critical thinking can indeed be suppressed, so that people believe that there are other values that are more important, such as harmony or preservation of the existing social order. But if it can be suppressed, then it can also be promoted. All that is required is a change in belief or mindset of the people. This sounds very difficult to do, but if we focus on the idea that it is human practical nature that is ultimately at work, then the task does not seem as difficult as it may look at first. For example, if it can be shown to the members of the Thai culture that they stand to gain a lot of benefits by actively internalizing the values associated with both human rights and critical thinking, and not merely paying lip service to them, then, people being naturally practical, they will adapt their ways on their own. But in order to achieve this, the force that has hampered their adoption, such as the conservatism of the elites, has to be done away with.

As the world changes, there is an ever increasing need for critical thinking; otherwise the country cannot survive. Regarding critical thinking and its values as contingent also has an advantage in that it is then possible to conceive of one and the same culture adopting critical thinking without having to change its identity. In other words, the culture can remain resolutely Thai even after internalizing the values of critical thinking.

There is, then, a way out of both universalism and relativism. Instead of viewing values such as those associated with liberal democracy or critical thinking as belonging essentially to Western culture, or as purely culture-transcending and universal values in the Platonic sense, one should view these values as just a means by which a culture responds to challenges, a set of tools that it uses to realize its goals, which certainly vary according to changing circumstances. In one historical context, the use of critical thinking by the general population might not be exactly advisable because expediency obtained from absolute obedience might be needed in that context, but no one can deny that in today's world not being able to think critically is detrimental to one's chance of success, and a country or a culture that avoids critical thinking as a set of general values risks losing out and becoming irrelevant. Thus, critical thinking is neither universal nor relative to a particular culture. It is only something that members of a culture can use and discard as they see fit, and all cultures can do the same. If this is the case, then the next task would be to search for ways in which critical thinking, in the case of Thai culture, could once again become a tool that the whole culture can wholeheartedly adopt and internalize.

COMMUNICATING ETHICS ACROSS CULTURES: POSSIBILITIES AND PITFALLS

Regarding values as sets of tools that one can pick and choose to accomplish one's varied goals goes a long way towards facilitating communicating ethics across cultures, and I believe that communicating ethics involves communicating how to do critical thinking too. In terms of critical thinking, then, this means that one culture believes that critical thinking and its associated values are home-grown within the confine of one's own culture, so the culture feels that it has the mission to spread critical thinking to all other cultures who are 'in the dark', so to speak. This sounds quite like the zeal that missionaries felt in the old days when they desired to spread the Gospel to people of other religions. One believes that critical thinking is the only way to be truly modernized and civilized, so one 'communicates critical thinking' or 'communicates ethics' to others believing that one is trying to benefit the whole world.

The examples of Indian and Buddhism logic, and Mohism in China should be enough to put this thought to rest for good. The zeal of the missionary results from deep conviction one has in the 'truth' of one's belief system, but others do not see things the same way as does the missionary. Confucius, for example, is also well known for the Golden Rule, which sounds very much that same as the same rule in Kant and Jesus. In Confucius the rule says: 'Do not impose on others what you do not wish for yourself,' and in Kant the Categorical Imperative says: 'Act only according to that maxim whereby you can at the same time will that it should become a universal law.' In both versions the core similarity is that any rule that we want to be adopted by others has to be adopted by ourselves too. It is only a short step from the Confucian Golden Rule to the Kantian Categorical Imperative, and vice versa. Thus, in communicating Kantian ethics to a Confucian culture, one should pay attention to this type of similarities and build upon mutual understanding from there.

This is very different from believing that one's own version or conception of the world is the only truth and that others have to follow this version as if they did not have any ethical thoughts or ethical traditions of their own. In any case, the communication has to be two ways; it has to be part of a constructive dialogue where both sides give and take, and learn from each other. This is supported by the fact that traditions in the East have their own knowledge of logic and critical thinking, which forms a basis on which communication is possible. Indeed cross-cultural communication requires that each side has to be adequate in background information, something that is recognized as being shared by both sides, which forms a basis on which communication and mutual understanding is possible. In order for the information to be shared in this way, there has to be a mutually intelligible language so that both sides of the sharing understand each other, and this has represented a rather serious challenge. It seems that there is a vicious circle here. In order for the mutual understanding and sharing of background to be possible, the languages of both sides have to be rather transparent to one another. That is, the languages need to be translatable into the other without much loss. But for that mutual translatability to be possible, there has to be adequate amount of shared information in the first place. This problem is also known as the hermeneutic circle, where understanding requires that the different languages be fully mutually translatable to each other, but for these languages to be so transparent, mutual understanding is already presupposed (See, e.g. Palmer 1969). Thus, in the case of communicating the value of critical thinking to Thai culture, there has to be first a mutually intelligible language in which the communication takes place. This language can be English or Thai. In either language, there has to be a set of vocabulary that covers topics in critical thinking, but if Thai culture does not have such a vocabulary, then it has to be translated, and the act of translation requires that there be already a mutually intelligible language. So we end up in a circle.

A way to break into the circle would be to find a starting ground where there are already mutual understandings, no matter how small it might be at first, and build up from there. In the case of Confucianism and Kantian ethics as described above, the mutual ground is certainly the similarities of the Golden Rule and the Categorical Imperative. This of course requires that the languages of Confucianism (i.e. Chinese) and of Kantian ethics (English or German) be translatable, but that has been achieved already as Chinese, English and German are all the world's major languages. Apart from the similarities, however, there are numerous differences between Chinese and English that prevent the languages from being perfectly translatable one to the other, and as regards to cultural beliefs, it is also well known that there are very many differences. Nonetheless, these represent a set of challenges to overcome, and should not lead one to conclude that the two or three languages and the two cultures can never be bridged.

Thus, the possibilities of communicating ethics across cultures lie precisely in finding shared background and information that serves as a starting ground towards deeper mutual understanding. However, the remaining differences among the two cultures certainly represent pitfalls that need to be identified and overcome. These differences are those that make the two cultures to be bridged different ones to begin with, and they range from differences in beliefs and values to those in practices. These differences are the standard fodder for the relativists to construct their argument.

Moreover, another pitfall against communicating ethics across the cultures is that, instead of focusing on extant similarities as in the case of the Mohism or the Indian logical tradition, which is largely very similar to Aristotelian logic as we have seen, one might choose to emphasize the differences instead. Focusing on cultural differences has a long tradition because it is necessary for a particular culture to assert its own unique identity. However, focusing too much on uniqueness means that it becomes more and more difficult for the culture to find common ground with others. We have seen that, for Thai culture at least, it is traditionally the elites who call the shot and decide whether a culture should adopt any ethical system proposed to them by the international community or not. Thus choosing what to preserve and what to change in order to accommodate the international community can become a kind of political conflict. The issue is not whether an ethical system, such as the one on which the Universal Declaration on Human Rights is founded, is a valid one or not; the issue is rather that, in order to decide on the validity of a system, more often than not, the Thai culture looks at how much direct benefit it would get by going one way or the other. And the arduous struggle that accompanies deep political transformation that Thailand is now experiencing can itself be a very serious obstacle against the project of communicating ethics globally (See, e.g. Hewison 1997 and McCargo 2005 for an overview of the current political conflict in Thailand).

To illustrate, a faction in Thai culture might argue that, instead of making Thai culture more open towards critical thinking, the culture should instead remain the same as before, and continue to live with its traditional attitude of not encouraging critical thinking in order to preserve its identity. This has been a strong argument by a powerful faction in Thai culture. Communicating ethics to this conservative faction would then be very difficult. As the faction views critical thinking and rationality, which are presupposed by modern ethical system, as 'foreign' to Thai culture as they see it, or only as something they are willing to put up only as a facade to show that Thailand is also modernized as we have seen, they will start with a negative attitude towards the attempt at communicating ethics from the beginning. This is really a serious pitfall.

A way out, as I see it now, is for the progressive elements within Thai culture itself to get their voices heard. In fact the famous political struggle that has been going on in the country for almost a decade is little more than a struggle between the conservative and the progressive. The one wants Thailand to remain static; the other wants it to go ahead and merge more with the world. The conflict is expressed in many levels, starting from raw political struggles for power to the more intellectual debates on which set of values is the most suitable one for the country at the moment. Only when the progressive force becomes dominant will the values inherent in critical thinking, human rights and liberal democracy be fully and sincerely respected and internalized, and not only paid lip service to as in the past.

One factor that has aided the progressive force is undoubtedly the global economy. Thailand has been much integrated into the global economy, thus it is almost inconceivable to find the country retreat into a kind of radical conservatism that would reject globalization and economic integration. Sooner or later the country has to find a way to get rid of their traditional sources of power and find a new source for both power and legitimacy from values such as those inherent in critical thinking and liberal democracy. However, the process may take years since the conservative force is still very strong and many Thai people have been brought up to believe that the rule by the traditional elites is the only possible option for the country. Furthermore, once the progressive faction gains the upper hand, there will be reforms in many sectors, such as in education, the judicial system, the mechanisms of voting, the military and so on, with the purpose of aligning the country more accurately with the requirements of an advanced and globalized economy. Here philosophical arguments can be crucial, because they are the key factor in helping the people understand the need for changing the set of values for the country and to see why there has to be change.

CONCLUSION

What I have said here sounds very much like mixing politics and ethics. However, if we are intent on laying the groundwork for communication of ethics across cultural boundaries, then political manoeuvring and struggles do not seem to be dispensable. The idea is that the global community can do little more than standing on the outside and providing moral support to those in Thailand who fight for more open society.

Nonetheless, the philosophical point that we can obtain from looking at the Thai example, which could be applicable everywhere else, is that culture is malleable and there is no trait that we can pinpoint at all times and say that it is necessary for that culture, and without it the culture will collapse and lack its identity altogether. I think the argument I have shown so far should put this belief to rest. Instead of regarding culture as rigid and dependent upon a small number of necessary and sufficient conditions – those without which the culture will cease to be the same – we should view culture as more fluid and as a collection of thoughts, beliefs and practices of a people who live together and share background information together (which they call their traditions or the stories that bind them together as a people). We have seen that practices such as critical thinking, as well as its associated values such as openness, rationality, healthy scepticism, preference for rational argumentation to brute force in settling disputes, do not belong to such necessary and sufficient conditions.

Moreover, critical thinking is not the sole prerogative of the West, as the historical evidence I discussed earlier in the paper clearly shows. This means that critical thinking is not a defining characteristic of any culture, and a consequence of this is that cultures which for the last few centuries might have shunned critical thinking can certainly come back to it without having to fear that they will lose their identities. In communicating ethics, it is clear that critical thinking and the values of openness are absolutely necessary, as communication and ethics both need rational argumentation to work. Furthermore, the communication between different cultures or between a culture and the rest of the world has to be in form of constructive dialogues too.

Chapter 7

Religious Transcendence

Hope for Global Communication Ethics

Peter Gan

There is a component of religion that can figure as a distinctive religious contribution to global communication ethics. In order to develop this thought, I shall first attempt to elicit the elements of transcendence and hope, which are embedded in the religious phenomenon. Following this I shall examine the challenge directed at moral universalism and discuss the role this universalism plays in global communication ethics. After piecing together religious transcendence, hope and other connected concepts to form a basis of global communication ethics, the next step would be to delve into the communication of ethics, particularly within the context of inter-religious dialogue. Religion is not a monolithic entity, and even within each tradition there is so much complexity and diversity that it is best not to assume that a sub-tradition represents the teachings of the main tradition. While religion as a generic concept is predominantly used in this chapter, I have also, in several places, inserted ideas extracted from specific strains or commentaries within religious traditions.

RELIGIOUS TRANSCENDENCE AND HOPE

The human person has the potential for transcendence. By virtue of human consciousness, there is already a capacity to mentally extract oneself from external reality. Moreover, the self as subject is also able to consciously dissociate itself from some of its contents of consciousness. Inherent to self-consciousness itself is the potential for transcendence. Consciousness of something specific indicates a form of finitude because this consciousness would be determined or limited by its object. However, as stated, the self as subject, that is, the 'I', has the ability to abstract itself from external objects and events as well as internal processes of consciousness. As such, it is, as Georg W.F. Hegel (1967, 1821, sections 4–5: 20–21) would say, free – implying the potential for freedom from finiteness. Apart from this negative sense of freedom ('freedom from ...'), the will also has a positive aspect of freedom: it has the capacity to direct its attention to that which is infinite – itself.

Notwithstanding the definitional problems assailing the concept of religion, let us assume that the fundamental orientation of religious traditions is to that which is regarded as the ultimate (see Tillich 1957: 1–3). Considering that the ultimate would not be so if it were limited, infinity would then be its key attribute. Religious doctrines contain statements that revolve around the belief that there is an ultimate reality and that a relational connection exists between this reality and the universe.[1] Religious faith is said to be inextricably bound to the notion of transcendence.[2] Ultimate reality as defined by the respective traditions of religion is not confined to the idea of total transcendence, but includes the feature of immanence. In other words, by virtue of this reality's relationship to the universe, the interface between these parties signifies immanence.

Even when we look exclusively at the self as subject, transcendence is already an inherent potential. I qualify this transcendence as a potential for it is not an empirical fact that the self has complete control over the exercise of abstracting itself from any external and internal phenomena that it so wishes. There are physical as well as psychological factors that impede the actual realization of the consciousness of one's liberation from limitations. For example, while in principle, it is conceivable that one can genuinely be aware of the capacity of transcending a strong sense of dread that presently engulfs oneself, frequently, the complete actualization of this capacity does not eventuate. Religious faith advocates a reliance upon an ultimate being that, contingent upon doctrinal teachings, may be personal, impersonal or both, transcendent to and immanent in humanity and the world, or regarded as a transpersonal self that includes the empirical or psychological self, and so forth. It is difficult to delineate the contours of the concept of ultimate reality, which would satisfy all religious traditions and their respective sub-traditions. Nevertheless, I postulate that integral to the major living religions is the orientation to the transcendent that is deemed ultimate. I also do not restrict the term 'ultimate' to a purely theistic sense.

While the capacity for transcendence exists within the self, the reliance upon an ultimate force endows the human person with a source of hope for negotiating life's many challenges. Hinduism's Patanjali Yoga understands hope as signifying an aspiration for something better, and given that there is always a desire and an opportunity for something better, the very possibility of hope is contingent upon the existence of that highest reality which exceeds all things empirical (Krishnananda n.d.: 291–292). In this chapter I do not intend to engage with the immense discourse surrounding the concept of hope. Instead, I wish to unravel a foundational and perhaps shared pattern of hope generated by the religious drive. Hope underpins petitionary prayer and this type of prayer is found in virtually all religions. As an example, in Judaism, some prayers, especially when made during harrowing circumstances such as that in Auschwitz, are an expression of an intimate relationship with God as the source of hope (see Fröchtling 2002 : 149–151). Hope is fused with desire and we have a natural desire to attain goodness for ourselves. Hence, in moments when the path towards such an attainment is perceived as closed off, the subject naturally hopes for a positive outcome.

Religious hope adds onto this natural passion for goodness the belief in an ultimate reality that offers the means to and constitutes the goal of utmost goodness (see Aquinas 1990, thirteenth century, part II of the second part quest. 17 artcl. 1: 457). The term 'goodness' has a distinct advantage over utilitarianism's 'happiness' because its significance extends beyond sentient beings capable of experiencing happiness or pleasure, to include the other things in nature. Religious hope, like the many expressions of hope, is inevitably rooted in human experience. However, being centred on ultimate or infinite reality, religious hope extends its grasp beyond humanity and thereby provides a way out of anthropocentrism in ethics. Undoubtedly, the list of things that one can hope for is endless. Nevertheless, it does not make sense to hope for something that will certainly come to pass, and to hope for an impossibility. I am hesitant to dismiss hoping for a highly improbable occurrence. For instance, the chance of my winning the lottery on a single ticket is one in a million, but this does not mean that it would be irrational of me to hope that my lottery ticket hits the jackpot. Similarly, no matter how despairing a situation may present itself, be it a personal adversity or a prodigious social crisis, to hope is an essential means to transcend the situation and direct the will to attain something better. It is not an irrational indulgence in delusion.

Gabriel Marcel (1951, 1945: 44–46) speaks about 'absolute hope' – to hope, without setting conditions for hope. He explains:

> We can, on the other hand, conceive, at least theoretically, of the inner disposition of one who, setting no condition or limit and abandoning himself in absolute confidence, would thus transcend all possible disappointment and would experience a security of his being, or in his being, which is contrary to the radical insecurity of Having. This is what determines the ontological position of hope – absolute hope, inseparable from a faith which is likewise absolute, transcending all laying down of conditions, and for this very reason every kind of representation whatever it might be.

A way to imagine this dynamic is to think of absolute hope as an attitudinal stance towards a challenging situation for the subject, in which the subject, though harbouring a desire for a favourable eventuality, at the same time, is open to whatever the future offers. In this mix of desire and surrender, there is in hope an engagement with that which transcends the self. The Christian mystic, John of the Cross (1991, sixteenth century, *The Dark Night*, bk. 2 ch. 21: 11–12: 448–49), tells us that at the deepest stage of self-detachment and complete intimacy with God, the experience is that of mystical death, and the only things left in the mystic's resources are faith, hope and love. In here, hope surrenders the familiar and reaches out for the radically unfamiliar. Some Buddhist teachings propose an abandonment of hope in the sense of not fixing set desirables to be attained, and instead be open to the unexpected.[3]

While the term 'absolute' in reference to hope implies a form of pure hope, it should be stated here that in the text that Marcel (1951, 1945: 45–47) treats this subject he speaks of a state in which there is *more* of hope without object than hope with object. In other words, it is not *just* a form of hope completely devoid of object. For the purposes of this chapter, 'absolute hope' involves an interplay between desiring a specific outcome and surrendering to a much larger dynamism. According to Marcel (1951, 1945: 93–94), hope cannot be dissociated from communion, especially when hope springs from a care for the welfare of others; and more notably, in absolute hope, there is this reliance upon a higher power. In essence, within the structure of hope is the orientation to the infinite that extends beyond the narrow self-centred interests of the person. Thus far, I have argued that the feature of transcendence can be considered a shared denominator for religions and that the phenomenon of hope is a vital expression of this transcendence. How then is this form of hope relevant to communication ethics in the global arena? The first task would be to examine the universal – particular aporia that troubles the ethics of communication.

SHARED UNIVERSAL PRINCIPLES

If the concerns of ethics revolve around values, norms and issues within morality, then communication ethics is concerned with the moral rightness and wrongness of acts of communication. As a philosophical subfield, communication ethics appeals to rational discourse. Ethics' reliance upon reason reflects the universality of reason as applied to morality. However, this aim of applying purportedly universal principles to morality has faced challenges dealing with the impugnment of the universality of such principles. In the postmodern era we see a crisis of validation of proposed universal moral principles (see Christians 1995: 60; Lyotard 1991, 1979: 30). In fact, the critique of universal norms had already been present among thinkers in the modern era, principally, in Friedrich Nietzsche (1966, 1887: 16, 85, 97–98). The caution raised is that proposed rationally supported moral norms deemed to be objectively real are actually constructed by particular societies. Is the existence of universally agreed moral principles necessary for global communication ethics? This question is not as straightforward as it appears. A moral relativist might argue that there are no universal moral precepts because what is morally right or wrong is determined by specific societies. On the other hand, the relativist might also tell us that there is a universal obligation for all societies to respect the moral systems created by each and every society, regardless of the presence or non-presence of common elements among them.

It is open to question whether the detractors of moral universalism have been successful in their endeavours. One can appeal to the shared traits of being human such as a desire for happiness and evading suffering as determining universal moral norms. The deep desires and experiences of people, though personal, are also universal. By and large, the sufferings and hopes of individuals are also the sufferings and hopes which are universal to the human race. Moreover, it is virtually impossible to do away with human reasoning when engaged in any form of philosophical discussion. Arguments raised to undermine moral universalism inevitably have to be grounded in reason. Even if reason can be subjected to manipulation by a group in order to rationalize the group's unjust deeds, the deliberate act of manipulating reason implies that the manipulator already recognizes the inherent wrongness of these deeds. Also, disclosing such a manipulation and opposing it require the applications of logic and empirical verification.

In sum, a viable global communication ethics requires a common denominator of shared universal values. At the least, some agreement to respect the individual sets of moral principles and practices promulgated by different societies can be attained. A whole gamut of actions under moral scrutiny may range from the most venial to the most severe. One of these actions should be able to elicit a commonly agreed judgement as to its goodness or evilness. Although orchestrated mass torturings and killings of defenceless and innocent people have taken place in history, it is difficult to imagine the construction of a robust ethical theory that endorses such egregiously evil acts. Contrary to the viewpoint that we should refrain from imposing any assumed universally applicable yardstick for moral judgements, it seems that there is a shared limit to our tolerance of moral transgressions. True, many issues of morality lend themselves to endless controversy and argumentation, but this does not mean that there is absolutely no moral agreement among people of different cultures. For humanity to sustain itself and flourish there must be some tacit agreement among its members to curtail their personal freedoms for the benefit of the collective (see Hobbes 1998, 1651: 82–89). Inevitably, some guidelines of conduct can be said to exist to ensure the smooth operation of living in this world, especially now, given that our world is made so much smaller through advanced media.

In the current global ethos where events have influential force across national boundaries, there is an increasing need to formulate a system of ethics capable of commanding general assent. Discourses on ethics are somehow compelled to seriously consider human welfare that is more cosmopolitan in its embrace. There are moral concerns that are more circumscribed in its scope of reference and application. Narrow parochial interests of one group may clash with the interests of a much larger population. While I am reluctant to suggest a made-for-all-cases theoretical model of moral analysis, I suppose that the broader a perspective stakeholders are able to take towards a matter of significant moral consequence, the better it is for optimal moral deliberation. While deliberations of this sort form the ideal instance, more often than not, a clash of thoughts and arguments may ensue. Still, it is important to maintain open lines of communication rather than hurriedly resort to dogmatic and authoritative means to end the moral discourse.[4] A moral discourse that is expansive, accommodative, yet discerning, is less likely to conduce to courses of action that infringe fundamental maxims of morality such as respect for human life and rights.

In his efforts to build arguments against moral relativism, Clifford Christians (2011: 6) appeals to an analogy with language:

> Among human beings are common understandings entailed by their creatureliness as lingual beings. All human languages are intertranslatable. In fact, some human beings in all languages are bilingual. All languages enable their users to make abstractions, draw inferences, deduce and induce when solving problems. All human languages serve cultural formation, not merely social function. All humans know the distinction between raw food and cooked.

Just as a shared common language and overlaps in structures of different languages enable communication, the presence of shared moral norms can serve as a set of rules for navigating human interactions. Moral objectivism claims that there is at least one moral judgement that is true or false, irrespective of the opinions of individuals or societies. Another way to view this is that there are some moral truths that exist amidst the interface between conscious subjects and physical events and entities. This idea is amenable to the belief that specific moral norms may change as sociocultural circumstances change. Additionally, interpretations of what is morally right and wrong may not always reflect what is actually and objectively the case. How are we to work out a coherent system of communication ethics for a globalized world?

ETHICS OF COMMUNICATION

When we look at how religious transcendence can form a basis of communication ethics, a likely starting point is the concept of the human person. As explained above, the human person or subject inherently possesses the capacity for transcendence. The subject can abstract itself from itself as object and from external objects and events. From this premise, Hegel (1967, 1821, sections 35–36: 37) sketches the concept of the person as being free and having the potential through self-consciousness to relate to himself or herself as pure consciousness, a form of consciousness that is devoid of determinations and thereby infinite. Hegel then argues that by virtue of this, the person has the right to be treated as a person, that is, with respect; and the person in turn has the duty to treat other persons with respect. The Abrahamic faiths believe that humans are created in the image of God (Koslowski 2001: especially 10). Imbued with this divinity, humans are sacred and they deserve to be treated as having intrinsic worth. The advantage the Hindu system of *Advaita Vedānta* has is that through one of its articles of faith – every creature, not just human beings, has its *atman* (soul), which is identical to *Brahman* (ultimate reality) – non-human beings too have a right to be treated with respect (Deutsche and Dalvi 2004, eighth century: 170).

Religious transcendence, which is characterized as an orientation to an infinite reality that is immanent in and transcendent to the self, is not confined to the compass of formal religious practices. Self-consciousness conceals a natural potential to access that which is infinite, itself as pure consciousness. However, in the recognition of and reliance upon an infinite being, a further transcendence of the self obtains.[5] The idea of the sacredness and interconnectedness of all things within infinite reality suggests that there ought to be a shared responsibility and care for our world. On top of this, if free will is regarded as the necessary precondition for moral responsibility, then the presence of human free will as located in the capacity to transcend determinations, affirms our inescapable moral responsibility towards ourselves and our world.

Transcendence and Communication

Human communication presupposes human beings' innate capacity for transcendence. The process of abstraction which is crucial in language acquisition and application is an engagement, whether spontaneous or conscious, with transcendence at a variety of levels, including that which involves the process of signification and its inevitable differences between signifier, signified, communicator and recipient. At a deeper level, the breadth and depth of the mutual exchange and interpretation among communicating participants are a function of these participants' ability for empathy, that is, the ability to transcend oneself and take the perspective of the other. In order for me to have an inkling as to how my message is interpreted by my audience, I need to be able to imagine being in the shoes of my audience. Communication is virtually impossible if there is absolute difference and otherness between two subjects attempting to communicate with one another. Hence, underlying the dynamic process of communication is the presence of a shared medium, generally, the medium of a commonly understood language, as well as a space in which some thoughts and sentiments resonate with the participants.

Communication in its many modalities pervades the interactions of people at diverse circumstances. When we think about it, virtually everyone has some influence, be it minuscule or monumental, on the current of global processes. Moreover, in the pragmatic character of our communicative acts, statements that we make have a performative element in them. For example, the statement – 'Only discussions amongst sharers of the same faith can be enriching' – might conceal a performative element of insisting that matters of faith in the speaker's religion cannot be challenged, especially by other traditions. Speech then functions like an act that attempts to affect the world and not just describe it.[6] Accordingly, the morality of communication is enmeshed within the whole setting of concrete instances of communication that encompass our conscious acts of acquiring, interpreting, modifying and relaying information, as well as influencing external events.

Communication Ethics as Informed by Infinity

Religious transcendence serves as a normative base that shapes the form in which one can be guided to ascertain some of the contents of global communication ethics. For example, religious transcendence as orientation to infinite reality informs the actors in global communication of the foremost need to maintain a cosmopolitan outlook and concern. This type of transcendence with its accompanying goal of attaining ultimate goodness, and its faith in ultimate reality can also be a source of inspiration for adhering to the moral maxims tied to global communication. It may be observed that the basis of ethics as delineated here shares a few features of normative ethical theories such as utilitarianism, deontology and contractualism. John Stuart Mill's (1969, 1861) universal utilitarianism, Immanuel Kant's (1998, 1785) universalizability principle and Thomas Scanlon's (1998) contractualism that is entrenched in our mutual recognition of one another as rational beings sharing the same moral status all involve abstraction from the limits of self-interest as well as the particularity of a moral circumstance in order to hold a relatively more comprehensive and universally applicable perspective on moral matters. Abstraction of this sort is a form of transcendence.

That which sets apart the 'religious transcendence' model of ethics is its firm footing in the notion of ultimate being as infinite. Although there is no perfect consensus among faith traditions on whether ultimate reality is infinite, and if so, its manner of being infinite, it is reasonable to assume that infinite ultimate reality has to include and be more than the totality of finite things. After all, if the infinite is completely other than the finite, then the infinite would be bounded by the finite and would paradoxically be finite. Human consciousness, in principle, has the potential to be directed towards that which is infinite. The realm of the mind is mathematically infinite (see Rucker 1995: 35–39). Undoubtedly, due to limitations of physical power, a person will not have the strength to actually think of an infinite number of thoughts, but potentially there can be an infinite number of thoughts. Although human consciousness' inherent infiniteness and natural capacity for transcendence may constitute a reason for the special moral status of the person, that is, as a being deserving respect, it is the religious orientation towards infinite reality, the greater reality surpassing the self, that configures a metaphysical validation for an imperative of enlarging the self's span of moral concern.

The 'religious transcendence' model of ethics extends beyond the anthropocentric character of traditional systems. Hypothetically speaking, let us say that the human race will end in a year's time and we happen to know this. No matter how slim a chance of averting this catastrophe, we can still hope for a better future, with or without us in it. Besides, do we not still shoulder a moral responsibility towards the non-human denizens of this world? This model does not run contrary to the larger schema of ethical pluralism in that it cannot claim to be the primary foundation for addressing all moral situations, and neither can it assert that there will be no occasion in which another theory would not do a better job of making moral assessments and decisions for action.[7] The key features to bear in mind are transcendence, infinity and hope.

Essentially, on account of infinity, both within and beyond me, my close connection to it, and my possession of faculties that can contribute to the betterment of this world, I am somehow obligated to have a latitudinous perspective and care. Any sectarianism in religion runs against the grain of the spirit of inclusivity as advanced here. When this spirit is put to use in global communication, there is little justification for imposing, pervasively and systematically, the doctrines and practices of any religion onto institutions of a multireligious society, especially if these doctrines and practices cannot command general assent. Undoubtedly, there are and will be challenging situations in discussions and negotiations where religion is involved. The tenet of religious transcendence may form the backbone of global communication ethics, yet the intricate dynamics that operate in actual interactions demand utmost consideration, openness, tolerance and even tact. At times, the way communication is conducted has greater practical import than the content communicated. For instance, disagreement and even anger can be communicated without being antagonistic. Sensitivity to diverse cultures goes a long way towards facilitating effective and harmonious discussions. The innate potential for natural and religious forms of transcendence not only supplies a rational impetus for participants in dialogue to subscribe to the spirit of universal solidarity and concern, it also is the means by which the moral ideals of communication can be attained.

The basis of ethics as developed here, like any theoretical support for concrete morality, suffers from being abstract, general and in some areas, ambiguous. On the one hand, it offers us plausible reasons for why one should be moral – (1) our capacity for transcendence endows us with free will (and thereby moral responsibility) and the ability to go beyond self-interest to possess a much larger span of concern; (2) there is an inherent connectedness among all beings; (3) the potential for absolute hope is a means towards being open to the larger dynamic of ultimate reality; (4) the preceding three statements impress upon us our contributive role towards the attainment of ultimate goodness. On the other hand, how are we to interpret the orientation to infinity as drawn from religious transcendence? It is not necessarily the case that, for instance, human life is good and therefore population expansion is the right way to reach ultimate goodness. Thus far, it appears that infinity is associated with goodness for the largest possible number of beneficiaries. But it can just as well refer to goodness to the highest degree and qualitative excellence attainable by a single individual. Then again, both of these representations of the orientation to infinity can, together, be the directed object of religious transcendence. Moreover, committed and sustained privileged treatment of the poor and less fortunate is not antithetical to the moral obligation to strive for infinite goodness. The big question is: how are we to calculate the course of action our moral efforts should take after weighing the rights of and justified beneficence deserved by the widest possible spectrum of beings? For certain concrete issues there might be no clear and definitive solutions that can be directly derived from the concept of infinity. Still, the principles of transcendence, absolute hope, and participative and progressive discourse, can serve as guidelines to reach a suitable course of moral action. In deciding whether a particular action is consistent with global communication ethics, one can examine whether the action originates from an intention to bring the greatest possible good to all beings, adopts an encompassing perspective and concern, and follows the route of multilateral participative and progressive discourse. Despite its shortcomings, this framework of ethics is generous enough to permit the employment of a plurality of ethical theories that can veritably be applied to situations within global communication. Its congeniality to including multiple relevant theories is in line with the concept of infinity's open-endedness. Given the significant influence religion has over populations of diverse cultures, religious transcendence coupled with the phenomenon of hope is able to form a valuable basis for global communication ethics.

The wide-ranging considerations to be factored into thought processes behind actions that have major consequences across cultural perimeters indicate that there is need for the building of relevant knowledge that can only be attained through collaboration. Arguably, the growth of knowledge through evolving multilateral discourse on the global platform can be said to be embedded within and sustained by the religious reference to infinite reality. Antonio Cua (1977: 313–314) argues that by relying on clarity of mind and connectedness to the infinite all-encompassing reality called Dao, it is possible to get above relative moral precepts and view moral situations from a Dao-imbued perspective. In the classical Chinese early Daoist tradition, the Dao is the all-pervading ultimate reality that is ineffable and mysterious. One way to understand 'clarity of mind' is to conceive it as clarity of awareness, awareness that is not obscured by selfish interests and is thereby able to stretch itself to incorporate other person's viewpoints and anticipated future outcomes of our actions (see Graham 1992: 21–27). Generally speaking, faith in this religious condition injects vital hope in continuing the project of striving for and maintaining the moral ideals of communication.

Communication Ethics as Informed by Hope

As related above, absolute hope, according to Marcel, is attached to communion. The desiderative essence of hope tends to characterize hope as a drive that is individual. However, when desire for a particular good is coupled with openness to the new, as what makes up absolute hope, in this absence of the imposition of one's particular wishes, and a presence of a willingness to surrender to the unexpected, the subject who hopes is drawn out of the boundaries of the self. To hope, without insisting on specific wants, parallels the orientation to infinite being that transcends specific determinations. In many respects, this kind of hope is congenial to all manner of communication with global repercussions. Absolute hope presupposes transcendence, both the natural and the religious forms. This is due to one of the paired constituents of absolute hope, that of pure hope without an object, which reflects a similar pattern to the self's potential to direct its awareness towards its pure consciousness and infinite being. To be sure, hope is a crucial ingredient in the global dialogue. A sense of solidarity or communion among agents engaged in global dialogue can help them manoeuvre through the labyrinth and dilemmas that sometimes permeate this kind of dialogue. And to an extent, absolute hope that entails a dialectic of particular hopes of different parties and the openness to the new without imposing expectations is conducive to building this solidarity. Absolute hope would suitably accommodate the ideal of willing for goodness that benefits all. Hence, it, like transcendence, by virtue of its pervasive presence, can contribute to forming a viable infrastructure for global communication ethics. Admittedly, there is no critique-free logical inference from the pervasiveness of this phenomenon to a solid imperative to adhere to moral maxims in the global context. Nonetheless, one can plausibly argue that given the pervasiveness of the potential for absolute hope and religious transcendence directed towards the infinite, our actions that have global consequences ought to adhere to sound moral maxims. Aside from this, hope also supplies the spirited force that sustains the challenging and ongoing discourse of global magnitude. Simply put, there is no more crucial need for hope than in actions that have the vested interests of the largest number of beings to reckon with.

COMMUNICATION OF ETHICS

The broad and abstract system of ethics that is sustained by religion's ideas of transcendence and hope can be of some help when trying to figure out concrete moral practices pertaining to global communication. Consistent with this, the communication of ethics (moral philosophies, values and norms), either by specific religious institutions or done in the name of religion as a general concept, should also observe the very principles sustained by religious transcendence and hope. In brief, the communication of ethics ought to be ethical. One of the most intriguing and significant aspects of religion that bears upon the communication of ethics is religion's inability to truly represent infinite reality. Karl Barth (1933, 1922: 136–137) goes to the extent of asserting that both religion and the opposition to religion lack certainty and security. Religion and anti-religion can only point beyond themselves to that which perpetually eclipses their conceptualizations. In Daoist philosophy, 'Dao can be talked about, but not the Eternal Dao' (Lao Tzu 1990, fifth century BCE: 1). Divine ineffability, despite being a notion that is plagued with difficulties, is stressed in many major religions including Islam (see Hewer 2006: 75–76). Barth's (1933, 1922: 136 and 184) caution below may seem exaggerated, but it can be taken to heart when pondering over actions initiated in the name of religion.

> No human demeanour is more open to criticism, more doubtful, or more dangerous, than religious demeanour. No undertaking subjects men to so severe a judgement as the undertaking of religion. ... In the same twilight men engage in anti-religious propaganda – which is but another form of religion. However much we may protest that our religion is free of misunderstanding; however

delicate may be the scepticism of those irreligious-religious men who stand outside; yet we and they still remain within the framework of history, unable to escape from the twilight of misunderstanding. We must therefore abandon our superiority and pride of difference.

Going by this major assumption in religion, one can draw the implication that any assertion of divine command and moral edict has to be made with heedful circumspection and a sense of tentativeness, rather than with absolute certainty. It does not follow from the above that inaction is the recommended response and that religion has nothing to contribute to the cause of morality. Initiatives embarked upon in the name of religion have spanned the range from the eminently noble to the horrifyingly contemptible. Although I quote Barth for the purpose of underscoring the epistemic chasm between divine reality and human capacity, I am aware that Barth has been widely considered as advocating Christocentric revelation and exclusivism (see McCarthy 2000: 76–77).

Perspectives on Religious Diversity and the Communication of Ethics

Organized interfaith efforts to communicate universal values such as peace, love and hope have been and will continue to be conducted with the intent of promoting unity and the awareness that collaboration is the crucial means towards addressing global crises such as war, hatred, injustice and environmental destruction. Religious diversity is differently perceived through the lenses of the exclusivist, inclusivist and pluralist. Basically, while the exclusivist takes his or her religious tradition as the sole custodian of true faith and salvation, and the inclusivist acknowledges the beliefs and teachings of all faiths, though still regarding his or her religion as superior and capable of generating truths that are present in the other religions, the pluralist considers all religions to be equally worthy and that no religion can claim ascendancy over the others.[8] Pluralists may view all faith traditions as pathways to a single mysterious ultimate reality (convergent pluralism), or that ultimate reality is actually constituted by the plurality of diverse properties stipulated by the various religions (non-convergent pluralism) (McCarthy 2000: 92). The non-convergent version will have to contend with the problem of accommodating ascriptions of God's attributes that are contrary to one another; for example, Christianity's doctrine of divine incarnation versus Islam's rejection of the notion of God becoming human.

Fundamentalism correlates with, but is not identical to, exclusivism. Exclusivist religious groups think that they have exclusive possession of truths of religion and ultimate being. If they do engage in inter-religious projects, frequently, conversion is topmost on their minds. Militant fundamentalist groups who resort to violence clearly run afoul of the basic moral injunction against harming and killing people. We should bear in mind that such extreme acts embarked upon by militant fundamentalists often spring from idiosyncratic interpretations of scripture, an irrational clinging to beliefs that either lack evidential support or patently fly in the face of facts, a sense of loss of cultural identity and of economic and political emasculation. In other words, religious fundamentalism is not just about religion (see Frey 2007: 106ff.). Those contributing factors do not attenuate the imputability of the perpetrators' depraved offence, but hopefully, being aware of them may help in preventing any future resurgence of such extremism. Not all religious exclusivists are militant fundamentalists, and some are keen on participating in inter-religious dialogues. Exclusivists may bring to the dialogue table an intention of communicating their ideas of the nature of ultimate reality and on salvation, and while doing so, they may implicitly or explicitly convey their repudiation of the other religious traditions' beliefs. In the spirit of openness, the exclusivist ought not to be excluded from dialogue. Guidelines for dialogue can be put in place to ensure an atmosphere of respect for one another amidst substantial critical discussion. After all, should there not be an ethics of communication of ethics?

Among the three perspectives on religious diversity, the pluralists are the most open. Unlike the inclusivist, who interprets the other religions as implicitly or unconsciously practising the inclusivist's tradition, the pluralist allows the other to be the other without assuming any tradition to be superior to the rest. However, the pluralist cannot impose this open and accommodating disposition onto other participants of inter-religious dialogue without compromising the pluralist position. Nevertheless, the pluralist approach is most in tune with the type of global communication ethics rooted in religious transcendence and hope, which espouses multilateral and progressive discourses.

Religion as a Source of Moral Motivation

Virtually anything can be discussed in an inter-religious forum. Even areas of faith, rituals and practices are up for exchanges of ideas, agreements and disagreements. On issues of ethics, constructive discourse can be built upon shared understandings of norms, rights and duties. Let us take the imperative: 'love unconditionally'. Is the essential value of this message different, depending on whether its messenger is the Buddha, Prophet Muhammad, Jesus Christ or an atheist? In itself, no. But, 'why love unconditionally?' elicits different answers from these representatives of their respective traditions. As long as it is agreed that we should love unconditionally, does it really matter if the motives behind this imperative differ? For practical purposes, accepting and striving to realize this noble virtue should suffice.

Religion should be able to inspire people to act morally. Its capacity to infuse hope in times of tribulation, offer consolation and meaning, craft a moral compass to order one's life, encourage non-attachment and self-giving service and promise eternal happiness for the virtuous person directly or indirectly encourages moral conduct. It is good though to note that many systems within major religions regard the adherence to moral precepts strictly in order to receive heavenly rewards and escape damnation as selfish and abhorrent. A commentator on Hinduism's sacred texts called *Upanishads* views such a self-serving motive as akin to an evil person attempting to be virtuous (Radhakrishnan 1927: 229). Rābi'a Basri, an eighth-century woman Muslim sufi, says that she wants to douse the fires of hell and set heaven alight so that our hopes for reward and fears of punishment will disappear and no longer hinder us from sincerely knowing and loving God (Smith 1984, 1928: 98–99).

Faith and Reason: Shared Morality

Apart from examining the religious motives behind morality, it is also important to consider moral imperatives strictly within its configuration of reasoning and empirical reference, rather than solely relying on specific faith dogmas that cannot be expected to summon the conviction of anyone save the faithful. What happens if I lose my present religious faith, and no other religion has yet to win me over, would I then abandon the call to love unconditionally? A crucial subject of inquiry which the diverse traditions can engage with is rational ethics. Numerous sets of interconnected propositions support a particular moral norm or value. The set for a faith-sustained moral norm includes propositions on matters of religious belief. And if the belief propositions constitute indispensable links in the whole argumentative chain leading to the moral norm, then non-believers may be left out of the conversation. However, if a set is capable of appealing to reason and premises with sufficient evidence, then it holds promise for evoking relatively greater assent. The numerous systems of secular ethics as well as those of religious ethics need not be inconsistent with one another. In fact, they do complement one another. The virtues of trust in a transcendent being, hope, love and forgivingness, and the rationality of ethics, coupled with honest and respectful inter-religious exchanges, can conjointly contribute to moral flourishing. Furthermore, acts of charity and outreach which cut across creedal boundaries can be subsumed under this category of dialogue, and they possess a tremendous capacity for forging ties among the different faiths.

CONCLUSION

Permit me to articulate a couple of closing remarks. Transcendence, absolute hope, infinity, goodness and the evolving discourse, which make up the framework developed here, can reasonably sustain the ethics of global communication, a communication with far-reaching implications. Religious transcendence serves as both a general principle of ethics as well as the inspiring force for attempting to reach infinite goodness. This is not just an abstract static principle, but one that is immersed in a process, especially an evolving process of dialogue amidst transformations of agents and situations. At the start of this chapter, I mentioned that transcendence is integral to religion. Tightly linked to the bearing towards the infinite is the virtue of universal love, which is found in many religious teachings (see Greenberg 2008: especially 5, 134, 229, 337 and 582). Intriguingly, Iris Murdoch (2001, 1970: 99–100) is convinced that while the 'good' is a sovereign concept over all other concepts, the only other concept that comes closest to it is 'love'. But exploring the links between religious transcendence and universal love will have to be left for a future essay.

NOTES

1. Andrzej Bronk (Internet source) defines religious truth as 'orientated towards the ultimate deepest reality called by various names: God, Dharma, Dao, the Sacred, etc.'

2. After exploring the family resemblance analogy as applied to defining religion, John Hick (1989: 5–6) homes in on the 'belief in the transcendent' as that which he considers to be the anchoring point for religions.

3. Pema Chödrön (2002: 51–55), in an intriguing way, links hope with wanting, clinging and fear, and says: 'If we're willing to give up hope that insecurity and pain can be exterminated, then we can have the courage to relax with the groundlessness of our situation' (51). I do not think that this advice proposes a complete submission to despair. Rather, it is part of an overall Buddhist doctrine of overcoming suffering. Thanissaro Bhikkhu (2006: 26) believes that the way of life as taught by the Buddha offers us hope of securing infinite happiness.

4. Refer to Habermas's 'discourse ethics', which is painstakingly developed in his *Moral Consciousness and Communicative Action*.

5. It is possible to imagine different levels of infinity, one connected to another. Between 0 and 1 lies an infinite series of real numbers, and likewise, the same applies for between 1 and 2; and that the number 1 connects both these infinite series.

6. In John L. Austin's *How to Do Things with Words,* Second Edition *(William James Lecture delivered at Harvard University in 1955)*, the author differentiates between the 'constative' element of utterances, that is, the content of utterances that professes to describe the world and is said to be truth evaluable, and the 'performative' element of utterances, that is, what utterances attempt to do, and this being a speech act, is not truth evaluable. Austin finds it difficult to identify utterances that are totally devoid of the performative. Since utterances, he concludes, are like actions done for a purpose, it is quite likely that all utterances are performatives.

7. The term 'ethical pluralism' covers both its types: intrapersonal – an agent's moral decisions and actions may be informed by several moral norms and theories – and interpersonal – different individuals and groups may adopt different moral norms and theories.

8. For an instructive synthesis and evaluation of these three perspectives on religious diversity, see McCarthy (2000).

Part III

ETHICS AND COMMUNICATION: CASE STUDIES

Chapter 8

Communication Ethics in Japan

A Sociocultural Perspective on Privacy in the Networked World

Kiyoshi Murata and Yohko Orito

While tremendous advances in information and communication technology (ICT) have allegedly created a 'globalized world', there is still no universally accepted definition of privacy (Introna 1997; Solove 2008). However, given that the ways of defining and protecting privacy in a society define societal relationships between individuals, organizations and individuals and organizations in that society, and that ICT-based systems and services allow (even non-technical) individual users and organizations to circulate personal information across borders at the speed of light, a formal concept of communication privacy that is locally effective and globally acceptable is now required. As a first step towards such a conceptualization, this study attempts to investigate traditional values concerning communication privacy in Japan from the viewpoint of Japanese sociolinguistic culture.

As Adams et al. (2009) have pointed out, Japan has traditional social norms of limits on the disclosure, circulation, sharing and use of personal information, that is, communication privacy. However, such norms have recently tended to break down, due, in particular, to the social changes that have taken place since the early 1990s, and the architectural changes wrought by networked information processing capabilities. In particular, the widespread use of social media, such as Twitter, Facebook and LINE, especially among young people, has dramatically changed the ways of communication and has caused problems associated with communication activities. It has often been observed that differences between an imagined audience and the actual audience of posts on social media bring about privacy issues and even online vigilantism or aggressive, but not legally authorized, actions of Internet users (online vigilantes) against one who exhibits online behaviour that is regarded as improper by them.

However, it has also been alleged that social awareness of privacy and personal data protection among the general public has been enhanced in Japan, and the Act on the Protection of Personal Information (APPI; Act No. 57 of 2003) went into force in April 2005 in response to that enhanced awareness. According to our research (Murata et al. 2014, 2015; Orito et al. 2013, 2014), typical Japanese Internet users

a. recognize the importance of privacy protection without clearly understanding what the right to privacy is, why protection of the right is important, who may infringe their privacy, and what technology can threaten their privacy,
b. do not read the terms of service and/or privacy policies when/before using an online service,
c. do not understand how and for what purpose the personal information they provide online is used by organizations in the public and private sectors,
d. underestimate the damage caused by invasions of their privacy,
e. have unfounded confidence in their online security, estimating that the public has a higher probability of suffering some kind of damage by misuse of their personal information in the current Internet environment than the probability of their own chances of suffering the same fate, and
f. have an intention to secure their privacy for personal reasons like for protecting their lives and property, but not for social reasons such as for assuring individual autonomy and protecting civil liberty,

although some of these may not necessarily be unique to the Japanese.

Investigations of the processes leading to the development of the APPI (Adams et al. 2010), and of the recent discussions about revisions to it, demonstrate that the Japanese personal data protection laws were enacted and revised for economic purposes, *not* for protecting people's privacy. Japanese policy and law makers have slickly avoided head-on discussions about the concept and social significance of a right to privacy. They have emphasized the importance of protecting information privacy without mentioning other dimensions of privacy such as bodily and decisional privacy. It seems that the right has simply an instrumental value for organizations both in the public and private sectors, as well as for policy makers. The situation surrounding communication privacy in Japan may stand in sharp contrast to that in other (especially EU member) countries.

JAPANESE TRADITIONAL COMMUNICATION STYLES

Sociolinguistic Characteristics of Japanese Communication

Do as Little Talking and Writing as Possible

Communication as a human act contains intrinsic difficulties. A particular difficulty is involved in the use of language, which is the only means of perceiving the chaotic real world in a (seemingly) orderly fashion (Suzuki 1973), for communication, because what one intends to communicate using language, or the referent of what one writes or speaks to communicate with someone else, is usually not a linguistic entity and it is very difficult to explain the whole meaning of a word or a term through language (Suzuki 1973). Idioms, rhetoric, wordage and ways of non-verbal communication have been developed to compensate for the limitations of language as a means of communication, reflecting the sociolinguistic culture in which the language is used, while at the same time functioning as determinants of that very same sociolinguistic culture.

It is often alleged that Japanese is one of the most difficult languages to learn due to its usage of a mixture of Chinese characters (*kanji*), most of which have both Japanese readings (*kun-yomi*) and Chinese-derived readings (*on-yomi*), and two sets of Japanese phonetic characters (*hiragana* and *katakana*); this said, these linguistic characteristics allow ordinary Japanese people to readily understand technical terms and to coin new words (Suzuki 1990). In fact, many new words have been coined, mainly by the youth of the country, often with a tendency to abbreviate those words. Moreover, there are many homonyms because only 23 kinds of phonemes are used in the Japanese language, and the meanings of words of Japanese origin (*wago*) are generally abstract; additionally, *wago* have different kinds of denotative meanings (Suzuki 1990). This requires people to judge what a homonym and a *wago* mean when conducting a spoken dialogue, where the Chinese characters of the homonym and *wago* are not visually displayed, based on the context of the dialogue. Japanese vocabulary is composed of *wago*, *kango* (words of Chinese origin and Japanese–Chinese words), *yōgo* (words of Western origin and Japanese *yōgo*, which are usually written using *katakana*), and hybrid words, and yet, at the same time, Japanese has been relatively free of influence from other languages in terms of grammar and pronunciation (Kindaichi 1988). Japanese words are spelt in several different ways. There are gender differences in spoken Japanese. However, the real difficulty is not in the linguistic characteristics of Japanese but in the Japanese sociolinguistic culture, a significant part of which is hard to perceive even for native Japanese speakers (Suzuki 1990).

Kindaichi (1975) pointed out that traditional Japanese language life is characterized by an attitude of doing as little talking and writing as possible. 'Deeds, not words' have been recognized as a norm of action in Japan. In fact, many Japanese people have empathy with the following phrases in the Analects of Confucius (Legge 1971): 'Fine words and an insinuating appearance are seldom associated with true virtue' (Xue Er 1: 3), and 'The firm, the enduring, the simple, and the modest are near to virtue' (Zi Lu 13: 27).

The Japanese tend to shy away from speaking at great length and eloquently justifying themselves. Those who are voluble and who make many excuses are often despised, and many Japanese people have the experience of being required to put things in a nutshell in the classroom as well as in a business setting. Subjects are often missing in Japanese sentences. In everyday speech, demonstratives are used a lot without making clear what they indicate and listeners are expected to understand what a speaker wants to say, playing their hunch (Kindaichi 1988). Haiku, a Japanese traditional seventeen-*haku* (syllables/morae) poem in which subjects and subjective complements are often missing, fits well within the aesthetics of the Japanese.

Understanding each other without talking or by telepathy and behaving considerately through attuning oneself to the minds of others are considered the optimal state of communication in Japan. Thus, it is not surprising, and actually not unusual, that the Japanese tend to obscure their statements, especially when they talk about important things with others. They are prone to communicate important things implicitly, assuming they appropriately share an understanding of the context in which the communication is being conducted with others. It is presumed that listeners or readers correctly comprehend the implied meaning of statements even when they are expressed obscurely or equivocally. As Hall (1976) described, the Japanese live in a culture where high-context messages are used a lot in routine communications.

Kindaichi (1975) stated that a primitive belief in the power of words was a foundation of Japanese linguistic behavioural tendencies at one time. That is, Japanese people were cautious about talking or writing because they vaguely felt that those who gave careless utterance and put too much into writing could get their just deserts. However, Suzuki (1972) pointed out that Japanese spirituality and lifestyle have much in common with Zen thought. This does not mean that Zen Buddhism unilaterally influenced the development of Japanese ways of thought and living. Instead, the idea that words are an obstacle to mutual understanding is indigenous to the Japanese (Aida 1972; Watsuji 2011) and, at the end of the twelfth century when Zen Buddhism started to spread throughout Japan, it was combined with the tradition of the spiritual life of the samurai, which had sufficiently matured to the extent that, thereafter, Zen lifestyles developed independently based on forms of Japanese spirituality, and gradually entered into every phase of the cultural life of Japanese people (Suzuki 1959, 1972). Indeed, the Zen mottos of 'no reliance on words', 'the one is always the same as the other, the two are never to be separated', and 'no discrimination is to be exercised [to arrive at the truth]' (Suzuki 1959) have shared values with Japanese sociolinguistic culture.

Communication in the Ie Society

Japanese people are traditionally very careful with their speech so as not to break the rules of courtesy in the *ie* society, where it is emphasized that a human being is an existence of self plus certain relationships with others, or *aidagara,* rather than an independent individual. The Japanese term *ie* (家) is usually translated as a family or house(hold). However, as Nakane (1970) has stated, this term has connotations beyond those of the English words 'family' or 'household'. She pointed out that *ie* constitutes a distinguishable social group that is constructed on the basis of an established frame of residence and/or of management organization, rather than on kinship or consanguinity, and that the human relationships, especially vertical ones with superiors and subordinates, within *ie* are thought of as more important than all other human relationships. This leads to a strong tie among *ie* members, as well as a strong awareness of *uchi* (inside) and *soto* (outside). These characteristics of social group structure are found in the majority of Japanese groups and organizations.

In such a society, similarity/difference or closeness/distance between people, located in a certain situation, is understood by them on the basis of how much they share their *aidagara.* This realization leads to their recognition of *ba* – the field, place or immediate social context – they are in and their awareness of whether they occupy an *uchi* or *soto* position in that *ba* (Murakami et al. 1979).

Generally, Japanese people are prone to hesitate when it comes to engaging in a candid and vigorous debate, even at an academic or business meeting. Making a candid negative remark about another's statement in public is usually avoided, so as not to cause a loss of face or to avoid bringing any shame upon him/her. Instead, making a subtle suggestion indicating criticism in a roundabout way is preferred, even at a get together. Making a great effort not to humiliate oneself, or another, is at the root of Japanese people's behavioural patterns (Kindaichi 1988).

In the social relationships of *aidagara,* as well as in *ba,* specific stations and associated roles are explicitly or implicitly assigned to the people involved. Benedict (1946) mentioned the importance of 'taking one's proper station' in Japanese vertical society. A person who has a conversation with others is expected to properly understand his/her station and role in the *ba* of the conversation. A speaker is required to immediately judge vertical relationships with listeners in the given conversational context. He/she is expected to use appropriate terms for self and terms of address, honorific/humble terminologies and formal/casual lines based on his/her understanding and judgement. Expressing his/her opinion candidly without knowing his/her station in the *ba* and/or reading the situation is regarded as inappropriate, and sometimes rude, behaviour. Personal pronouns are used as little as possible and addressing others using pronouns is considered impolite in some cases (Kindaichi 1988). Instead, different kinds of terms for self and terms of address are used, depending on the context in which a conversation is undertaken. That usage needs to reflect the role each person involved is expected to play in the conversation, based on the vertical personal relationships among those who take part in it (Suzuki 1973).

Knowing their station and reading the situation or sensing the atmosphere in the *ba* of communication is an important art that Japanese people are expected to develop as they grow up, to avoid causing unnecessary friction in their social lives. However, this Japanese communication style has its downside. Those who recognize their lower stations in a *ba* tend to hold back from sharing their thoughts. Once a dominant atmosphere is developed in a *ba*, it is hard for anyone in the *ba* to behave so as to upset the atmosphere and, thus, unrestricted discussion in the *ba* becomes more difficult (Yamamoto 1983).

Awareness of *Uchi/Soto* and *Seken*

Figure 8.1 shows the in-group/out-group or *uchi/soto* model, depicting the Japanese people's understanding of the relationships between self and others and other related concepts. The innermost regions are the individual self or *watashi* and the close family/*miuchi*. The outermost region consists of *tanin*, those persons who can never be inside one of the individual's in-groups. The

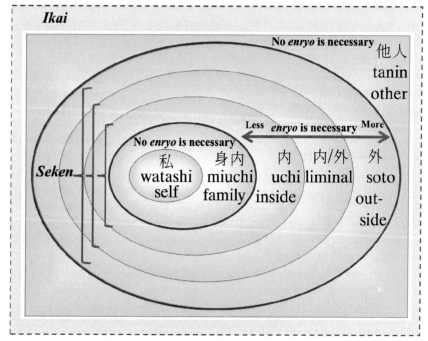

Figure 8.1 *Uchi/soto* Model. *Source*: With kind permission from Springer Science + Business Media: AI & Society, The Japanese Sense of Information Privacy, 24(4), 2009, 334, Andrew A. Adams, Kiyoshi Murata and Yohko Orito, Fig. 2 (with additions).

separation between *uchi* and *soto* is not a fixed measure but a sense of the relative psychological distance between people. Japanese people's judgement about whether someone is in their *uchi* or *soto* zone reflects their perception of the 'density of *aidagara*' or the level of closeness to him/her. However, this perception is neither fixed nor stable but depends on the context. To clearly illustrate the relative nature of the *uchi/soto* border, the liminal zone is explicitly included (Adams et al. 2009).

Doi (1973) attempted to examine Japanese behavioural patterns from the viewpoint of *amae*, which means presuming the good will of others. According to him, the presence or absence of *enryo*, restraint or holding back, is a way of distinguishing between the types of human relationships, which are referred to as *uchi* and *soto*. In the parent–child relationship, there is no *enryo* because the relationship is permeated with *amae*. With respect to other relationships, *enryo* decreases (because *amae* increases) proportionately with closeness, whereas *enryo* increases (because *amae* decreases) with distance. Interestingly, however, there is no need for *enryo* with *tanin*, with whom *amae* is completely missing, on the assumption of a lack of continuing contact.

Abe (1995, 1999) insisted that the ordinary Japanese person lives, at least mentally, not in society but in *seken*, which is a small world defined by the relationships with those towards whom the person feels mutual obligation (*giri*) and empathy (*ninjō*). Thus, in Japan, a human being tends to be regarded as *aidagara*, not as an independent individual or citizen, and people carefully behave so as not to be excluded from their *seken*. Inoue (2007) pointed out that the Japanese sense of morality is closely related to norms in this small world; one's behaviour is disciplined so that it conforms to the norms of one's *seken*, or is honourable in the eyes of people in the *seken*. According to Nakada and Tamura (2005), Japanese people believe that disaster, illness, war and crime come from *ikai*, a different world from that of their *seken*, which constitutes their normal world. People living in a *seken* feel that the *seken* is a secure and safe world where it is permitted to introduce *amae* because it is assumed that all the people in the *seken* have long-term, mutually interdependent relationships or *giri*. Indeed, *seken* often have an exclusive nature and people tend to remain aloof from *tanin* or those outside their *seken*. *Seken* may be recognized narrowly in one situation and broadly in others, based on one's perception of the context one is in. The narrowest *seken* can be the close family/*miuchi*, whereas *tanin* can never be in one's *seken*.

In terms of communication, generally, the further away one moves from the self, the less information is communicated (Orito and Murata 2008). To those in the *uchi-soto* liminal zone (i.e. those who are sometimes in *uchi* and sometimes in *soto*), less information is revealed than to those always within the *uchi* zone. Japanese people have a tendency to share personal information, such as health conditions, family issues and personal histories, with each other in the *uchi* or *miuchi* zone based on the feeling of *amae*, which causes a sense of trust among people in those groups. Identity numbers that can lead to financial loss, such as bank or credit card numbers, are occasionally shared among *miuchi*/family members.

It is interesting to note that, reflecting their perceptions of there being no need for *enryo* for *tanin* and no possibility of *tanin*'s coming into their lives or *seken*, Japanese people tend to have no interest in whether their personal information, except that which can be used to harm the victim financially, are disclosed to and/or circulated among *tanin*. The Japanese proverb, 'One loses all sense of shame, when he/she is away from home', illustrates this well. In fact, *tanin* may receive significant private information, including sensitive information; however, in such a case, they are expected to hear it and, once they leave the situation in which they have heard it, to behave as if they had not heard it at all or totally forgot it.

In contrast, Japanese people are quite cautious about revealing their personal information to those who are in the liminal zone. In fact, personal information revealed to them is carefully selected because it is nearly impossible to predict when they will move into the *uchi* zone. For example, because the Japanese tend to stress situational position in a particular *ba* or frame within which they belong, rather than experiencing a social life as a universal attribute (Nakane 1970), personal information concerning their frames, such as their companies, old school and hometowns, is usually revealed to others even in the liminal zone. However, sensitive personal information, like health conditions, is rarely disclosed to others in the liminal zone (Orito and Murata 2008).

Tactful Use of *Hon'ne* and *Tatemae*

The *uchi/soto* awareness is directly related to Japanese insular collectivism (Adams et al. 2009). The term 'insular collectivism' refers to a particular form of Japanese collectivism, which is sometimes referred to as 'groupism'. The Japanese form of groupism forms hierarchies, based on strong vertical personal relationships with superiors and subordinates, weak horizontal relationships with fellow subordinates of a common superior, and very weak ties to other members of the organization. The strong identification of the individual with the group in Japanese society, expressed principally in terms of vertical relationships up and down, suppressing horizontal links, leads to a fragmentation of society into competing islands. In the insular collectivism society, Japanese people tend to place more importance on the interests of the *uchi* group to which they belong than on their personal interests or the good of society as a whole (Orito and Murata 2008).

In speaking to members of one's *uchi* group, one uses *hon'ne* speech; that is, one speaks the bare truth or one's real intentions. When speaking to members of one's *soto* group, one uses *tatemae* or courteous speech; that is, one communicates just what one politely says on the surface to casual acquaintances. For example, instead of saying 'no' in a business negotiation with a customer, Japanese businesspeople often say, 'We will carefully consider your request'. Their *hon'ne*, or what they truly want to say, is that the customer's request is not acceptable at all (Orito and Murata 2008). In a situation where people from one's *soto* group interact with those from one's *uchi* group, one uses *tatemae* speech, expecting that the *uchi* members can correctly understand the *hon'ne* meanings behind the speech. The tactful use of *hon'ne* and *tatemae* is considered a matter of course for normal adults in Japan.

SOCIAL ATTITUDES TOWARDS COMMUNICATION PRIVACY IN JAPAN

Traditional Social Norms of Communication Privacy

It has been alleged by many academics that the Japanese lack, or at least used to lack, a sense of privacy. For example, Benedict (1946) stated that:

> Because there is little privacy in a Japanese community, too, it is no fantasy that 'the world' knows practically everything he does and can reject him if it disapproves. Even the construction of the Japanese house, the thin walls that permit the passage of sounds and which are pushed open during the day, makes private life extremely public for those who cannot afford a wall and garden. (p. 288)

Ito (1964), who was a Supreme Court judge, stated that a sense of respect for the private life of the individual was lacking in Japan, and Horibe (1988), who is practically the first Japanese privacy commissioner (the first chairperson of the Specific Personal Information Protection Commission), pointed out the Japanese people's lack of sensitivity to privacy.

Contrary to these allegations, Adams et al. (2009) demonstrated that there is a strong sense of information privacy in Japan, which has long been a part of the culture. While 'puraibashī' as a recently imported word may represent a relatively new categorical concept in Japan, the concept of information privacy has been in the culture for a considerable time, and is still evolving to take account of changes in the world such as networked computer processing and globalization.

In fact, it is clear that the awareness of *ba* with associated stations and roles, and of *uchi/soto* and the use of *hon'ne* and *tatemae*, deeply relate to how Japanese people control the disclosure and flow of information, including personal information. Social norms to protect communication privacy are embedded in Japanese sociolinguistic culture in several ways.

In addition, traditionally, the construction of Japanese houses has used paper and light wooden sliding doors called *fusuma* or *shoji* for room dividers. This provides little restriction on the access to spoken information among those residing in the houses. This lack of an architectural (Lessig 1999) limit on the sharing of information has been solved by the development of social norms requiring people to appreciate the sections as a sound barrier and to behave as if they heard nothing of overheard, but not explicitly given, information. As Watsuji (1979) noted, *fusuma* can function as a barrier when people using *fusuma* mutually appreciate it as a barrier. At the very least, the illusion of privacy and also a restriction on the spread of information beyond those who join the chatter are required. This is reflected particularly in the as-if tradition (Mizutani et al. 2004) in the culture of sympathy (Aida 1972), which allows, for example, spouses to have arguments without the rest of the household treating them as though their marriage is in trouble unless one or both partners approach a third party for help or advice in the matter, and still has a strong influence on social practices of information sharing in Japan today. While Japan may be at or near an extreme of information revelation, the concept of communication privacy does exist, and it is a key part of the Japanese sociolinguistic culture (Adams et al. 2009).

Japanese Perception of Self

Privacy, in the West, is usually presented as dependent on a strong individualist core of selfhood, where the self is defined within a clearly defined shell. Information within that shell is private, as is information that implies a structure within the shell (Adams et al. 2009).

However, based on an etymologic analysis of the Japanese term *ningen*, corresponding to the English concept of a human being, Watsuji (2007) concluded that *ningen* is a term used to express the *seken* a person lives in and, simultaneously, a person who lives in the *seken*. He insisted that people become human beings when they reside in a *seken* and are recognized as human beings because they represent the whole *seken*, and that human existence is definitely inseparable from *aidagara*.

The idea that *ningen* means self plus his/her *aidagara* is broadly accepted in Japan. For example, beyond Abe's (1995; 1999) insistence described above, Kimura (2006) mentioned that the personal identity of an individual is usually determined based on his/her perception of relationships with others. Doi (1973) noted that the Japanese mentality of *amae* reflects Japanese people's realization that their lives are ruled by interdependent relationships with others:

> It is surely significant ... that the Japanese term *uchi* (inside), as used in words such as *miuchi* (family circle) or *nakamauchi* (circle of friends or colleagues),

refers mainly to the group to which the individual belongs and not, as with English terms such as 'private,' to the individual himself. In Japan, little value is attributed to the individual's private realm as distinct from the group. (p. 42)

This idea affects the Japanese perception of what kind of information is private and to be protected. In fact, as Adams et al. (2009) pointed out, rather than being the poor cousin of the Western sense of information privacy, Japanese social interactions and linguistics demonstrate that the Japanese have a broader definition of information privacy, allowing a fuzzy boundary to the self and the definition of private information and, thus, of privacy. In Japan, privacy has tended to be regarded as being relational and contextual, though it is sometimes considered a universal value.

COMMUNICATION PRIVACY IN THE ICT-DRIVEN NETWORKED SOCIETY

The Transformation of *Seken*

After losing in the Second World War, Japan rose from being a devastated state to become one of the world's top economic powers. Heavy industry was a driving force of this miraculous economic growth, at least until the early 1990s, and industrialization caused significant social transformations. For example, urbanization, accompanied by the development of commuter towns, eroded traditional local communities. Moreover, Japanese employment systems based on lifelong employment promoted the centripetal force of companies. Employees came to feel a sense of belonging to their companies, and communities centred on businesses such as the 'business castle towns' and company housing, which are still numerous today, furthered this sense of belonging. These transformations can be understood as a transition from traditional rural collectivism, based on rice-growing agriculture, to urban collectivism through industrialization (Murata and Orito 2010).

Through the process of industrialization in Japan, as Murata and Orito (2010) stated, the *seken* concept was modernized. Urban society, by nature a cluster of strangers, was reconstructed as a collective *seken* entity, defined primarily by long-term business relationships, and the Japanese sense of morality was maintained in this modernized *seken*. Mutual trust between members of a modernized *seken* has been sustained by rituals, as suggested by Giddens (1994), such as presenting year-end (*oseibo*) and midsummer gifts (*ochūgen*), sending New Year's cards (*nengajō*), and exchanging business cards (*meishi*).

However, the burst of the bubble economy in 1991 caused the Koizumi administration to adopt economic policies intended to shrink the government and revitalize private-sector economic activity. The resulting changes in employment systems in the private sector caused latent risks, created during industrialization, to manifest. The social functions of both traditional and modernized *seken*, and consequently of families as well, deteriorated, causing people to adopt individualistic attitudes more than ever, as exemplified by the new and increasing trends of job-hopping, divorce and suicide. Long-term relationships with individuals and organizations have not necessarily been assumed. The rituals described above are falling into disuse. Unabashedly avaricious behaviour among businesspeople, previously deterred by the *seken* concept, is now more prevalent. The maturation of the domestic economy and arrival of globalization have stimulated these tendencies. Considering Lessig's (1999) model of four modalities for the regulation of human behaviour, it may not be surprising that a decline in the idea of the *seken* as an institution of social norms has prompted the enactment of laws and the construction of a technological architecture, which are expected to compensate for the malfunctioning of *seken* (Murata and Orito 2010). However, the fact that the technical problem of *kanji* processing was solved in the mid-1990s, and that significant processing of personal information about Japanese individuals became both commonplace and fully interoperable between commercial organizations and between private and public bodies, overwhelmed existing social norms regarding communication privacy in Japan (Adams et al. 2010).

APPI as a Poor Cousin of a Western Personal Data Protection Law

Historically, in Japan, when individuals gained knowledge about others through overhearing conversations, they were expected to follow the 'as-if' tradition. Urbanization in Japan did not undermine the original as-if expectations, upheld by the strong social norms insisting on *hon'ne/tatemae* distinctions. The creation of personal information databases, the ease with which information about individuals may be transmitted between *soto* entities, and the requirements to deal with such entities have resulted in a rapid awakening among the Japanese that social norms are no longer sufficient to regulate the protection of information privacy (Adams et al. 2009). Simultaneously, the demise of the modernized *seken* has made the boundary between *uchi* and *soto* more vague and fluid.

In such circumstances, a government announcement of the introduction of a citizen numbering system called the Basic Resident Register Network System (*Juki* Net) in 1999, full-scale operation of which started in August 2003, gathered the attention of the media, and media reports made the general public aware of the malfunction of social norms, leading to increased concern about communication privacy issues. Additionally, the Japanese business community, which had strongly asserted that self-regulation was the most efficient means of protecting personal information in the private sector, to avoid negative impacts on the business activities of Japanese firms, significantly changed its public position, issuing a new policy on constructing a secure and safe Net society in the face of the stagnation of domestic markets and the progress of economic globalization (Nippon Keidanren 2003).

Consequently, APPI was passed in 2003 and went into force in April 2005. Although this legal development was a response to the failures of social norms that had previously guaranteed communication privacy, the act failed to compensate for those failures. APPI corresponds to the OECD guidelines (OECD 1980), which were developed based on the Westin (1967) conception of the right to information privacy. Directive 95/46/EC (The European Parliament and the Council of the European Union 1995) had a particularly significant effect on APPI because it includes the following clause: business activities in the global business environment in which personal information is shared among business organizations beyond national borders will not be permitted unless some form of regulation on the protection of personal information exists in each nation in which the business organizations are based. In these respects, APPI has the appearance of a Western-style personal information protection law while actually being a pro-economic law, not a pro-privacy law. The act presumes the usefulness of personal information and intends to promote the use of personal information, counterbalanced with its protection, while avoiding a clear reference to privacy. However, Japanese policy and law makers failed to recognize, or ignored the existence of, traditional social norms concerning communication privacy in Japan, which were not reflected in the letter of the act or in the revised APPI, which passed in September 2015.

APPI's introduction and its associated penal provisions (Articles 56 and 57) raised awareness among both individuals and organizations of the need to address personal information protection and to spread awareness about the protection act. This response resulted in excessive rigidity in interpreting APPI. This was highlighted by the JR Fukuchiyama Line train disaster on 27 April 2005, in which 107 were killed and 562 were wounded. To abide by the act, hospitals refused to disclose information on the names and conditions of the victims, even though Article 16 of APPI describes that personal information about an individual can be handled without obtaining prior consent in cases where the handling of personal information is necessary for the protection of the life, body, or property and where it is difficult to obtain the individual's consent. Consequently, victims' relatives were unable to acquire vital information about their loved ones (Murata and Orito 2008).

APPI also caused a degree of confusion. Some citizens, students and parents have refused to provide personal information for community membership lists or student lists (National Consumer Affairs Centre of Japan 2005).

These people arbitrarily assumed that they had the right to refuse to provide personal information based on APPI. Some people have refused to fill out the census form on the authority of the act, although APPI does not apply to the census. Moreover, to comply with APPI, several local governments have refused to reply to enquiries of defendants who are engaged in lawsuits although, again, APPI does not apply to this sort of enquiry (Murata and Orito 2008).

Generally, a written contract and legislation tend to be regarded as *tatemae* in Japan (Nakane 1970; Uchida 2000). However, regarding APPI, it seems that a significant number of people have struggled to comply with the act, although some of them have made false attempts. Business people who take the act seriously have been prone to comply with the act in a 'cold feet' fashion; they seem to hesitate to do anything that is questionable, even though it would be legal (Murata and Orito 2008). There are some business people who feel strong resentment towards the unnecessary legislation for protecting personal information, labelling APPI as a curse of 'compliance depression'.

Simultaneously, however, even after the enforcement of the act, many personal information leakage incidents occurred, which gave the appearance that APPI had failed to function well in promoting the proper handling of personal information. In fact, a series of personal information leakage cases revealed that many organizations in the public and private sectors have not built effective frameworks for compliance with the act despite the fact that most of them declare on their websites that they abide by the act or the relevant acts or ordinances enacted based on APPI. Additionally, no one who has been responsible for a personal information leakage case has ever been brought to trial under the Act. These situations can be considered to reflect the *hon'ne/tatemae* tradition; for many people, APPI is just *tatemae* (Murata and Orito 2008; Orito and Murata 2008). In July 2014, it became known that personal information of at least 20.7 million people was leaked from the Benesse Corporation, which is engaged in correspondence education and publishing. It was found that the main causes of this incident were rudimentary defects not only in technological but also in organizational security systems; the company behaved as if they had taken no notice of APPI.

The overzealous interpretation of APPI, and taking little or no account of the act, are two sides of the same coin. A personal information protection act not rooted in Japanese sociolinguistic culture cannot compensate for the malfunctioning of Japanese traditional communication ethics. Using Brey's (2007) terminologies, in Japan, protection of information privacy at the institutional (legal) level based on the Western conception of it has been implemented without regard to the traditional ways of dealing with personal information at the behavioural level, and this has caused the problems and tensions.

Illusion of the Emergence of E-*seken*

Social media are usually considered a useful way for people to stay connected with their family, friends and acquaintances, allowing them to overcome time and spatial limitations. As in other industrialized countries, many people in Japan started to use social media in the late 2000s, and Twitter, Facebook and LINE are popular, especially among the younger generations. Because social media demonstrated their usefulness in supporting victims of the Great East Japan Earthquake in March 2011, enabling the victims to transmit information about their safety and to make contact with their families in a chaotic situation in which existing traditional media such as phones, TV, radio and newspapers did not work, the systems have been expected to play a significant role in promoting bonding between people in Japan (Asai and Kavathatzopoulos 2012). Decrepit *seken* may be able to be revitalized in cyberspace through social media use.

The proliferation of social media has been remarkable in Japan. According to the results of a questionnaire survey on social media usage, which the authors conducted in November 2013 using an online survey site and to which 368 valid responses were provided by university students aged 18–23 years at Meiji (110) and Ehime (258) Universities (Orito et al. 2014),

a. more than 30% (111/366) of respondents always connected with social media and frequently checked posts by others, and more than 40% (158/366) connected more than three times per day,

b. using mainly smart phones (294/324, 90.7%) and/or laptop PCs (138/324, 42.6%),

c. to mainly view articles, photos and videos posted by other users, click 'Like', comment and repost (193/303, 63.7%) and/or post articles, photos and videos (154/303, 50.8%), and

d. fewer than 3% (10/366) of respondents did not use social media at all.

As stated above, when Japanese people recognize that their personal information is collected and used by others in the *soto* or liminal zone, they should have serious concerns about potentially harmful effects. In contrast, when they consider that people in the *tanin* zone collect and use their personal information, they do not care about it. However, owing to the expansiveness and elusive features of Internet space, it can be difficult for anyone to imagine who collects his/her personal information on the Internet, and in what way, and how those who collect the information could use it. Ordinary Japanese people might expect complete strangers or *tanin* to collect and use their personal information during their social media usage, and they might consider that they do not need to have any concerns about harm caused by (mis)use of the collected information and that the risk of the collection is nothing much to worry about, based on the logic of *seken*. However, neither of the above expectations or considerations is appropriate.

Table 8.1 shows a result of the questionnaire survey regarding respondents' imagined audiences. More than a half of the respondents (146/288, 50.7%) posted information on social media, assuming that people who had some relationship with them, in both their real life and online, saw or read it. However, inappropriate postings on social media, which have often been made due to users' lack of knowledge about the nature of social media and prudence, have many times resulted in online vigilantism. For example, three baseball players at Kosei Gakuin High School in Aomori Prefecture in Japan, whose baseball team took second place in the 2011 Koshien High School Baseball Tournament, each separately posted on their mobile blogs about their underage drinking at Japanese-style pubs. One of them posted salacious details of his dates with a female student who acted as an assistant manager to the team. Someone reported these posts to officials at both the high school and the prefecture's high school baseball federation. As a consequence, the players were suspended from school. All local events to celebrate their second place were cancelled due to the scandals (Adams et al. 2011). In another case, a thoughtless Japanese college woman broadcasted live coverage of a date between a famous professional football player and a fashion model at a ritzy restaurant for which she worked as a part-time food server using Twitter in January 2011. Soon after the tweets, a human flesh search started and her name, home address, university and other personal information were investigated and exposed online by many anonymous Internet users. Given a situation in which such inadvertent use of social media is detected, numerous instances like those above have led to social media being known as a 'fool detector' in Japan.

Online vigilantism demonstrates that people in the *tanin* zone can easily intervene in *uchi* communication in the social media sphere and can exert a significant influence over the life of a target through aggressive behaviour, in both real space and cyberspace, whereas those who commit online vigilantism would

Table 8.1 Imagined Audience of Social Media

Q14 When you post information (articles, pictures, videos, etc.) on social media, who do you imagine will see or read it? (n = 288)		
	Number	*Percentage (%)*
1. People who have some relationship with me both in my real life and online	146	50.69
2. People who have some relationship with me only online	45	15.63
3. Any social media users including people unknown to me	90	31.25
4. Just I will	3	1.04
5. Others	4	1.39

usually never attack their *uchi* people. Grimmelmann (2009) pointed out that social-network-site profiles are social artefacts crafted by users for a specific audience, and Facebook's design sends mutually reinforcing signals that it is a private space, closed to unwanted outsiders. Given this understanding, social media users tend to play a character expected by their imagined online audience or put on the persona they suppose their imagined online audience identifies. In the real world, one can show different personae to different people, but in cyberspace one can hardly do so. An unimagined audience can suddenly barge into a user's private space, where foolish behaviour which is presented to regale the imagined audience is detected. People can no longer assume the traditional communication ethics in *seken* or be indifferent as to whether *tanin* obtain their personal information in an ICT-driven networked world. In the social media sphere, *tanin* can suddenly barge into the *uchi* area without any *enryo*.

Acquisti and Gross (2006) showed in their research results that a significant minority of Facebook users vastly underestimate the reach and openness of their own profile. This suggests that there are Facebook users who underestimate how many people can read their postings on the SNS and do not recognize the presence of *tanin* in their Facebook sphere. Marwick and boyd (2011) described how Twitter users conceptualized their audiences in diverse and varied ways. Those users who imagine their audience as people they already know consider Twitter to be a social space where they can communicate with pre-existing friends, whereas for those who recognize their audience as themselves Twitter is a personal space where other people's reactions do not matter. However, both types of expectations about the Twitter sphere are unrealistic and can sometimes lead to serious situations for users.

Lack of knowledge regarding the nature of social media as a communication space among users, especially among young and reckless people, will mean that social media continue to function as a fool detector. Anyone who conducts open and honest postings without thoughtfulness and prudence may be detected as a fool on social media. For the Japanese, it is urgently necessary to re-examine traditional communication ethics, which have permeated Japanese people's communication behaviour heretofore, to clearly understand the risks entailed in an ICT-driven networked world. Based on this understanding, the right to communication privacy, and protection of this right, should be properly conceptualized and a law to protect that privacy right appropriately has to be developed.

CONCLUSIONS

It is often alleged that Japanese is one of the most difficult languages to learn due to its linguistic characteristics such as the usage of a mixture of *kanji*, *hiragana* and *katakana* and the existence of many homonyms. However, the real difficulty is not in such characteristics but in the Japanese sociolinguistic culture, a significant part of which is hard to perceive even for native Japanese speakers. As part of the culture, Japan has traditional social norms governing communication with others, and limits on the disclosure, circulation, sharing and use of personal information, that is, communication privacy, which were based on an awareness of *uchi/soto* and *ba*.

Given the existence of self plus *aidagara*, a Japanese person is expected to behave in a way that maintains the dignity of his/her *seken*. However, following changes in the economic situation in the early 1990s, the social functions of both traditional and modernized *seken* have deteriorated and, consequently, social norms have been undermined. Simultaneously, significant processing of personal information about Japanese individuals since the mid-1990s has overwhelmed the previous social norms.

APPI failed to compensate for the malfunctioning of social norms relating to communication privacy because it was enacted and revised for economic purposes, not to protect privacy, ignoring, in the process, the Japanese traditional social norms regarding communication. The widespread use of social media has worsened the circumstances surrounding communication privacy in Japan. A re-examination of traditional Japanese communication ethics, proper conceptualization of the right to communication privacy based on such a re-examination and the development of appropriate measures to protect that right taking the characteristics of the current networked world into account are pressing issues in Japan. Considering the global nature of ICT and the local nature of human beings, both the concept of the right and the measures should be locally effective and globally acceptable. Those who deal with the issues have to take the position of 'moral pluralism': while values and moral principles may differ between cultures (either on the surface or more deeply), such differences can be perceived by each side and there exist social conditions under which those differences can be accepted and respected, with diverse values and moral principles coexisting in circumstances developed through civilized discussion.[1]

NOTE

1. The authors appreciate really helpful comments and suggestions provided by the reviewers. This study was supported by the MEXT (Ministry of Education, Culture, Sports, Science and Technology, Japan) Programme for Strategic Research Bases at Private Universities (2012–16) project 'Organisational Information Ethics' S1291006 and the JSPS Grant-in-Aids for Scientific Research (B) 25285124 and for Young Scientists (B) 24730320.

Chapter 9

What Is the Critical Role of Intercultural Information Ethics?

Elin Palm

INTRODUCTION

Intercultural Information Ethics (IIE) has emerged as a research field within which the ethical relevance of cultural differences in the design, implementation and use of Information and Communication Technologies (ICT) are researched. A common claim by IIE scholars is that a globalization of information and communication processes, originally stemming from Western engineering, entail a cultural component and a Western bias (cf. Ess 2006; Capurro 2008), rendering export of ICT/ICT systems a form of 'value colonialism'.[1] A broad range of services are provided by technical systems with 'cultural components'. One example of the way in which ICT is said to be biased is that the 'genetic makeup of ICT', the very structures of both computer hardware and software of ICT are expressions of Western culture (Bielby 2014). Computer code is typically programmed in Latin characters and expressed in English language, even if programming is taking place outside the anglophone world (Bielby 2014).[2] Although non-English based programming languages exist, they have not been influential internationally. Another example of an alleged Western cultural leaning in ICT is that of privacy seals necessary for the usage of certain online services. These seals are also the result of Western programming and said to presuppose an understanding of a concept that is alien to many non-Western users. For instance, it has been argued that these seals prevent Japanese users from consenting to certain online services in an informed manner (Orito and Murata 2007, chapter 8 of this volume). Even if ICT has brought the world together in the sense of facilitating cross-national communication and data transfer, biases built into the technology are taken to influence and steer information transmission, reception, processing and retrieval in certain directions. In order to overcome problems with implementation and use of technology that may carry 'alien' values and an undue impact, it has been stressed that potential differences between 'sending' and 'receiving cultures' must be properly recognized. Following one of the founders of IIE – Rafael Capurro – the main challenge of global intercultural ethical research is to 'critically analyse the traditions in which ICT systems are implemented and used, to compare them, to look at similarities and differences particularly concerning the reasons given (or not) for moral principles and value hier-archies ruling human action' (Capurro 2010). A frequently raised question within the IIE discourse is whether values embedded in the usage of ICT are *culture specific* or universal. Tools and models for constructivist (Evanoff 2006) and systematic *intercultural* comparisons have been proposed (Hiruta 2006; Brey 2007). Furthermore, the claim has been made that IIE studies should contribute to foster dialogue between applied ethics and computer science as well as *between cultures* (Ess and Thorseth 2006). Without dis-puting the need for cross-cultural studies, here the case will be made that, before *systematic* comparative analyses can be undertaken in a meaningful way, a better understanding for the key concepts of 'culture' and 'cultural' is needed. And, it is argued that scholars within the field of IIE should be more explicit regarding what this cultural component integrated in technol-ogy is taken to mean and how the implications thereof should be dealt with. Despite the many different meanings and definitions attached to the term as well as the controversies regarding 'culture' within, for example, sociology and ethnography, this notion is seldom specifically defined by IIE scholars. Hence, this paper aims to provide a critical discussion of common aims and methods within the field of IIE with a particular focus on the meaning and ethical relevance of 'culture' and 'cultural'. An overview of how culture is defined and discussed by IIE scholars will be made together with an analysis of what it is taken to mean to investigate how cultures respond to or are influ-enced by ICT. Arguably a greater sensitivity to the complexity of culture is needed within IIE, and in order to respect the many influential and diverging perspectives, it becomes necessary to question what characteristics, manifes-tations or layers are considered relevant when comparing cultures within IIE studies. Equally important, what should be considered ethically relevant and why? Against this backdrop, an attempt will be made to draft a reasonable understanding and role of 'culture' in critical studies of social and ethical implications of ICT.

The next section describes the development of intercultural studies within the domain of Information Ethics (IE), discussing aims and methods within IIE. The following section portrays and problematizes the notion of culture and the relevance of this notion for the field of IE. Then a discussion on the role of cultural in IIE is offered and the chapter ends with a conclusion.

THE ADVENT OF IIE

Before entering a discussion regarding the meaning and role of 'culture' in IE, a brief overview of the fairly recent development of IIE as a research field will be offered.

In the 1960s, studies on social and ethical implications of ICT emerged, foremost in the West, and developed into the field of IE (cf. Moor 1985; Bynum 2008) investigating – almost exclusively – Western conditions and interests. Approaches with a broader scope, addressing the global impact of ICT, appeared in the mid-90s with discussions on the equity and fairness of the global ICT-development such as a 'Digital divide' (cf. Moss 2002) or a split between information rich and poor (cf. van den Hoven 1995; Britz 2006). During the past decade, a more inclusive approach focusing the ethical implications of ICT on non-Western cultures has emanated (for an informative overview, see: Bielby 2014) from the insight that ICT, originally developed in the Western world, now exported and used worldwide, 'embed and foster specific Western values and communications preferences' (Ess 2002). Concerns have been raised that the problems and solutions identified in IE may have little bearing in other parts of the world (Ess 2005). Since Western and First World cultures are initially responsible for the invention and proliferation of ICTs, it has been argued that a certain accountability and responsibility regarding the effects of ICT – or at least stewardship – follow (Bielby 2014). In a general sense, researchers and technology developers can be considered morally responsible for the consequences of the knowledge that they produce, and hence, expected to, as far as possible, foresee and alleviate negative implications (cf. Shamoo and Resnik 2009). In the case of already existing technology, it can be expected that attempts are made to disclose values that are assumed or (more or less consciously) embedded in the technologies and systems under development as suggested by Philip Brey in his diclosive ethics approach (Brey 2009).[3]

The more inclusive approach to ICT stressed that implications of ICT should be assessed at a global rather than at a local level. Questions are addressed if the ICT-related ethical issues discussed in the West would be the same, similar or completely different in other cultures and whether or not solutions to such issues could be reached that are relevant within the Eastern as well as Western philosophical tradition. A broadening of the scope of IE and opening up a global dialogue were warranted in order to better respect different cultural identities and in order to avoid 'imperialistic homogenisa-tion' (Ess 2005). As a result of more or less concerted initiatives to explore ICT from a cross-cultural perspective, IIE has become a research field of its own within which ICT-related moral issues and the use of information are 'reflected on in a comparative manner on the basis of different cultural traditions' (Capurro 2007). The Internet is recognized as a particular challenge to IIE. Investigations (often of an empirical nature) explore how far 'traditional cultures and their moral values communicate and transform themselves under the impact of the digital "infosphere" in general and of the Internet in particular' (Capurro 2007). Examples of questions under analysis are the extent to which the Internet alters the life and culture in traditional societies and what the impact may be on future societies in global and local senses (Capurro 2007). Studies focus on reactions to the introduction of Internet in developing nations like Thailand (Lü 2005) and on different attitudes towards file sharing in ICT-saturate countries like Japan and Sweden, related to the notion of privacy (Murayama et al. 2014). Moreover, a significant number of cross-cultural research projects have investigated potential commensurability between Western normative concepts and Eastern counterparts such as the notion of privacy (cf. Hongladarom 2001, 2007; Kitiyadisai 2005; Lü 2005; Nakada and Takanori 2005; Nishigaki 2006; Adams et al. 2009). In particular, possible counterparts and matches to the Western notion of privacy have been sought in the Japanese language (cf. Capurro 2005; Cullen 2007; McRobb et al. 2007; Mizutani, Dorsey and Moor 2004; Nakada and Tamura 2005; Murata and Orito 2008; Adams et al. 2009).

AIMS AND METHODS IN IIE/CRITICAL ROLE

This chapter aims to provide a critical discussion of common aims and methods within the field of the newly established IIE with a particular focus on the meaning and (ethical) relevance of 'culture' and 'cultural'. A brief account of key ambitions and methods within IIE is offered, intended as a basis for an ensuing discussion on the critical role of this 'research program' (however eclectic IIE may be).

While there is a broad agreement among IIE scholars regarding that which IIE should be concerned with – investigate the global impact of ICT, promote equal representation and strengthen the inclusion of marginalized voices in order to prevent homogenization – there is less agreement about the desirability of more ambitious aims like the development of a globally shared code of ICT ethics or one globally shared ethics of information (Ess 2006) and yet weaker synopsis concerning how the aims should be achieved, by what methods and what standards. Several methodological approaches sort under the panoply IIE. It includes descriptive studies on the impact of ICT on customs, languages and social stability in different countries as well as normative analyses of how ICT ought to be implemented and used together with systematic analyses of cultural differences (cf. Bielby 2014). Rafael Capurro suggests that the critical task of IIE is to compare information moralities both at an ontological/structural level and at an ontic/empirical level of analysis. In the programme that he devised for IIE, it is suggested that: 'A future intercultural philosophy should look for textual basis from literature, art, religion and everyday culture paying attention to complex phenomena and to the interaction between moods and understanding' (Capurro 2006). The respective roles of empirical and normative analyses within IIE have been further explicated. Empirical studies should describe 'existing patterns of beliefs, values and behaviour through the use of statistical data, interviews, case studies and from theoretical studies, which attempt to make generalizations about cultural differences and how people respond to them by abstracting from such data' (Evanoff 2006), while normative studies should be concerned with beliefs, values, and forms of behaviour that could be adopted in response to ICT. Issues like how such decisions could be justified (or not) and critically discussed across cultures are dealt with in meta-ethical analyses (Evanoff 2006). Philip Brey suggests that a descriptive analysis could contain interpretations of attitudes towards ICT usage and implications within and between moral systems of different cultures. Normative analyses should critically discuss standards and practices in different cultures, including the own culture. It should also investigate what compromises cultures should make and provide moral principles that can govern the interaction between cultures (Brey in Ess 2007). Following Brey, irrespective of if intercultural analyses of ICT are of a descriptive or normative nature, they should adhere to a certain structure/format (Brey in Ess 2007). IIE should 'interpret, compare and critically evaluate moral systems in different cultures regarding their moral attitudes towards and behaviour towards information and information technology' (Brey 2007). Below, three different suggestions regarding how these critical analyses should be conducted will be (briefly) discussed.

Implied in a *pros hen* ('towards one' or unity) account formulated as a model for IIE by Charles Ess is a search for a pluralist interpretation and application of shared ethical norms (Ess 2006). Ess seeks to pave the way for a 'global information ethics' that can avoid imperialistic homogenization while simultaneously preserving 'the irreducible differences between cultures and peoples' (Ess 2006). He employs his *pros hen* pluralistic account when exploring Eastern and Western conceptions of privacy and data privacy protection. Since critical reasoning and questioning of foundations and conceptualizations are essential in his approach, this kind of pluralism, Ess argues, is the opposite to a purely *modus vivendi* pluralism that recognizes differences without problematizing them, leaving tensions and conflicts unresolved, without any ambition to move further beyond such digressions and contradictions. The reasonableness of this approach has been critically discussed by, for example, Key Hiruta (Hiruta 2006) questioning the merits of an ambition to move towards value unity. Is it not clear, Hiruta argues, what role shared ethical agreements play in Ess's programme, why they are important and in particular, if at all the desired unity can be aligned with the quest for diversity concerning judgements of ethical perspectives (Hiruta 2006). Capurro recognizes the merits of this critique (Capurro 2007) and stresses that there are pitfalls of *prima facie* convergences, analogies and family resemblances that may be oversimplified by a *pros hen* strategy. Instead, Capurro advocates a *hothen* ('from which') approach focusing the question of the source(s) of ethical norms including the how such source(s) are understood (the cognitive-emotional experience thereof) (Capurro 2007). In order to understand where these claims originate, more in-depth analyses are required. Following Capurro, the task of IIE is not only to describe the foundations of norms and mores, but to translate between them. In order to achieve this, a form of 'communicative ethics' is suggested. In order to identify whether conflicting views regarding ICT are incommensurable or in some ways compatible and if different cultures require their own IE, it has been suggested that attention should be paid to differences on three levels. Philip Brey offers a triptych model containing: (1) conceptual, (2) institutional and (3) behavioural levels (Brey 2007). In intercultural comparisons, he argues, scholars ought to distinguish between differences along these three dimensions. Each level is explicated as follows:

1. Conceptual level: the extent to which there are moral concepts across cultures with similar meanings,
2. Institutional level: the extent to which there is a similarity between codified rules expressing moral principles and codified statements expressing moral judgements about types of situations,
3. Behavioural level: similarities between morally guided behaviours, for example, blaming and praising of certain behaviour (Brey in Ess 2007).

Diverging perspectives between cultures, Brey argues, are likely to be found on each of these levels. It is sometimes assumed that differences at the behavioural and the institutional level automatically will imply differences, at times even 'incommensurability', on the conceptual level. For example, when questioning the feasibility and desirability of the ambition to develop a global code of ICT ethics anchored in globally accepted principles, Peter Malcouronne stresses:

Ethnic diversity in the Asia Pacific region is unequalled. We have hundreds of millions of Muslims, Christians, Hindus, Shinto, Sikh and Buddhists; we live under feudal kings, socialist prophets and capitalist roaders. Our differences pose unique regional challenges to reaching a consensus on Information Society Ethics. Would we be able to reach a consensus amongst ourselves? And if we did so, the concerns of our region are likely to be very different to those, say, of Europe. Indeed is a meaningful International Code of Ethics possible, even desirable? (Malcouronne 2008)

In this example, the potential for (encompassing) conceptual unity is questioned by reference to existing varieties regarding institutional arrangements and religious and ethnic plurality. Yet, even if different expressions are recognized at the behavioural level, for instance, in the form of traditions, and at the institutional level, in the shape of laws and directives, when a phenomenon like privacy is compared in different regions of the world, discrepancies may but must not necessarily be reflected at an ethical theoretical level. Despite divergence in moral conduct and legally codified principles, it may still be possible to, by means of translation and systematic reasoning, reach a shared understanding at the conceptual level. While perfect conceptual correspondence and encompassing unity regarding all notions and values may be a utopian aspiration, acceptance may be reached regarding some notions. Attempts can be made to reveal how profound the discrepancies are and to explore the deeper meanings of concepts. In the initial studies on privacy in Japan, no obvious conceptual counterparts were found (Orito and Murata 2007). Lack of perfect conceptual correspondence however, it was argued, should not be taken to mean that privacy would have no room in Japan (cf. Collste 2008). On the basis of a further articulation of the meaning and value of the Western notions of private and privacy, it has been proposed that privacy can be universally shared if understood as a means to protect the more fundamental value autonomy. Although there are contextual differences concerning what kind of information is considered privacy sensitive in different regions, the suggested conceptualization could find universal acceptance (Collste 2008). Most importantly, using the case of the implementation of the EU-inspired privacy protection legislation 'APPI' in Japan, it has been shown that translation is necessary prior to the incorporation of a foreign concept like privacy (cf. Murata and Orito in chapter 8 of this volume).

TOWARDS A REASONABLE USAGE OF CULTURE IN INTERCULTURAL COMPARISONS

Irrespective of which method that is applied, it is of central importance to explicate how the controversial and much debated notion of culture is understood in IIE studies. Culture has even been discarded by some as an impossible notion (Freilich 1989). So far, articulations of what 'culture' means in intercultural comparisons are lacking. Despite the many studies that have been conducted on the meaning of culture, cultural diffusion and convergence, and despite the many controversies surrounding the concept within the fields of sociology and anthropology – fields where culture is one of the most well-researched themes – IIE scholars often take the notion as 'uncontroversial' without need for further explication. In order to illustrate the variety/range of ideas, some ways of depicting culture will be mentioned. Some descriptions stress the immanent aspects of culture over manifest and 'measurable' aspects. Within social psychology, culture has been defined as 'the enduring behaviours, ideas, attitudes and traditions shared by a large group of people and transmitted from one generation to the next' (Myers et al. 2012: 12). Similarly, culture has been described as 'an historically transmitted pattern of meanings embodied in symbolic systems of inherited conceptions expressed in symbolic forms by means of which men communicate, perpetuate, and develop their knowledge about and attitudes toward life' (Geertz 1993: 89) and as 'a matter of ideas and values, a collective cast of mind' (Kuper 1999: 227). More traditional definitions within sociology stress that culture is the ensemble of symbolic codes used by members of a society and in various ways manifested in society. Reference is made to the ways of life in the society, including customs and religious ceremonies, language and family life, work patterns and leisure pursuits (Giddens 2005). In addition to visible or in some sense 'tangible' expressions of culture, such as social institutions, artefacts, symbols and language, there are less obvious expressions in the form of values, ideals, norms and beliefs influencing and directing social living. In IIE research, however, culture is often used as if it is synonymous with a nation or a large geographical region and invoked in ethical assessments of ICT in order to *explain* differences in *attitudes and in behavior.* Given the many different understandings of the notion of culture, scholars conducting research within the field of IIE should make clear what culture is taken to mean and not assume *one* shared understanding of culture as a starting point for analyses.

Important lessons regarding the difficulties surrounding the notion of culture and the need to formulate definitions and delimit the scope of the assessment can be learned from the many perplexities surrounding comparative studies on cultures, such as George Peter Murdock's *Ethnographic Atlas* (Murdock 1967) and his *Atlas of World Cultures* (Murdock 1981) and from Geert Hofstede's (and his research team) contrasting studies on corporate culture worldwide. These projects are examples of attempts to make large-scale comparisons revolving on (different) understandings of culture. Merits and drawbacks could inform how culture should be understood in comparative studies on ICT.

Following Murdock (1967, 1981), culture varies, not only across regions such as Europe, but within countries and certainly, cultures may be found within societies in the form of exile cultures. That is, countries *may* have one distinct culture but can also comprise of several cultures. This thesis is illus-trated in Mordock's Encyclopaedia of World cultures, where Europe that is made up by 32 nation states host 82 different cultures (Murdock 1967, 1981).[4] Murdock's Ethnographic Atlas from 1967 is a database containing data on 1167 societies organized around a standard set of 89 parameters (Murdock 1967: 3), including qualities such as community organization (Murdock 1967: 48), games that are played (Murdock 1967: 52), presence of male genital mutilation (Murdock 1967: 53), the institution of slavery (Murdock 1967: 58) and the roofing material employed for housing (Murdock 1967: 60). The set of specific cultural characteristics have been extracted from a meta-analysis of a vast collection of anthropological research on cultures and from Murdock's extensive fieldwork. These characteristics have been coded alpha-numerically for a great number of cultures worldwide, allowing cross-cultural comparisons and correlation studies using mathematical approaches. A central aim behind the operationalization of the concept of culture is the ambition to facilitate systematic comparative research on cultures. While influential, Murdock's *Atlas of World cultures* is a rather controversial way of representing culture and there are many debates surrounding the multifac-eted phenomenon (cf. Giddens 2005). Even if his construct is based on an encompassing collection of traits, the relevance of the inclusion/exclusion of characteristics has been called in question as well as the limitations of attempts to quantify culture by numeric indices and matrices. The case has been made that the numerical approach is likely to capture and underscore the more manifest and measurable aspects of culture, to the detriment of immanent features. Also, the status of the observer outside the culture can be questioned – to what extent can culture be understood and analysed from outside? (Baskerville 2003).

Geert Hofstede and his colleagues have offered a highly influential dimensional model for comparative studies of corporate culture (Hofstede 2011, Hofstede et al. 2010). Hofstede's model has been used extensively by corporate managers trying to understand the differences between workforces in different environments. Although frequently used and reproduced, this model has been criticized for a lack of clarity regarding the meaning, range and scope (cf. Baskerville 2003; McSweeney 2002). Even if Hofstede offers a definition of culture, 'the collective programming of the mind distinguish-ing the members of one group or category of people from others'[5] (Hofstede et al. 2010), underlining that culture only becomes relevant in comparison (Hofstede 2011); the definition is too broad to be meaningful as a basis for the comparisons to be undertaken and the case has been made that none of the large number of contrastive studies conducted (on the basis of ver-sions of the dimensional model) deal with culture in any meaningful sense (Baskerville 2003). Importantly, the basis for Hofstede's model of analysis is sprung from his work within one multinational corporation – IBM – and has been further developed and applied on corporate organizations world-wide. Covered by the (four to six) dimensions are, for instance, power distance, collectivism versus individualism, femininity versus masculinity, uncertainty avoidance and long-term versus short-term orientation – aspects that have their genesis in and are of particular interest for corporations. Rather than searching for parameters that could serve to characterize *culture* in a broader sense, Hofstede and his research teams employ dimensions that correlate with socio-economic aspects such as Gross Domestic Product and provide a limited account of 'corporate culture' (Baskerville 2003: 210). Framed in this way, the comparisons undertaken will inevitably measure socio-economic characteristics. A most problematic aspect is that in which the model-for-analysis should be explained is assumed and built into the assessment tool. A more promising model would, according to Baskerville, incorporate important explanatory factors such as ethnicity. Moreover, a serious problem underlying the analyses conducted by Hofstede and colleagues is that each nation is considered to be one culture even if culture not necessarily equates with nation (Baskerville 2003: 6). Hence, that which Hofstede's model can explain is limited to *socio-economic aspects* of *nations* (Baskerville 2003: 10).

Unfortunately, methodological problems of the kind described above are also found within the field of IIE. Similar to Hofstede's studies on corporate cultures, scholars conducting IIE research tend to conflate culture with nations or geographical regions, for instance, when conducting cross-cultural studies on concepts such as privacy, liberty and autonomy. Rather than offering definitions of what 'culture' means, and information that clarifies this elusive concept, or delimiting particular expressions or features that should be compared, it is assumed that the meaning of culture is self-evident beyond the need for further articulation. Worse still, the undefined notion of culture is included when differences in attitudes to ICT are to be explained. Many IIE scholars start out from a classical divide between a Western and an Eastern philosophical tradition comparing the use of certain notions/concepts or values within one specific nation in the Eastern hemisphere against the meaning and value of the same notion within a whole tradition like the Western philosophical tradition. Such constructs find homogeneity where Murdock finds myriads of cultures. For instance, Japanese notions (or absence of notions) of privacy are typically contrasted with 'a Western conception of privacy', lumping together a multitude of 'rivalling' conceptualizations (Palm 2008). Without disputing significant differences between philosophy in East and West, and important similarities within these regions, it should be recognized that there are important differences within the respective philosophical tradition and region that deserve due attention when analysing specific phenomena.

Often, the comparisons undertaken within IIE fail to recognize the limitations of too broad categorizations.

This problem can be illustrated with examples from the privacy debate. Privacy is one of the most well-researched notions within ICT ethics (Brey 2009) and has been defined in a multitude of ways by scholars within the Western philosophical tradition (cf. Palm 2008). When employing constructs like 'Western privacy' in order to make comparison with the understanding of privacy in a specific non-Western country, there is a significant risk that important differences in reasoning between the many privacy scholars of Western origin are neglected/glossed over. In comparisons of this kind, research within the Western philosophical tradition is typically considered far more homogenous than what it actually is. Western philosophy is treated as if it sprung from one culture. It is important to recognize the multitude of conceptions within the Western philosophical tradition. Otherwise, shared features and interests may be obscured (Palm 2008). For instance, traditional IE is said to revolve around values becoming individual agents like autonomy and privacy (complimented by democratic and capitalist concerns of ownership and rights). It assumes a fundamental and existential self and a Western founded philosophy (Bielby 2014).

Subjectivity understood as a stable, autonomous identity has been identified as a basic assumption underpinning the Western notion of privacy (Capurro 2005). However, the description of the Western self as an atomistic, autonomous and coherent self is not fully adequate. 'Counter to the tendency within IIE to treat the stable self as if it had unchallenged dominance in the West, there are important philosophical work that opposes this view' (Palm 2008). Although the Western legal system may have contributed to foster a general idea of individual selves and responsibility, the conception of the self is a manifold, complex and contested tradition of thought, that of Hume being one example (Murray 1993), Derek Parfit's discussion on identity being another (1984). While IIE scholars have framed the Western concept of personal identity as rather static, referring to one identity from birth to death, there are significant differences within the Western philosophical tradition. The idea that the subject is a fixed entity over time is at least disputed by some philosophers. Importantly, there are philosophers within the analytical philosophical tradition who offer perspectives on identity that are closer to the Eastern thinking than what the intercultural studies referred to admit (Palm 2008).

Likewise, the commonly invoked divide between individualistic and collectivistic is a rather rough construct to be treated with caution. Even if individual rights are more prevalent in Western societies than Asian and African societies, there are significant differences within the Western philosophical tradition. Communitarians ascribe individual rights and interest less weight than liberals. The assumed differences were further highlighted by a closer look at the meaning and value of privacy typically viewed as an individualistic interest with little bearing in non-Western cultures. And, better than describing privacy as a static concept is to view this value as contextually dependent, changing between and within cultures, over time and among individuals. These aspects that increase the chances of a shared understanding have typically been overlooked in comparative studies within IIE. Yet, it seems more reasonable to aim for acceptability regarding normative concepts central to ICT than for full conceptual commensurability.

Unfortunately, the conceptual constructs used within IIE are often too simplistic, leaving aside significant external and internal differences. Certainly, Capurro is aware of the problem of extrapolations, making reference to Karl Baier who warns against attempts to construct stereotypes in order to be able to, more effectively, explore and unmask differences between East and West (2006).[6] In response to such cautions, Capurro states that 'if there is a danger of building stereotypes, there is also one of overlooking not only concrete or ontic but also structural or ontological differences by claiming a single world culture that mostly reflects the interests and global life style of a small portion of humanity' (2007). Arguably, both dominating perspectives and stereotypization must be avoided in IIE. One way of combating domination is that of inclusion of unrepresented or poorly represented perspectives. Marginalization can be avoided by – continuously – including analyses of ICT from as many parts of the world as possible. Although broad coverage is advocated here, it should also be stressed that demands must be raised on the quality of the analyses in order to enable meaningful comparisons. And, even if an important factor, inclusion will not in itself eliminate the risk of domination of one perspective over another. No region or culture must get the prerogative of interpretation. In particular, it is important that economically dominant North American and Western European societies that traditionally have had a strong influence on other societies and that have benefitted from a prerogative of interpretation in IIE are moderated rather than allowed to trump. Although the main concern has been to disclose Western values embedded in ICT, it could be useful to investigate the relevance of non-Western principles like Ubuntu and Motteinai (discussed by Collste in the Introduction) for the information society, rather than exclusively focusing Western constructs. More to the point, the inclusive ambition of IIE may carry a risk that one or few studies conducted in a region that previously was exempt from analysis, are taken to be representative (enough) of that country or region and that the pioneers doing this studies become *the* (often exotic) voice of the marginalized region, preventing other voices from the same country or region from being heard.

These are some of the problems that IIE must recognize and seek to alleviate. Rather than assuming homogeneity in vast geographical regions, a better starting point for cross-cultural *conceptual* comparisons would be one that (1) clearly specifies the level of investigation and (2) is open for conceptual dis/similarities within and between cultures (Palm 2008). For reasons of comparability and coherence, the three levels suggested by Philip Brey can be useful. If the interest is potential conceptual correspondence, legal and behavioural aspects should be left aside, and treated separately. Certainly, the three levels are not always clear-cut. Religiously motivated ethical principles and religiously coloured traditions can be interrelated. Nevertheless, by striving to differentiate between these levels as far as possible, it is more likely that comparisons of the right categories are made. A minimum criterion for intercultural comparisons is that such studies are based on/related to a critical discussion of how culture should be understood and the limits/risks of this notion. Certainly, categorizations will always be rough and imperfect, but any study of cross-cultural comparisons must address the following two problems: (i) classification and definitions (ii) the problems of sampling and units of comparison (Baskerville 2003). What is warranted is a better recognition of the complexity of the notions 'culture' and 'cultural' and the need for an attempt to define how the notion is understood when undertaking comparisons of particular aspects of ICT.

CONCLUSIONS

The discussion in this chapter has been exploring an often overlooked aspect of ethics and communication, namely the role of 'culture' in IIE concerned with the effects of information and communication technology/systems. Certainly, some scholars within IIE have warranted a more nuanced understanding of similarities and dissimilarities beyond the simple dichotomy between 'East' and 'West' (cf. Nakada and Tamura 2005) but for the most, this divide is used as a starting point rather than being problematized.

ICT and Internet have enabled an unprecedented global interconnectedness. ICTs dissolve borders both literally and metaphorically including national geographical borders to intellectual borders of nationalism (Bielby 2014). IIE is concerned with ethically relevant effects of the proliferation of ICT worldwide and benefits and burdens of this development. Importantly, 'ICT is not simply computer hardware, software, and telecommunications connections. ICT, like all technology, is combinations of artifacts, social practices, social institutions, and social and cultural meanings associated with the artifacts' (Johnson 2007: 10). Viewed as sociotechnical systems or sociotechnical ensembles, as Deborah Johnson suggests, a plethora of questions unfold which concern the character of the social practices, relationships and institutions that together with hardware and software constitute ICT. Within the field of IIE, empirical and normative analyses are conducted on the role of such systems in other parts of the world than the Western hemisphere from which both ICT and critical studies of ICT originate. In the beginning of the new century, Rafael Capurro warranted an IIE outside of the so-called developed world (2004). Only one decade later, IIE has become an established area of research, and several cross-cultural studies have been undertaken in regions where IIE previously did not exist. Still 'an ethical consideration of ICTs external from a Western ethical worldview certainly exists, albeit in many cases only in its infancy or in some cases, as in Africa, barely at all' (Britz 2013). Since the field is under development, there is still room for improvement.

In this contribution, an overview of how 'culture' has been defined, or rather not been defined, and discussed by IIE scholars has been offered together with a brief analysis of what it has taken to mean to investigate how cultures respond to or are influenced by ICT. It has been stressed that countries may have distinct cultures, but that culture also can vary within a region, society or subgroup. We may, for instance, find exile cultures within cultures. Given the many different conceptualizations of culture, it is of utmost importance to specify and motivate what manifestations or layers are considered ethically relevant in IIE studies. Certainly, in his conclusions, Capurro briefly mentions that there are partly contradictory traditions and stories within Europe (2006: 46). Still, to a large extent, such differences are glossed over in comparative studies, contrasting a Western perspective – including Europe and larger regions.

In this section, the case has been made that homogenizations should be avoided and that such contradictions should be highlighted rather than downplayed. There are important differences regarding norms and mores within what is described as one culture. By framing values, norms and mores as Western, significant differences within the Western culture may be obscured. For instance, when looking at privacy protection and mechanisms to safeguard informational privacy (the institutional level) in the Western hemisphere, significant differences protrude. This is true even within the Northern part of Europe with significant differences between, for example, Germany and Sweden.

Another issue that merits further consideration is the responsibility of 'dominant cultures' when it comes to influences on this new research domain IIE. Although the ambition behind cross-cultural comparisons has been to prevent and balance value colonialism and value monism, IIE has been initiated and directed from the economically dominant societies of the world. Despite good intentions, these attempts come at the risk of reproducing Western ideas and values by asking to what extent Western constructs exist in other cultures. Equivalent values may be found in non-Western cultures but preferably, the stage for comparative work should ideally not be set by those initiating the debate. Arguably, the different – and at times conflicting – conceptions and constructs within the Western philosophical tradition should inform cross-cultural research. Although simplifications may be necessary at times, a reduction of conflicts and diverging perspectives and economic presentations of concepts to be compared are likely to obscure similarities and convergence. That said, one hopes that the diversity within the Western philosophical tradition will be better represented and respected in future studies. A failure to recognize relevant differences will stand in the way of effective communication regarding values and principles.

NOTES

1. Even if the level of ICT saturation differs between nations and regions across the globe (Britz 2013), to an increasing extent, information technology makes up an important part of the infrastructure worldwide.

2. More than a third of all programming languages have been developed in the United States, United Kingdom, Canada and Australia. Programming languages developed in non-English speaking nations often use English keywords for reasons of broad usability (in order to appeal to an international audience). Even if ICT, to an increasing extent, is designed and assembled in countries like India, China, Korea and Japan, English remains the main programming language.

3. It can be asked whether or not ICT is different from other technologies with respect to value colonialism and if it poses unique ethical problems and responsibilities. Is ICT different from other types of technologies that have been exported from one part of the world to another? Does this type of technology draw on/transmit values in ways different than previous technologies?

4. Similarly geographical regions like The Americas and South East Asia are made up of impressive numbers of cultures. These differences are generated from analyses based on 89 different parameters (that in turn have been extracted from anthropological research and taken to be of significance for culture) (Murdock 1967: 3).

5. Each of the dimensions has been measured for a large number of countries, and cross-country comparisons have been made.

6. For instance when analysing the search for harmony as a feature characteristic of Asian cultures or the opposition between collectivity and individuality.

Bibliography

Abdarraziq, A. 1933/1934. L'islam et les bases du pouvoir, *Revue des Études Islamiques* Vol. VII (1933), and Vol. VIII (1934).

Abe, K. 1995. *What Is "Seken"?* Tokyo: Kodansha (in Japanese).

Abe, K. 1999. *Theory of "Seken": Love and Individuality in Medieval Europe.* Tokyo: Asahi Shimbunsha (in Japanese).

Abu-Sahlieh S. 1994. Les Musulmans faxe aux droits de l'homme: religion & droit & politique. Étude et documents. Bochum: Dr. Winkler.

Acquisti, A. and R. Gross. 2006. Imagined Communities: Awareness, Information Sharing, and Privacy on the Facebook. In Golle, P. and Danezis, G. (eds.), *Privacy Enhancing Technologies: 6th International Workshop, PET 2006, Cambridge, UK, June 28–30, 2006, Revised Selected Papers.* Berlin Heidelberg: Springer, pp. 36–58.

Adams, A. A., K. Murata, and Y. Orito. 2009. The Japanese Sense of Information Privacy. *AI & Society* 24(4): 327–41.

Adams, A. A., K. Murata, and Y. Orito. 2010. The Development of Japanese Data Protection. *Policy & Internet* 2(2): 95–126.

Adams, A. A., K. Murata, Y. Orito, and P. Parslow. 2011. Emerging Social Norms in the UK and Japan on Privacy and Revelation in SNS. *International Review of Information Ethics* 16: 18–26.

Aida, Y. 1972. *The Japanese Consciousness Structure.* Tokyo: Kodansha (in Japanese).

al-Ashmasy M. 1989. *L'islamisme contre l'islam.* Paris: la découverte.

Alfredsson, G. and E. Asbjörn, eds. 1999. *The Universal Declaration of Human Rights.* The Hague: Martinus Nijhgoff Publishers.

American Philosophical Association. 2013. Minorities in Philosophy. APA Online: https://c.ymcdn.com/sites/www.apaonline.org/resource/resmgr/data_on_profession/minorities_in_philosophy.pdf (Retrieved October 1, 2015).

Anderson, J. N., 1979. *Law Reform in the Muslim World,* London: Athlone.

An-Na'im, A. 1990. *Toward an Islamic Reformation. Civil Liberties, Human Rights, and International Law.* New York: Syracuse University Press.

Anonymous. 2015. Civil Discourse and Civil Society: The dysfunctional culture of Thai academia. *Kyoto Review of Southeast Asia* 17. http://kyotoreview.org/yav/dysfunctional-thai-academia/ (Retrieved October 27, 2015).

Aquinas, T. 1990. 13th cent. *The Summa Theologica, Book II* (*Great Books of the Western World*, ed. Mortimer Adler). Trans. Laurence Shapcote. Chicago: Encyclopaedia Britannica, Inc.

Arendt, H. 1974. *Elemente und Ursprünge totaler Herrschaft.* Munich: Piper.

Asai, R. and I. Kavathatzopoulos. 2012. Do Social Media Generate Social Capital? *Proceedings of ICT, Society and Human Beings 2012*, 133–36.

Aurelius, M. A. 1987. *The Communings with Himself.* Revised Text and Translation into English by C. R. Haines, Cambridge/MA: Harvard University Press.

Austin, J. L. 1975. *How To Do Things With Words,* Second Edition (*William James Lecture delivered at Harvard University in 1955*), ed. J. O. Urmson and M. Sbisà. Cambridge, MA: Harvard University Press.

Baier, K. 2006. Welterschliessung durch Grundstimmungen als Problem interkultureller Phaenomenologie. *Daseinsanalyse* 22: 99–109.

Barnes, E. 2015. Biographical interview on *What is it like to be a philosopher*, http://www.whatisitliketobeaphilosopher.com/#/elizabeth-barnes/ (Retrieved December 6, 2015).

Baron, S., T. Dougherty, and K. Miller. 2015. Why is There Female Underrepresentation among Philosophy Majors? Evidence of a Pre-University Effect. *Ergo: An Open Access Journal of Philosophy* 2(14): 329–65.

Barr, M. 2007. Lee Kuan Yew and the 'Asian Values' Debate, in *Asian Studies Review*, 24(1): 309–34.

Barry, B. 1988. Equal Opportunity and Moral Arbitrariness, in *Equal Opportunity*, ed. N. E. Bowie, pp. 23–44. Boulder: Westview Press.

Barth, K. 1933, 1922. *The Epistle to the Romans.* Trans. Edwyn C. Hoskyns. London: Oxford University Press.

Baskerville, R. 2003. Hofstede Never Studied Culture. *Accounting, Organizations and Society* 28(1): 1–14.

Beauchamp, T. L. and J. F. Childress. 2013. *Principles of Biomedical Ethics.* Oxford: Oxford University Press.

Beckwith, C. 2015. *Greek Buddha: Pyrrho's Encounter with Early Buddhism in Central Asia.* Princeton, NJ: Princeton University Press.

Bell, D. A. 2006. *Beyond Liberal Democracy, Political Thinking for an East Asian Context.* Princeton: Princeton University Press.

Bell, D. A. 2015. *The China Model – Political Meritocracy and the Limits of Democracy.* Princeton: Princeton University Press.

Benedict, R. 1946. *The Chrysanthemum and the Sword: Patterns of Japanese Culture.* Boston, MA: Mariner Books.

Bernstein, R. J. 2005. *The Abuse of Evil – The Corruption of Politics and Religion since 9/11.* Cambridge: Polity Press.

Bhargava, R. 2013. Overcoming the Epistemic Injustice of Colonialism. *Global Policy* 4(4): 413–17.

Bielby, J. 2014. Information Ethics III: Concerning Intercultural Information Ethics, The History of Information Ethics. http://www.academia.edu/7416977/Information_Ethics_III_Concerning_Intercultural_Information_Ethics (downloaded December 5, 2015).

Bielefeldt, H. 1996. Secular Human Rights: Challenge and Opportunity to Christians and Muslims. *Islam and Christian-Muslim Relations* 7(3): 311–25.

Bielefeldt, H. 1997. Autonomy and Republicanism. Immanuel Kant's Philosophy of Freedom. *Political Theory* 25: 524–58.

Bielefeldt, H. 2000. 'Western' versus 'Islamic' Human Rights Conception?: A Critique of Cultural Essentialism in the Discussion on Human Rights. *Political Theory* 28(1): 90–121.

Bilimoria, P. 1991. Indian Ethics, in *A Companion to Ethics*, ed. P. Singer, pp. 43–57, Oxford: Blackwell.

Brecher, B. 2007. *Torture and the Ticking Bomb*. Malden, MA: Oxford and Melbourne: Blackwell Publishing.

Brey, P. 2007. Is Information Ethics Cultural-relative? *International Journal of Technology and Human Interaction* 3(3): 12–24.

Brey, P. 2009. Values in Technology and Disclosive Computer Ethics. *The Cambridge Handbook of Information and Computer Ethics,* Ed. L. Floridi. Cambridge: Cambridge University Press.

Britz, J. J. 2013. Understanding Information Ethics. *Information Ethics in Africa: Cross-cutting Themes*. Pretoria: ACEIE, pp. 1–6. http://www.africainfoethics.org/pdf/ie_africa/manuscript.pdf (Retrieved December 5, 2015).

Bronk, A. Truth and Religion Reconsidered: An Analytical Approach. Available from https://www.bu.edu/wcp/Papers/Reli/ReliBron.htm (Retrieved August 17, 2015).

Buchanan, T. 2012. *East Wind: China and the British Left 1925-1976*. Oxford: Oxford University Press.

Burke, E. 1910. *Reflections on the Revolution in France*. With an Introduction by A. J. Grieve, London: Dent.

Bynum, T. 2006. Flourishing Ethics. *Ethics and Information Technology* 8: 157–73.

Cairo Declaration. 1991. *Conscience and Liberty. International Journal of Religious Freedom* 3: 1.

Capurro, R. 2005. Privacy. An Intercultural Perspective. *Ethics and Information Technology* 7: 37–47. Online: http://www.capurro.de/privacy.html (Retrieved December 5, 2015).

Capurro, R. 2006a. Ethik der Informationsgesellschaft. Ein interkultureller Versuch. Online: http://www.capurro.de/parrhesia.html (Retrieved December 5, 2015).

Capurro, R. 2007. Intercultural Information Ethics. In: Capurro, Rafael/Frühbauer, Johannes/Hausmanninger, Thomas (eds.): *Localizing the Internet. Ethical Aspects in Intercultural Perspective*. Munich: Fink, pp. 21–38. Online: http://www.capurro.de/iie.html (Retrieved December 5, 2015).

Capurro, R. 2008. Intercultural Information Ethics: Foundations and Applications. *Journal of Information, Communication and Ethics in Society* 6(2): 116–26.

Capurro, R. 2010. Global Intercultural Information Ethics from an African Perspective. Keynote address at the 2nd African Information Ethics Conference September

6–7, 2010, Gaborone, Botswana. http://www.capurro.de/botswana.html (Retrieved December 5, 2015).

Chang, P. C. 1914. The Gospel in China. *Students and the World Wide Expansion of Christianity*. London: Forgotten Books, reprint 2013.

Chang, P. C. 1933. Education and Scientific Research. *The Open Court*, nr 7.

Chang, P.C. 1936b. Intercultural Contacts and Creative Adjustment, *Progressive Education*, November, nr 13.

Chang, P. C. 1939a. Universities and National Reconstruction in China, in Edward Bradby, red. *The University Outside Europe*. New York: Oxford University Press.

Chang, P. C. 1948. Statment by Dr. P. C. Chang before the Plenary meeting of the General Assembly of the Declaration of the Human Rights, Roosevelts Library, New York City.

Chang, P. C.1936a. *China at the Crossroads*. London: Evan Brothers Ltd.

Chang, P. C. 1939b. The Second Phase of China's Struggle. *International Affairs* 18(2).

Chang, P. C. 1923. *Education for Modernization in China*. New York: Columbia University.

Cheng, R. H. C. and S. Cheng, red. 1995. *Peng Chun Chang: Biography and Collected Works* (Private printing).

Chödrön, P. 2002. *When Things Fall Apart: Heart Advice for Difficult Times*. Boston: Shambala.

Christians, C. 1995. The Problem of Universals in Communication Ethics. *Javnost - The Public: Journal of the European Institute for Communication and Culture* 2(2): 59–69.

Christians, C. 2011. Primordial Issues in Communication Ethics. In *The Handbook of Global Communication and Media Ethics, Vols. I and II*, eds. R. S. Fortner and P. M. Fackler. Chichester, West Sussex: Wiley-Blackwell, 1–19.

Coady, D. 2012. *What to Believe Now: Applying Epistemology to Contemporary Issues*. Malden, MA: Wiley-Blackwell.

Coleman, N. A. T. 2014. Philosophy is Dead White – and Dead Wrong. *The Times of Higher Education*: https://www.timeshighereducation.com/comment/opinion/philosophy-is-deadwhite-and-dead-wrong/2012122.article (Retrieved October 7, 2015).

Collste, G. 2011. Specifying Rights: The Case of TRIPS, *Public Health Ethics* 4: 63–69.

Collste, G. 2008. Global ICT-ethics: The Case of Privacy. *Journal of Information, Communication and Ethics in Society* 6.

Commission on Global Governance (CGG). 1995. *Our Global Neighbourhood*. Oxford: Oxford University Press.

Commission on Intellectual Property Rights. 2002. *Integrating Intellectual Property Rights and Development Policy*. Report of the Commission on Intellectual Property Rights, London.

Commonwealth of Australia. 1997. *Bringing Them Home: Inquiry in the Separation of Aboriginal and Torres Strait Islander Children from their Families*. https://www.humanrights.gov.au/sites/default/files/content/pdf/social_justice/bringing_them_home_report.pdf (Retrieved October 3, 2015).

Coulson, N. J. 1964. *A History of Islamic Law*. Edinburgh: Edinburgh University Press.

Cua, A. 1977. Forgetting Morality: Reflections on a Theme in Chuang Tzu. *Journal of Chinese Philosophy* 4(4): 305–28.

Cullen, R. 2007. Citizens' concerns about the privacy of personal information held by government: A comparative study, Japan and New Zealand. Proceedings of the 41st Hawaii International Conference on System Sciences. IEEE Computer Society Press, 2007, 1–10.

Cushman, F., L. Young, and M. Hauser. 2006. The Role of Conscious Reasoning and Intuition in Moral Reasoning: Testing Three Principles of Harm. *Psychological Science* 17(12): 1082–89.

Daniels, N. 1997. *Justice and Justification. Reflective Equilibrium in Theory and Practice*. Cambridge: Cambridge University Press.

Dennett, D. 1984. *Elbow Room: The Varieties of Free Will worth Wanting*. Oxford: Oxford University Press.

Dershowitz, A. 2002. *Why Terrorism Works: Understanding the Threat, Responding to the Challenge*. New Haven and London: Yale University Press.

Deutsche, E. and R. Dalvi, eds. 2004, 8th cent. *The Essential Vedānta: A New Source Book of Advaita Vedānta*. Bloomington, IN: World Wisdom.

Doi, T. 1973. *The Anatomy of Dependence*. Tokyo: Kodansha International.

Donnely, J. 2003. *Universal Human Rights in Theory and Practice*, 2nd edn. Ithaca: Cornell University Press.

Dotson, K. 2012. How Is This Paper Philosophy? *Comparative Philosophy* 3(1): 3–29.

Dower, N. 1998. 2n edn. 2007. *World Ethics - the New Agenda*. Edinburgh: Edinburgh University Press.

Dworkin, R. 2011. *Justice for Hedgehogs*. Cambridge, MA: Belknap Press.

Dyzenhaus, D. 1996. *Legality and Legitimacy. Carl Schmitt, Hans Kelsen and Hermann Heller in Weimar*. Oxford: Clarendon Press.

Ebeling, H. 1994. *Der multikulturelle Traum. Von der Subversion des Rechts und der Moral* Hamburg: Europäische Verlagsanstalt.

Ehrenreich, N. and M. Barr. 2005. Intersex Surgery, Female Genital Cutting, and the Selective Condemnation of 'Cultural Practices'. *Harvard Civil Rights-Civil Liberties Law Review* 40: 71–140.

Encyclopedia Britannica. http://global.britannica.com/topic/communication, (Retrieved November 24, 2015).

Engelhard, P. 1993. Was kann die Ethik des Thomas von Aquin zur kritischen Klärung und Begründung der Menschenrechte beitragen? in Johannes Schwartländer, ed., *Modernes Freiheitsethos und christlicher Glaube. Beiträge zur Bestimmung der Menschenrechte* Mainz: Grünewald.

Esposito, J. L. 1991. *Islam and Politics*. 3rd edn. New York: Syracuse University Press.

Ess, C. and M. Thorseth. 2006. Neither Relativism Nor Imperialism: Theories and Practices for a Global Information Ethics. *Ethics and Information Technology* 8(4): 91–95.

Ess, C. 2006. Ethical Pluralism and Global Information Ethics. *Ethics and Information Technology* 8(4): 215–26.

Ess, C. 2006. Ethical Pluralism and Global Information Ethics. *Ethics and Information Technology* 8: 215–26.

Ess, C. 2007. Can the Local Reshape the Global? Ethical Imperatives for Humane Intercultural Communication Online. In Capurro, Rafael/Frühbauer, Johannes/ Hausmanninger, Thomas (eds.) *Localizing the Internet. Ethical Aspects in Intercultural Perspective.* Munich: Fink, 153–69.

European Parliament and the Council of the European Union. 1995. Directive 95/46/ EC of the European Parliament and the Council of 24 October 1995 on the Protection of Individuals with Regard to the Processing of Personal information and on the Free Movement of Such Data. Available at: http://eur-lex.europa.eu/Lex UriServ/LexUriServ.do?uri=CELEX:31995L0046:en:HTML (Retrieved October 21, 2015).

Evanoff, R. 2006. Intercultural Ethics – A Constructivist Approach. *Journal of Intercultural Communication* 9: 89–102.

Faath, S. and H. Mattes, eds. 1992. *Demokratie und Menschenrechte in Nordafrika*, Hamburg: edition wuquf.

Feder, E.-K. 2014. *Making Sense of Intersex: Changing Ethical Perspectives in Biomedicine.* Bloomington and Indianapolis: Indiana University Press.

Fikentscher, W. 1987. Die heutige Bedeutung des nicht-säkularen Ursprungs der Grundrechte, in: E. W. Böckenförde, and R. Spaemann, eds., *Menschenrechte und Menschenwürde. Historische Voraussetzungen — säkulare Gestalt — christliches Verständnis.* Stuttgart: Klett-Cotta.

Finnis, J. 1980. *Natural Law and Natural Rights.* Oxford: Oxford University Press.

Fishkin, J. 1983. *Justice, Equal Opportunity, and the Family.* New Haven: Yale University Press.

Foot, P. 1978. The Problem of Abortion and the Doctrine of Double Effect, in *Virtue and Vices and Other Essays in Moral Philosophy*, 19–32. Cambridge: Cambridge University Press.

Fraser, Chris. 2014. Mohism. In The Stanford Encyclopedia of Philosophy (Summer 2014 Edition), edited by Edward N. Zalta. http://plato.stanford.edu/archives/ sum2014/entries/mohism/. (Retrieved October 13, 2015).

Fraser, N. 2001. Recognition Without Ethics? in *Theory, Culture and Society* 18(2– 3): 21–42.

Freilich, M. 1989. *The Relevance of Culture.* South Hadley, MA: Bergin and Garvey.

Frey, R. J. 2007. *Global Issues: Fundamentalism.* New York: Infobase Publishing.

Fröchtling, A. 2002. *Exiled God and Exiled Peoples: Memoria passionis and the perception of God during and after apartheid and shoah.* Münster: LIT Verlag.

Fu-Chang, D. 1999. Ancient Chinese Medical Ethics and the Four Principles of Biomedical Ethics. *Journal of Medical Ethics* 25: 315–21.

Geertz, C. 1993. 'Ethnic Conflict': Three Alternative Terms. *Common Knowledge* 2(3): 54–65.

Giddens, A. 1994. Living in a Post-traditional Society. In U. Beck, A. Giddens, and S. Lash, (eds.), *Reflexive Modernization: Politics, Tradition and Aesthetics in the Modern Social Order.* Cambridge: Polity Press.

Giddens, A. 2005. *The New Egalitarianism.* Cambridge: Polity.

Gillon, R. 1994. Medical Ethics: Four Principles plus Attention to Scope. *British Medical Journal* 309: 184–88.

Glendon, M. A. 2002. *A World Made New – Eleanor Roosevelt and the Universal Declaration of Human Rights.* New York: Random House.

Graham, A. C. 1992. *Unreason Within Reason: Essays on the Outskirts of Rationality.* La Salle, IL: Open Court.

Greenberg, Y. K., ed. 2008. *Encyclopedia of Love in World Religions.* Santa Barbara, CA: ABC-CLO.

Greene, J., B. Sommerville, L. Nystrom, J. M. Darley and J. D. Cohen. 2001. An fMRI Investigation of Emotional Engagement in Moral Judgment. *Science* 267: 2105–08. DOI: 10.1126/science.1062872.

Griffin, J. 2008. *On Human Rights.* Oxford: Oxford University Press.

Grimmelmann, J. 2009. Saving Facebook. *Iowa Law Review* 94: 1137–206.

Gutmann, A. and Thompson, D. 2012. *The Spirit of Compromise: Why Governing Demands It and Campaigning Undermines It.* Princeton: Princeton University Press.

Habermas, J. 1990, 1983. *Moral Consciousness and Communicative Action.* Trans. C. Lenhardt and S. W. Nicholsen. Cambridge: Polity Press.

Habermas, J. 1992. *Faktizität und Geltung. Beiträge zur Diskurstheorie des Rechts und des demokratischen Rechtsstaats.* Frankfurt: Suhrkamp.

Hall, B. J. 2005. *Among Cultures: The Challenge of Communication.* Belmont: Thomson/Wadsworth.

Hall, E. T. 1976. *Beyond Culture.* New York: Anchor Books.

Harris, J. 1975. The Survival Lottery. *Philosophy* 50: 81–87.

Haslanger, S. 2008. Changing the Ideology and Culture of Philosophy: Not by Reason (Alone). *Hypatia* 23(2): 210–23.

Hassan, R. 1982. On Human Rights and the Qur'anic Perspective, in: Swidler, A., ed., *Human Rights in Religious Traditions*, New York: The Pilgrim Press.

Hauerwas, S. 1974. *Vision and Virtue: Essays in Christian Ethical Reflection.* Notre Dame: Fides Publishers, Inc.

Hegel, G. F. W. 1986. *Vorlesungen über die Philosophie der Geschichte.* Werke 12, Frankfurt: Suhrkamp.

Hegel, G. W. F. 1967, 1821. *Philosophy of Right.* Trans. T.M. Knox. Oxford: Oxford University Press.

Helsinki Declaration, 2013, World Medical Association, http://www.wma.net/en/30publications/10policies/b3/17c.pdf, (Retrieved November 24, 2015).

Hewer, C. T. R. 2006. *Understanding Islam: The First Ten Steps.* London: SCM Press.

Hewison, K. (Ed.). 1997. *Political Change in Thailand: Democracy and Participation.* London: Routledge.

Hicks, J. 1989. *An Interpretation of Religion: Human Responses to the Transcendent.* London: Palgrave Macmillan.

Hilpert, K. 1991. *Die Menschenrechte. Geschichte – Theologie – Aktualität.* Düsseldorf: Patmos.

Hiruta, K. 2006. What Pluralism, Why Pluralism, and How? A Response to Charles Ess. *Ethics and Information Technology* 8: 227–36.

Hobbes, T. 1998, 1651. *Leviathan (Oxford World's Classics).* Oxford: Oxford University Press.

Hobbes, Th., 1651. *Leviathan.* In R. Tuck, (ed.). Cambridge: Cambridge University Press.

Höffner, J. 1972. *Kolonialismus und Evangelium. Spanische Kolonialethik im Goldenen Zeitalter,* 3rd edn. Trier: Paulinus.

Hofstede, G. 2011. Dimensionalizing Cultures: The Hofstede Model in Context. *Online Readings in Psychology and Culture* 2(1).

Hofstede, G., J. Hofstede, and M. Minkov. 2010. *Cultures and Organizations: Software of the Mind.* 3rd edn. McGraw-Hill, USA.

Hongladarom, S. 2001. Cultures and Global Justice. Online: http://www.polylog.org/them/3/fcshs-en-htm (Retrieved December 5, 2015).

Hongladarom, S. 2007. Analysis and Justification of Privacy from a Buddhist Perspective. In S. Hongladarom, C. Ess, (eds.): Information Technology Ethics: Cultural Perspectives. Hershey, Pennsylvania: Idea Group, pp. 108–22.

Hongladarom, S. 2002. *Science in Thai Society and Culture.* Bangkok: Institute of Academic Development [in Thai].

Hongladarom, S. 2002a. *Science in Thai Society and Culture.* Bangkok: Institute for Academic Development [in Thai].

Hongladarom, S. 2002b. Cross-cultural Epistemic Practices. *Social Epistemology* 16(1): 83–92.

Hongladarom, S. 2006. Asian Philosophy and Critical Thinking. In *Critical Thinking: Concepts and Applications* edited by Nasreen Taher and Swapna Gopalan. Hyderabad: ICFAI University Press. http://pioneer.chula.ac.th/~hsoraj/web/APPEND.html. (Retrieved October 13, 2015.)

Hongladarom, S. Forthcoming. Intercultural Information Ethics: A pragmatic consideration. In a Festschrift volume on the occasion of Rafael Capurro's 70th birthday, edited by J. Bielby and M. Kelly.

Horibe, M. 1988. *Privacy and the Advanced Information Society.* Tokyo: Iwanami Shoten (in Japanese).

Howard, R. E. 1995. *Human Rights and the Search for Community.* Boulder: Westview Press.

Human Rights in Islam. 1982. Report of a seminar held in Kuwait, December 1980, published by the *International Commission of Lawyers.*

Hume, D. 2000. *A Treatise of Human Nature,* ed. D. F. Norton and M. J. Norton. Oxford: Oxford University Press.

Huntington, S. 1998. *The Clash of Civilizations and the Remaking of World Order,* London: Touchstone Books.

Ingelhart, R. and Wezel, C. 2005. *Modernization, Cultural Change and Democracy.* Cambridge: Cambridge University Press.

Inoue, T. 2007. *The Structure of 'Seken-tei': A Socio-Psychological Approach.* Tokyo: Kodansha (in Japanese).

International Review of Information Ethics (IRIE). 2004. International ICIE Symposium. Online: http://www.i-r-i-e.net (Retrieved December 5, 2015).

Introna, L. D. 1997. Privacy and the Computer: Why We Need Privacy in the Information Society. *Metaphilosophy* 28(3): 259–75.

Ito, M. 1964. Issues in the 'After the Banquet' Decision. *Jurist* 309: 47–51 (in Japanese).

Ivanhoe, P. 2009. Pluralism, Toleration, and Ethical Promiscuity. *Journal of Religious Ethics* 37(2): 311–29.

Jellinek, G. 1974. Die Erklärung der Menschen- und Bürgerrechte, in: Schnur, R., ed., *Zur Geschichte der Erklärung der Menschenrechte*, 2nd edn. Darmstadt: Wissenschaftliche Buchgesellschaft.

Johansen, B. 1986. Staat, Recht und Religion im sunnitischen Islam. Können Muslime einen religionsneutralen Staat akzeptieren? in *Essener Gespräche zum Thema Staat und Kirche*, vol. 20.

John of the Cross. 1991, 16th cent. *The Dark Night.* In *The Collected Works of St. John of the Cross*, trans. K. Kavanaugh and O. Rodrigues. Washington, DC: Institute of Carmelite Studies Publications, pp. 353–457.

Johnson, D. G. 2007. Democracy, Technology, and Information Societies in IFIP International Federation for Information Processing. *The Information Society: Innovations, Legitimacy, Ethics and Democracy*, eds. P. Goujon, S. Lavelle, P. Duquenoy, K. Kimppa, V. Laurent. Boston: Springer.

Kahane, G. 2013. The Armchair and the Trolley: An Argument for Experimental Ethics. *Philosophical Studies* 162: 421–45.

Kamm, F. 2007. *Intricate Ethics: Rights, Responsibilities, and Permissible Harm.* Oxford: Oxford University Press.

Kant, I. 1998, 1785. *Groundwork of the Metaphysics of Morals.* Trans. and ed. M. Gregor. Cambridge: Cambridge University Press.

Kant, I. 1785. *The Groundwork of the Metaphysic of Morals.* In H. Paton, (trans.). *The Moral Law.* London: Hutcheson, 1949.

Kao, Y. G. 2011. *Grounding Human Rights In A Pluralist World.* Washington, DC: Georgetown University Press.

Karkazis, K. 2008. *Fixing Sex: Intersex, Medical Authority, and Lived Experience.* Durham and London: Duke University Press.

Kaviraj, S. 1993. Universality and the Inescapability of History. How Universal is a Declaration of Human Rights, in May, H. and Fritsch-Oppermann, S. eds., *Menschenrechte zwischen Universalisierungsanspruch und kultureller Kontextualisierung*, Loccumer Protokolle 10/93, Rehberg-Loccum: Evangelische Akademie Loccum.

Kelsay, J. and S. B. Twiss, eds. 1994. *Religion and Human Rights.* New York: The Project on Religion and Human Rights.

Keown, D. 2005. *Buddhist Ethics: A Very Short Introduction.* Oxford University Press.

Kimura, B. 2006. *Self, Relationship and Time: Phenomenological Psychopathology.* Tokyo: Chikumashobo (in Japanese).

Kindaichi, H. 1975. *Japanese Linguistic Expression.* Tokyo: Kodansha (in Japanese).

Kindaichi, H. 1988. *Japanese Language (Vol. 1).* Tokyo: Iwanami Shoten (in Japanese).

King, S. 2000. A Global Ethic in the Light of Comparative Religious Ethics. In *Explorations in Global Ethics: Comparative Religious Ethics and Interreligious Dialogue*, ed. S. B. Twiss and B. Grelle. Boulder, CO: Westview Press, pp. 118–40.

Kitiyadisai, K. 2005. Privacy Rights and Protection: Foreign Values in Modern Thai Context. *Ethics and Information Technology* 7: 17–26.

Klein, N. 2005. The Real Purpose of Torture. *The Guardian*, published May 14, 2005 at: http://www.theguardian.com/world/2005/may/14/guantanamo.usa (Retrieved on October 7, 2015).

Klug, F. 2015. *A Magna Carta for all Humanity – Homing in On Human Rights.* London: Routledge.

Kneale, W. C. and M. Kneale. 1962. *The Development of Logic.* Oxford.

Komparic, A. 2015. The Ethics of Introducing GMOs Into Sub-Saharan Africa: Considerations From the Sub-Saharan African Theory of Ubuntu. *Bioethics* 29(9): 604–12.

Koslowski, P., ed. 2001. *The Concept of God, the Origin of the World, and the Image of the Human in the World Religions.* Dordrecht, the Netherlands: Springer.

Kovacs, J. 2010. The Transformation of (Bio)ethics Expertise in a World of Ethical Pluralism. *Journal of Medical Ethics* 36: 767–70. DOI: 10.1136/jme.2010.036319.

Krauss, Michael E. 1992. The World's Languages in Crisis. *Language* 68(1): 4–10.

Krishnananda, S. n.d. *The Study and Practice of Yoga: An exposition of the Yoga Sutras of Patanjali Vol. 1.* Rishikesh, India: The Divine Life Society, E-book edition.

Krumbein, F. 2015. P. C. Chang – The Chinese Father of Human Rights. *Journal of Human Rights* 1.

Kukathas, C. 1994. Explaining Moral Variety, in *Cultural Pluralism and Moral Knowledge*, eds. E. F. Paul, et al. Cambridge: Cambridge University Press.

Küng, H. and K.-J. Kuschel. 1993. *A Global Ethic: The Declaration of the Parliament of the World's Religions.* London: SCM Press.

Kuper, A. 1999. *Culture: The Anthropologists' Account.* Harvard: Harvard University Press.

Lao Tzu. 1990, 5th cent. BCE. *Tao Teh Ching.* Trans. J.C.H. Wu. Boston: Shambhala.

Lao, Rattana. 2015. *A Critical Study of Thailand's Higher Education Reforms: The Culture of Borrowing.* London: Routledge.

Legge, J. 1971. *Confucius: Confucian Analects, the Great Learning and the Doctrine of the Mean.* New York: Dover Publishing.

Lessig, L. 1999. *Code and Other Laws of Cyberspace.* New York: Basic Books.

Liao, S. M. 2008. The Loop Case and Kamm's Doctrine of Double Effect. *Philosophical Studies* 146: 223–31.

Linklater, A. 1992. What is a Good International Citizen? In Keal, P. (ed.). *Ethics and Foreign Policy.* London: Allen and Unwin.

Liu, L. H. 2014. Shadows of Universalism: The Untold Story of Human Rights around 1948. *Critical Inquiry* 40.

Li, X. 1996. "Asian Values" and The Universality of Human Rights, Report from the Institute for Philosophy and Public Policy, Vol. 16: 2.

Li, X. 2006. *Ethics, Human Rights, and Culture: Beyond Relativism and Universalism.* Basingstoke: Palgrave.

Løgstrup, K. E. 1997. *The Ethical Demand.* Notre Dame: University of Notre Dame Press.

Lü, Y. 2005. Privacy and Data Privacy in Contemporary China. *Ethics and Information Technology* 7: 7–15.

Luban, D. 2008. Unthinking the Ticking Bomb. Georgetown Law Faculty Working Papers: http://scholarship.law.georgetown.edu/fwps_papers/68/ (Retrieved October 3, 2015).

Lutheran World Federation. 1977. *Theological Perspectives on Human Rights.* Geneva: Lutheran World Federation.

Lyotard, J. 1991, 1979. *The Postmodern Condition: A Report on Knowledge.* Trans. G. Bennington and B. Massumi. Minneapolis: University of Minnesota Press.

MacIntyre, A. 1988. *Whose Justice? Which Rationality?* London: Duckworth.

Mahmasani, S. 1982. Adaption of Islamic Jurisprudence to Modern Social Needs, in Donohue, J. J. and J. L. Esposito, eds., *Islam in Transition. Muslim Perspectives.* Oxford: Oxford University Press.

Malcouronne, P. 2008. The First Regional Conference for the Asia and Pacific Region on the Ethical Dimensions of the Information Society, 12–14 March 2008, Hanoi, Vietnam.

Malik, C. 2000. *The Challenge of Human Rights.* Oxford: the Centre for Lebanese Studies.

Marcel, G. 1951, 1945. *Homo Viator: Introduction to a metaphysic of hope.* Trans. E. Craufurd. Chicago: Henry Regnery Company.

Maritain, J. 1949. *Human Rights: Comments and Interpretations.* New York: Columbia University Press.

Marwick, A. E. and D. Boyd. 2011. I Tweet Honestly, I Tweet Passionately: Twitter Users, Context Collapse, and the Imagined Audience. *New Media & Society* 13(1): 114–33.

Marx, K. 1970. Zur Judenfrage, in *Marx-Engels-Werke*, Vol. 1, Eastern Berlin: Dietz.

Matilal, B. K. 1990. *Logic, Language and Reality: Indian Philosophy and Contemporary Issues.* Delhi: Motilal Banarsidass.

Matthews, B. M. 2000. The Chinese Value Survey: An interpretation of Value Scales and Consideration of Some Preliminary Results. *International Education Journal* 1(2): 117–26.

Mawdudi, A. A. 1976. *Human Rights in Islam.* Leicester: The Islamic Foundation.

Mayer, A. E. 1993. A Critique of An'Na'im's Assessment of Islamic Criminal Justice, in T. Lindholm, and K. Vogt, eds., *Islamic Law Reform and Human Rights. Challenges and Rejoinders*, Kopenhagen et al.: Nordic Human Rights Publications.

McCargo, D. 2005. Network Democracy and Legitimacy Crises in Thailand. *The Pacific Review* 18(4): 499–519.

McCarthy, K. 2000. Reckoning with Religious Difference: Models of Interreligious Moral Dialogue. In *Explorations in Global Ethics: Comparative Religious Ethics and Interreligious Dialogue*, eds. S. B. Twiss and B. Grelle. Boulder, CO: Westview Press, pp. 73–117.

McRobb, S., Y. Orito, K. Murata, and A. A. Adams. 2007. 'Towards an Exploration of Cross-Cultural Factors in Privacy Online', *Proceedings from the ETHICOMP conference,* Meiji University, Tokyo.

McSweeney, B. 2002. Hofstede's Model of National Cultural Differences and Their Consequences: A Triumph of Faith – A Failure of Analysis'. *Human Relation* 55(1): 89–118.

Mill, J. S. 1969, 1861. *Utilitarianism*, ed. Mary Warnock. London: Collins.

Mills, C. 1997. *The Racial Contract.* Ithaca, NY: Cornell University Press.

Mizutani, M., J. Dorsey, J. H. Moor. 2004. The Internet and Japanese Conception of Privacy. *Ethics and Information Technology* 6(2): 121–28.

Moltmann, J. and J. M. Lochmann, eds., 1976. *Gottes Recht und Menschenrechte. Studien und Empfehlungen des Reformierten Weltbundes,* Neukirchen-Vluyn: Neukirchener Verlag.

Moontime W. 2014. Good Philosophers Don't Have Anxiety Attacks: On Mental Health, Race, and Belonging in the Classroom. http://moontimewarrior.com/2014/03/27/good-philosophers-dont-have-anxiety-attacks/ (Retrieved October 7, 2015).

Morsink, J. 1999. *Universal Declaration of Human Rights: Origins, Drafting and Intent.* Philadelphia: University of Pennsylvania Press.

Morsink, J. 2009. *Inherent Human Rights – Philosophical Roots of the UN Declaration.* Philadelphia: University of Pennsylvania Press.

Mottahedeh, R. P. Toward an Islamic Theology of Toleration, in T. Lindholm, and K. Vogt, eds., *Islamic Law Reform and Human Rights. Challenges and Rejoinders,* Kopenhagen et al.: Nordic Human Rights Publications.

Moyn, S. 2010. *The Last Utopia: Human Rights in History.* Cambridge, MA: Harvard University Press.

Müller, L. 1996. *Islam und Menschenrechte. Sunnitische Muslime zwischen Islamismus, Säkularismus und Modernismus.* Hamburg: Deutsches Orient-Institut.

Mulligan, K., P. Simons and B. Smith. 2015. What's Wrong with Contemporary Philosophy? Preprint for a special issue of *Topoi,* https://www.unige.ch/lettres/philo/files/6514/2644/4477/mulligan_whatiswrongwithcontemporaryphilosophy.pdf (Retrieved November 10, 2015).

Murakami, Y., S. Kumon, and S. Sato. 1979. *The Ie Society as Civilisation.* Tokyo: Chuokoron Shinsha (in Japanese).

Murata, K. and Y. Orito. 2008. 'Rethinking the Concept of the Right to Information Privacy: a Japanese Perspective'. *Journal of Information, Communication and Ethics in Society* 6(3): 233–45.

Murata, K. and Y. Orito. 2008. Rethinking the Concept of the Right to Information Privacy: A Japanese Perspective. *Journal of Information, Communication and Ethics in Society* 6(3); 233–45.

Murata, K. and Y. Orito. 2010. Japanese Risk Society: Trying to Create Complete Security and Safety Using Information and Communication Technology. *Computers and Society* 40(3): 38–49.

Murata, K. 2008. Rethinking the Concept of the Right to Information Privacy: A Japanese Perspective. *Journal of Information Communication and Ethics in Society* 6(3).

Murata, K., Y. Orito, and Y. Fukuta. 2014. Social Attitudes of Young People in Japan towards Online Privacy. *Journal of Law, Information and Science* 23(1): 137–57.

Murata, K., Y. Orito, Y. Fukuta, A. A. Adams, and A. M. Lara Palma. 2015. So What If the State Is Monitoring Us? – Snowden's Revelations Have Little Social Impact in Japan. *Computers and Society* 45(3): 361–68.

Murayama, K., T. Lennerfors, and K. Murata. 2010. Comparative Analysis of P2P Software Usage in Japan and Sweden from a Socio-Cultural Perspective. *International Review of Information Ethics* 13(10).

Murdoch, I. 2001, 1970. *The Sovereignty of Good (Routledge Classics)*. London: Routledge.

Murdock, G. 1967. *Ethnographic Atlas*. Pittsburgh: University of Pittsburgh Press.

Myers, D., J. Spencer, and C. Jordan, 2012. *Social Psychology*, Third Canadian Edition, Toronto: McGraw-Hill Ryerson.

Nagel, Th. 2005. The Problem of Global Justice. *Philosophy & Public Affairs* 33: 113–47.

Nakada, M. and T. Tamura. 2005. Japanese Conceptions of Privacy: An Intercultural Perspective. *Ethics and Information Technology* 7: 27–36.

Nakada, M. and T. Tamura. 2005. Japanese Conception of Privacy: An Intercultural Perspective. *Ethics and Information Technology* 7(1): 27–36.

Nakane, C. 1970. *Japanese Society*. Berkeley and Los Angeles, CA: University of California Press.

National Consumer Affairs Center of Japan. 2005. A Trend and Problems Observed in a Recent Consultation Example Concerning Personal Information. Available at: http://www.kokusen.go.jp/pdf/n-20051107_2.pdf (Retrieved October 21, 2015) (in Japanese).

Needham, J. 1978. *The Shorter Science and Civilization in China: An Abridgement of Needham's Original Text, Volume 1*. Cambridge University Press.

Nickel, J. W. 2014. What Future for Human Rights? *Ethics & International Affairs* 28(2).

Nietzsche, F. 1966, 1887. *Beyond Good and Evil: Prelude to A Philosophy of the Future*. Trans. W. Kaufmann. New York: Vintage Books.

Nippon Keidanren. 2003. Towards Constructing a Secure and Safe Net Society. Available at: www.keidanren.or.jp/japanese/policy/2003/023/index.html (Retrieved October 21, 2015) (in Japanese).

Nishigaki, T. 2006. The Ethics in Japanese Information Society: Consideration on Francisco Varela's The Embodied Mind from the Perspective of Fundamental Informatics. *Ethics and Information Technology* 8: 237–42.

Nozick, R. 1974. *Anarchy, State and Utopia*. Oxford: Blackwell.

Nussbaum, M. C. 2000. *Women and Human Development: The Capabilities Approach*. Cambridge, UK: Cambridge University Press.

Nussbaum, M. 2006. *Frontiers of Justice. Disability, Nationality. Species Membership*. Cambridge: Belknapp Press.

Nygren, A. 1982. *Agape and Eros: The Christian Idea of Love*. Chicago: University of Chicago Press.

O'Connor, J. 2012. The Trolley Method of Moral Philosophy. *Essays in Philosophy* 13(1): 242–55.

O'Neill, O. 1989. *Faces of Hunger*. London: Allen & Unwin.

OECD. 1980. OECD Guidelines on the Protection of Privacy and Transborder Flows of Personal Information. Available at: http://www.oecd.org/sti/ieconomy/oecdguidelinesontheprotectionofprivacyandtransborderflowsofpersonaldata.htm (Retrieved October 21, 2015).

Oestreich, G. 1978. *Geschichte der Menschenrechte und Grundfreiheiten im Umriss*. Berlin: Duncker & Humblot.

Orend, B. 2002. *Human Rights – Concept and Context*. Peterborough, ON: Broadview Press.

Orito, Y. and K. Murata. 2008. Socio-cultural Analysis of Personal Information Leakage in Japan. *Journal of Information, Communication and Ethics in Society* 6(2): 161–71.

Orito, Y., Y. Fukuta, and M. Murata. 2014. I Will Continue to Use This Nonetheless: Social Media Survive Users' Privacy Concerns. *International Journal of Virtual Worlds and Human Computer Interaction* 2: 92–107.

Orito, Y., K. Murata, Y. Fukuta, S. McRobb, and A. A. Adams. 2008. Online Privacy and Culture: Evidence from Japan. *Proceedings of ETHICOMP*, pp. 615–22.

Orito, Y., Murata, K. and Fukuta, Y. 2013. Do Online Privacy Policies and Seals Affect Corporate Trustworthiness and Reputation? *International Review of Information Ethics* 19: 52–65.

Othman, N. 1994. The Sociopolitical Dimensions of Islamisation in Malaysia: A Cultural Accomodation of Social Change? in: same author, ed., *Shari'a Law and the Modern Nation-State. A Malaysian Symposium*, Kuala Lumpur: Sisters in Islam Forum.

Otsuka, M. 2008. Double Effect, Triple Effect, and the Trolley Problem: Squaring the Circle in Looping Cases. *Utilitas* 20: 1, 92–110.

Palm, E. 2007. The Ethics of Workspace Surveillance Doctoral Thesis. Royal Institute of Technology, Stockholm.

Palm, E. 2010. Privacy and Identity in Intercultural Information Ethics. *Applied Ethics Challenges for the 21st Century*. Centre for Applied Ethics and Philosophy, Hokkaido, pp. 98–108.

Palmer, R. E. 1969. *Hermeneutics: Interpretation Theory in Schleiermacher, Dilthey, Heidegger, and Gadamer*. Evanston, IL: Northwestern University Press.

Parekh, B. 2005. Principles of a Global Ethic. In J. Eade, and D. O'Byrne, (eds.). *Global Ethics & Civil Society*. Aldershot: Ashgate.

Parfit, D. 1984. *Reasons and Persons*. Oxford: Oxford University Press.

Park, E. S. 2014. Why I Left Academia: Philosophy's Homogeneity Needs Rethinking. Hippo Reads: http://read.hipporeads.com/why-i-left-academia-philosophys-homogeneity-needs-rethinking/ (Retrieved October 1, 2015).

Pateman, C. and C. Mills. 2007. *Contract & Domination*. Cambridge: Polity Press.

Pateman, C. 1988. *The Sexual Contract*. Stanford: Stanford University Press.

Paxton, M., C. Figdor, and V. Tiberius. 2012. Quantifying the Gender Gap: An Empirical Study of the Underrepresentation of Women in Philosophy. *Hypatia* 27(4): 949–57.

Picht, P. 1980. Zum geistesgeschichtlichen Hintergrund der Lehre von den Menschenrechten, in: same author, *Hier und Jetzt. Philosophieren nach Auschwitz und Hiroshima*, Stuttgart: Klett-Cotta.

Pogge, Th. 2003. *World Poverty and Human Rights*. Cambridge: Cambridge University Press.

Pollis, A. and P. Schwab. 1979. Human Rights: A Western Construct with Limited Applicability, in: same authors, eds., *Human Rights: Cultural and Ideological Perspectives* New York: Praeger.

Pollis, A. and P. Schwab. 1979. Human Rights: A Western Construct with Limited Applicability. In *Human Rights: Cultural and Ideological Perspectives* edited by Adamantia Pollis and Peter Schwab, pp. 1–18. New York: Praeger.

Purdy, M. 1991. "What is listening?" In *Listening in everyday life: A Personal and Professional Approach*, Edited by: Borisoff, D. and Purdy, M., pp. 3–19. Lanham, MD: University Press of America.

Rachels, J. and S. Rachels. 2012. *The Elements of Moral Philosophy*. 7th edn., New York: McGraw-Hill.

Radhakrishnan, S. 1927. *Indian Philosophy, Vol. 1*. London: George Allen and Unwin.

Rahman, F. 1966. *Islam*. Chicago: Chicago University Press.

Rahman, F. 1982. *Islam & Modernity. Transformation of an Intellectual Tradition*. Chicago: University of Chicago Press.

Rawls, J. 1971. *A Theory of Justice*. Oxford: Oxford University Press.

Rawls, J. 1993. *Political Liberalism*. New York: Columbia University Press.

Rawls, J. 1999. *The Idea of Public Reason Revisited*, in A Law of Peoples, Cambridge: Harvard University Press.

Richmond, Jonathan E. D. 2007. Bringing Critical Thinking to the Education of Developing Country Professionals. *International Education Journal* 8(1): 1–29.

Roosevelt, E. 1961. *The Autobiography of Eleanor Roosevelt*. New York: Harper.

Roth, H. I. 1999. *The Multicultural Park – A Study of Common Values at School and in Society*. Stockholm: Liber/Skolverket.

Roth, H. I. 2012. *Är religion en mänsklig rättighet?* (Is Religion a Human Right?). Stockholm: Norstedts förlag.

Rucker, R. 1995. *Infinity and the Mind: The Science and Philosophy of the Infinite*. Princeton: Princeton University Press.

Sandel, M. 1981. *Liberalism and the Limits of Justice*. Cambridge: Cambridge University Press.

Sandel, M. 1982. *Liberalism and the Limits of Justice*. Cambridge: Cambridge University Press.

Scanlon, T. M. 1998. *What We Owe to Each Other*. Cambridge, MA: The Belknap Press of Harvard University Press.

Schabas, W. A. 2013. *The Universal Declaration of Human Rights*. Cambridge: Cambridge University Press.

Schacht, J. 1964. *An Introduction to Islamic Law*. Oxford: Clarendon Press.

Schmitt, C. 1963. *Der Begriff des Politischen*. Berlin: Duncker & Humblot.

Schwitzgebel, E. 2014a. The 267 Most-cited Authors in the Stanford Encyclopedia of Philosophy. http://schwitzsplintersunderblog.blogspot.se/2014/08/the-266-most-cited-contemporary-authors.html (Retrieved November 10, 2015).

Schwitzgebel, E. 2014b. Citation of Women and Ethnic Minorities in the Stanford Encyclopedia of Philosophy. http://schwitzsplinters.blogspot.se/2014/08/citation-of-women-and-ethnic-minorities.html (Retrieved November 10, 2015).

Sen, A., 1999. *Development as Freedom*. New York: Anchor Books.

Sen, A. 2009. *The Idea of Justice*, Cambridge, MA: Belknap Press.

Senghaas, D. 1994. *Wohin driftet die Welt? Über die Zukunft friedlicher Koexistenz* Frankfurt: Suhrkamp.

Shafer-Landau, R. (ed.), 2012. *The Ethical Life: Fundamental Readings in Ethics and Moral Problems*. 2nd edn. Oxford: Oxford University Press.

Shamoo, A. and D. Resnik. 2009. *Responsible Conduct of Research, 2nd edn*. New York: Oxford University Press.

Shiva, V. 2001. *Protect of Plunder? Understanding Intellectual Property Rights.* London and New York: Zed Books.

Shklar, J. N. 1992. *The Faces of Injustice.* New Haven: Yale University Press.

Shue, H. 1996. *Basic Rights: Subsistence, Affluence and US Foreign Policy.* 2nd edn. Princeton: Princeton University Press.

Shue, H. 2006. Torture in Dreamland: Disposing of the Ticking Bomb. *Case Western Reserve Journal of International Law* 37: 231–39.

Shun, K. and D. Wong. 2004. *Confucian Ethics, A Comparative Study of Self, Autonomy and Community.* Cambridge: Cambridge University Press.

Singapore Statement. 2010. 2nd World Conference on Research Integrity. http://www.singaporestatement.org/downloads/singpore%20statement_A4size.pdf, (Retrieved November 24, 2015).

Singer, P., ed., 1994. *Ethics.* Oxford: Oxford University Press.

Singer, P. 1972. Famine, Affluence and Morality. *Philosophy & Public Affairs*, I, 1972, 229–43, and, extended, 1979. Rich and poor. In Singer, P. *Practical Ethics.* Cambridge: Cambridge University Press, 1979.

Singer, P. 2002. *One World – The Ethics of Globalisation.* London: Yale University Press.

Smith, M. 1984, 1928. *Rābi'a the Mystic and Her Fellow-Saints in Islam.* Cambridge: Cambridge University Press.

Solove, D. J. 2008. *Understanding Privacy.* Cambridge, MA: Harvard University Press.

Stahmann, C. 1994. Islamische Menschenrechtskonzepte, in: *Zeitschrift für Evangelische Ethik* 38.

Stiglitz, J. 2006. *Making Globalization Work.* London: Allen Lane.

Stourzh, G. 1987. Die Begründung der Menschenrechte im englischen und amerikanischen Verfassungsdenken des 17. und 18. Jahrhunderts, in: Böckenförde and Spaemann, eds., *Menschenrechte und Menschenwürde.*

Stout, J. 2001. *Ethics after Babel – The Languages of Morals and their Discontents.* Princeton: Princeton University Press.

Suzuki, D. T. 1959. *Zen and Japanese Culture.* Princeton, NJ: Princeton University Press.

Suzuki, D. T. 1972. *The Japanese Spirituality.* Tokyo: Iwanami Shoten (in Japanese).

Suzuki, T. 1973. *Language and Culture.* Tokyo: Iwanami Shoten (in Japanese).

Suzuki, T. 1990. *Japanese and Foreign Languages.* Tokyo: Iwanami Shoten (in Japanese).

Svensson, M. 2002. *Debating Human Rights in China.* New York: Rowman and Littlefield.

Talbi, M. 1991. Religious Liberty: A Muslim Perspective, in *Conscience and Liberty*, 3rd year, No. 1.

Tamir, Y. 2006. Hand Off Clitoridectomy. *The Boston Review*, published June 1, 2006 at: http://bostonreview.net/yael-tamir-hands-off-clitoridectomy (Retrieved October 7, 2015).

Tännsjö, T. 2013. *Understanding Ethics.* 3rd edn., Edinburgh: Edinburgh University Press.

Taylor, C. 1994. "The Politics of Recognition," in *Multiculturalism*, ed. A. Gutmann, 25–74. New Brunswick, NJ: Princeton University Press.

Thanissaro Bhikkhu. 2006. *Purity of Heart: Essays on the Buddhist Path*. Valley Centre, CA: Metta Forest Monastery.

Thomson, J. J. 1986. Killing, Letting Die, and the Trolley Problem, in *Rights, Restitution, and Risk: Essays in Moral Theory*, ed. William Parent, 78–93. Cambridge, MA: Harvard University Press.

Tibi, B. 1994. *Im Schatten Allahs. Der Islam und die Menschenrechte*. Munich: Piper.

Tillich, P. 1957. *Dynamics of Faith*. New York: Harper & Brothers.

Troeltsch, E. 1911. *Die Bedeutung des Protestantismus für die Entstehung der modernen Welt*. Munich: R. Oldenbourg.

Truth and Reconciliation Commission of Canada. 2015. *Honouring the Truth, Reconciling for the Future: Summary of the Final Report of the Truth and Reconciliation Commission of Canada*. http://www.trc.ca/websites/trcinstitution/File/2015/Findings/Exec_Summary_2015_05_31_web_o.pdf (Retrieved October 3, 2015).

Turner B. and H. Khondker. 2010. *Globalization East and West*. Los Angeles: Sage.

Twiss B. S. 2009. Confucian Contributions to the Universal Declaration of Human Rights: A Historical and Philosophical Perspective, in Sharma, A. (ed.) *The World's Religions after September 11,* Westport: CT.

Uchida, T. 2000. *The Age of Contract*. Tokyo: Iwanami Shoten (in Japanese).

Udeani, C. 2007. Cultural Diversity and Globalisation: An Intercultural Hermeneutical (African) Perspective. *International Review of Information Ethics* 7(9). http://www.i-r-i-e.net/inhalt/007/05-udeani.pdf (Retrieved December 5, 2015).

UNESCO. 2010. *The Ethical Implications of Climate Change*. Report by the World Commission on the Ethics of Scientific Knowledge and Technology. http://unesdoc.unesco.org/images/0018/001881/188198e.pdf, (Retrieved November 11, 2015).

Valadier, P. 1994. Aktuelle Gefährdungen der Menschenrechte, in: Odersky, W. ed., *Die Menschenrechte. Herkunft – Geltung – Gefährdung*. Düsseldorf: Patmos.

Van den Hoven, J. 1995. Equal access and social justice: information as a primary good, *Proceedings from the ETHICOMP conference*.

Vidyabhusana, S. C. 2006. *A History of Indian Logic: Ancient, Mediaeval and Modern Schools*. Delhi: Motilal Banarsidass.

Walpola, R. 1962. *What the Buddha Taught*. NY: Grove.

Watsuji, T. 1979. *A Pilgrimage to Ancient Temples*. Tokyo: Iwanami Shoten (in Japanese).

Watsuji, T. 2007. *Ethics as the Study of Human Beings*. Tokyo: Iwanami Shoten (in Japanese).

Watsuji, T. 2011. *The History of Japanese Thought of Ethics (Vol. 2)*. Tokyo: Iwanami Shoten (in Japanese).

Wen, H & Keli'i Akina, W. 2012. Human Rights Ideology as Endemic in Chinese Philosophy: Classical Confucian and Mohist Perspectives. *Asian Philosophy* 22(4).

Westin, A. F. 1967. *Privacy and Freedom*. New York: Atheneum.

Wielandt, R. 1982. Zeitgenössische Ägyptische Stimmen zur Säkularisierungsproblematik, in *Die Welt des Islams* XXII.

Will, P.-E. 2007. La Contribution chinoise à la déclaration universelle des droits de l'homme, Delmas-Marty M., *La Chine et la démcratie: Tradition, droti, institutions,* Paris.

Wong. D. B., 1984. *Ethical Relativism.* Oakland, CA: University of California Press.

Woods, K., 2015. *Human Rights.* New York: Palgrave Macmillan.

Wright, D. and P. De Hert. 2012. Introduction to Privacy Impact Assessment, in *Privacy Impact Assessment*, ed. D. Wright and P. De Hert, 3–32. New York: Spinger Science+Business.

Yamamoto, S. 1983. *The Study on "Atmosphere".* Tokyo: Bungei Shunju (in Japanese). Bull, H., 1977. *The Anarchical Society.* London: Macmillan.

Yancy, G. and Mills, C. 2014. Lost in Rawlsland. *The Stone*, of the *New York Times,* published November 16, 2014 at: http://opinionator.blogs.nytimes.com/2014/11/16/lost-in-rawlsland/?_r=0 (Retrieved October 7, 2015).

Zaid, N. H. A. 1996. *Islam und Politik. Kritik des religiösen Diskurses.* Trans. from Arabic to German by Chérifa Magdi, Frankfurt: dipa.

Index

Abdarraziq, Ali, 85
Abduh, Mohammed, 80
Abu Ghraib prison, 52
Abu Zaid, Nasr Hamid, 83
Act on the Protection of Personal
  Information (APPI), 164, 175–76,
  187
Advaita Vedānta, 149
agape, 7
ahimsa, 7
aidagara, 167, 169, 172, 180
Al-Ashmawy, Muhammad Said, 81, 85
Alexander the Great, 128
amae, 169–70, 172
amana (trust), 82
Analects of Confucius, 165
Anderson, James Norman, 80
An-Na'im, Abdullahi, 82
Antigone (Sophocles), 66
Apostasy, 76, 80
APPI. *See* Act on the Protection of
  Personal Information (APPI)
Aquinas, Thomas, 67
Arendt, Hannah, 69
Aristotelianism, 34
Aristotle, 126, 128, 132
art of living, 106, 108, 117–18
Asian values, 9
as-if tradition, 172, 174

Atlas of World Cultures (Murdock),
  188–89
atman (soul), 149
Austin, John L., 158n6
autonomy, 11, 14

ba, 167–68, 170, 180
baby lottery, 51–52
Baier, Karl, 192
Barnes, Elizabeth, 48, 58n4
Barth, Karl, 154–55
Basic Resident Register Network
  System (*Juki* Net), 174
Basri, Rābi'a, 157
Beckwith, Christopher, 128
Bhargava, Rajeev, 3, 13
Bhikkhu, Thanissaro, 158n3
Bible, 65, 72, 74, 89
binary thinking. *See* empty dichotomies
bioethics, 53
Bombs on China (short film), 101
Boxer Rebellion, 99
brahman (ultimate reality), 149
Brey, Philip, 183, 185–86, 193
bricolage, 120
Bronk, Andrzej, 158n1
Buddhism, 9–11, 131, 133–34
  logic, 128
  philosophy, 128, 131–32, 146

Burke, Edmund, 68
business ethics, 36, 40–41

Cairo Declaration on Human Rights in
    Islam, 77–78
capabilities approach, 8, 34–35
Capurro, Rafael, 182, 184, 186, 192,
    194
Carter, Jimmy, 104
Cassin, René, 95, 104, 107–8, 110,
    112–13
Categorical Imperative, 29, 138–39
Chang, Peng Chun, 8, 17, 95–123
Chang, Po-ling, 99, 101
Chao, Y. R., 103
Chiang Kai-Shek, 99, 102
China, critical thinking in, 128–30
Chödrön, Pema, 158n3
Christianity, 63, 66–69, 71–73
Christian Reformation, 71
church/churches, 69, 71, 87
civilization argument, 5, 107
The Clash of Civilizations and the
    Remaking of World Order
    (Huntington), 5
climate justice, 35
Cold War, 33–34, 105
communication, 3, 143, 146–56, 158;
    communicating ethics, 137–40;
    of ethics, 154–57;
    ethics as informed by hope, 153–54;
    ethics as informed by infinity,
        150–53;
    and global ethics, 23–27, 29, 30, 31;
    global perspectives, 1–14;
    intercultural, 114–15;
    limits of, 53–54, 57;
    and listening, 12–14;
    non-verbal, 165;
    possibility of, 8–12;
    privacy, social norms of, 171–72;
    transcendence and, 149–50
communicative action, 14
communitarianism, 38
community, 11
compliance depression, 176

comprehensive doctrine, 7, 9, 19n3, 88
Confucian ethics, 96, 98, 108
Confucianism, 138–39
Confucius, 9, 89, 105, 108, 118–20,
    129, 138, 165
conscience, 66
conscious/consciousness, 143–44,
    148–51, 153
contextual value, 10
Convention of Biological Diversity, 13
cosmopolitanism, 27, 29, 32, 34, 36,
    38–41
creative adjustment, 114–15
critical thinking, 128–37;
    in China, 128–30;
    contingency, 135–36;
    in India, 128–30;
    practical nature, 135–37;
    in Thailand, 130–35
cross-cultural overlapping consensus, on
    human rights, 86–89
Cua, Antonio, 153
culture/cultural, 3, 5, 9, 181–84, 187,
    189, 190, 192–94
cultural relativism, 63–93, 106

Daoist philosophy, 153–54
A Declaration toward a Global Ethic,
    25, 28
Dennett, Daniel, 59n9
Development as Freedom (Sen), 9
Dewey, John, 100, 117
dialogue, 143, 152–53, 156–58
difference principle, 8
Digital divide, 183
Dignitatis humanae, 71
dignity, 65, 68, 71–72, 77–78
discourse, 145–46, 148, 152–54, 156–
    57, 158n4
diversity, religious, 155–56
Dotson, Kristie, 44
Dworkin, Ronald, 106, 123

Earth Charter, 25
Eastern values, 9
Ebeling, Hans, 70

e-medicine, 2
empty dichotomies, 49, 54–55
Encyclopedia Britannica, 3
Enlightenment, 9–10, 29, 71, 108, 119
enryo, 169
epistemic injustice, 3, 13–14
equality, 14
e-*seken*, 177–79
Esposito, Joseph, 80
Ess, Charles, 46, 185–86
ethical laboratories, 50
The Ethical Life, 59n13
ethical relativism, 36–37
ethics of communication, 149–54
ethics of globalization, 25, 26
Ethnographic Atlas (Murdock), 188–89
European history, of human rights, 73–75
evil, 147, 157
exclusivism/exclusivists, 155–56

Faath, Sigrid, 75
Facebook, 18, 163, 177, 179
Falun Gong, 120
female genital cutting, 55–56
feminist philosophy, 46–48
Fikentscher, Wolfgang, 63–64
fiqh (jurisprudence), 81–82
fool detector, 178
Foot, Philippa, 48
Fraser, Chris, 129
Fraser, Nancy, 14
freedom/free will, 9, 144, 147, 149, 152
French Enlightenment, 96, 108, 120
French Revolution, 68–69
fundamentalism, 155–56
The Fundamentals of Ethics, 59n13
fusuma/shoji, 172

gender equality, 3, 9, 75–76
giri (obligation), 169
Glendon, Mary Ann, 104, 119, 124n1
global economy, 30–31, 140
global ethics, 143, 145–58;
    and business ethics, 40–41;
    and capabilities approach, 34;

challenges to, 36–41;
and communication, 23–26;
and communitarianism, 38;
contrast with a global ethic, 23–24, 26;
description, 26–27;
and ethical relativism, 36–37;
global by consent and by assent, 33;
global in scope of acceptance, 23, 27–29;
global in scope of content, 23, 27–29;
and global justice, 34–35;
global perspectives, 1–14;
and human rights theory, 33–34;
and internationalism, 39–40;
and international scepticism, 38–39;
and Kantianism, 29–30;
and libertarianism, 31–32;
with or without its source story, 28–29;
sources of interest in, 27;
and utilitarianism, 30–31
globalization, 1–3, 10–15, 18, 24–27, 39–40, 89, 125, 127, 140, 171, 174, 175, 181
global justice, 34–35
global warming, 1, 3
Golden Rule, 138–39
good/goodness, 145, 147, 150, 152–54, 157–58
Green, T. H., 32

Habermas, Jürgen, 14, 70
Haslanger, Sally, 58n1
Hassan, Riffat, 82, 84
Hauerwas, Stanley, 11
Hegel, Georg W. F., 64, 66, 68–69, 72, 144, 149
hermeneutics, 16, 72–73, 83, 89, 138
Hick, John, 158n2
Hilpert, Konrad, 69, 71
Hiruta, Key, 185
Hobhouse, L. T., 32
Hofstede, Geert, 188–90
Holocaust, 110
homogeneity, 16, 190, 192;

of professional philosophy, 43–45;
    religious, 91
hon'ne speech, 170–71, 174, 176
hope, 143–47, 151–57, 158n3
hothen ('from which') approach, 186
Howard, Rhoda, 87
How to Do Things with Words (Austin),
    158n6
humanization of man, 106, 112, 116,
    121–23
human rights, 10, 63–93;
    cross-cultural 'overlapping
        consensus' on, 86–89;
    European history of, 73–75;
    and global ethics, 33–34;
    Islamization of, 76–78;
    and political secularism in Islam,
        84–86;
    and *sharia* Islam, 75–76, 78–84
Human Rights Commission, 101–2,
    108, 111, 116, 122
Human Rights in Islam (Mawdudi), 76
Hume, David, 11, 59n6
Humphrey, John, 95, 102, 104, 116, 120
Huntington, Samuel, 5–6, 63–64

ICT. *See* information and
    communication technology (ICT)
IE. *See* Information Ethics (IE)
ie society, communication in, 166–68
Ignatieff, Michael, 89
IIE. *See* Intercultural Information Ethics
    (IIE)
IMF. *See* International Monetary Fund
    (IMF)
immanence/immanent, 144, 149
imperialistic homogenisation, 183
inclusivist/inclusivism, 155–56
incommensurability, 5–7, 12
India, critical thinking in, 128–30
Indian Residential Schools, 51
Indian syllogism, 128
infinite/infinity, 144–46, 149–54, 157–
    58, 158nn3
informed consent, 4

information and communication
    technology (ICT), 163, 181–83
Information Ethics (IE), 182
innate goodness, 112
insular collectivism, 170
intellectual property rights (IPR), 13
intercultural communication, 114–15
intercultural comparisons, 182, 187, 193
intercultural ethics, 6, 95–123
Intercultural Information Ethics (IIE),
    181–94
interfaith dialogue, 28
internationalism, and global ethics,
    39–40
International Monetary Fund (IMF), 31
international scepticism, 38–39
intuition pump, 49, 59n9
IPR. *See* intellectual property rights
    (IPR)
Islamic Council of Europe, 77, 93n8
Islam/Islamism, 10, 64, 70, 75–86
Islamization, of human rights, 76–78
Ivanhoe, Philip, 46

Jainism, 7
Japan, 18, 99, 104, 110
Japanese communication;
    awareness of *uchi/soto* and *seken*,
        168–70;
    emergence of e-*seken*, 177–79;
    in *ie* society, 166–68;
    overview, 163–64;
    perception of self, 172–73;
    social norms of privacy, 171–72;
    and sociolinguistic characteristics,
        164–68;
    tactful use of *hon'ne* and *tatemae*,
        170–71;
    transformation of *seken*, 173–74;
    Western personal data protection
        law, 174–76
Japanese Mottainai principles, 14
Jellinek, Georg, 66
Jesus, 65, 138
Jewish-Christian Holy Scriptures, 65

John of the Cross, 146
Johnson, Deborah, 193
justice as fairness, 8
Juki Net, 174

kango, 165
Kant, Immanuel, 29–30, 74, 128, 138,
  150
Kantianism, 29–30, 35, 74, 82, 138–39
karma, 11
Kaviraj, Sudipta, 67, 71
khalifa (deputy), 82
King, Martin Luther, 120
Kukathas, Chandran, 11–12
Küng, Hans, 28
Kuomintang, 102
Kurdi, Aylan, 2
Kyoto Review, 127

Lang, Cosmo, 101
language, 148–50;
  Japanese, 165–66
Lao, Rattana, 126–35
Las Casas, Bartolomé de, 66
The Last Utopia (Myon), 104
Levi, Primo, 111
Li, Xiarong, 12
liberalism, social, 32, 34, 121
libertarianism, 24, 31–32, 36
LINE, 163, 177
listening, and communication, 12–14
listicle ethics, 53–54
Liu, Lydia, 107
logos, 66
love, 146, 155–58
Luban, David, 59n10
Lutheran World Federation, 71

Maathai, Wangari, 14
MacIntyre, Alasdair, 6–7, 11
Maestre, Joseph de, 68
Magna Charta, 72
Mahatma Gandhi, 14
Mahmasani, Subhi, 81
Maistre, Joseph de, 68

Malcouronne, Peter, 186
Malik, Charles, 95–96, 104–5, 107,
  112–13
Malik, Habib, 107, 124n1
man's inhumanity against man, 111, 121
Mao Zedong, 99, 102
Marcel, Gabriel, 145–46, 153
Marcus Aurelius, 65, 67
Marx, Karl, 68–69
Mattes, Hanspeter, 75
Mawdudi, Abul A'la, 64, 76, 78, 84
Mayer, Ann Elizabeth, 79–80
migration, 3
Mill, John Stuart, 150
mission civilisatrice, 70
miuchi (close family), 168, 170
Mo Di, 129–30, 132
modus vivendi pluralism, 86, 185
Mohism, 129–30, 132–33, 138–39
*Moral Consciousness and
  Communicative Action*
  (Habermas), 158n4
moral *lingua franca*, 16, 89, 92, 95, 98
moral objectivism, 147–48
moral particularism, 4
moral pluralism, 180
moral relativism, 147–48, 153
moral responsibility, 1
Morsink, Johannes, 104
Moyn, Samuel, 104
Muhammad, 64
Murdoch, Iris, 158
Murdock, Rupert, 188–90

Nankai University, 99, 101
natural law, 27
natural law tradition, 67
Needham, Joseph, 130
  Needham's Question, 130
New Testament, 65
Nietzsche, Friedrich, 147
ningen, 172
ninjō (empathy), 169
non-verbal communication, 165
Nussbaum, Martha, 8, 34, 58n1

Nygren, Anders, 7;

occidentalism, 63, 65–66, 69–70, 72–73, 76, 86
O'Connor, James, 49
Oestreich, Gerhard, 65
O'Neill, Onora, 30, 35
Onesimus, 67
One World – The Ethics of Globalisation (Singer), 26
online vigilantism, 163
Organization of the Islamic Conference, 77
Othman, Norani, 83
Ottoman Law of Family Rights (1917), 80, 93n9
Our Global Neighbourhood, 25
overlapping consensus, 7–8, 16, 65, 86–89, 96, 121
overreliance on principles, 53

Parekh, Bhikhu, 28, 33
Parfit, Derek, 191
Park, Eugene Sun, 44
parochialism, 8
Patanjali Yoga, 144
Paul, 65, 67, 92n3
PBD. *See* privacy by default (PBD)
Philemon, 67
philosophical theory, 28
philosophy, professional, 43–45
PIA. *See* privacy impact assessments (PIA)
Picht, Georg, 63
Pius IX (Pope), 69
Pius VI (Pope), 69
Plato, 6, 9, 137
pluralism, 45–48, 55–56, 151, 155–56, 159n7
pluralistic tolerance, 17, 115, 117, 122–23
Pogge, Thomas, 35
political secularism, in Islam, 84–86
Pollis, Adamantia, 63–64, 73
polygamy, 80

posttraditional human rights, 70–71, 73–74
poverty, 27, 28, 30, 31, 38
principle of human dignity, 5
principle of informed consent, 4
principle of utility, 5
privacy, 54–55, 171–72, 190, 191, 194
privacy by default (PBD), 54
privacy impact assessments (PIA), 54
professional philosophy, 43–45
programming languages, 181, 195n2
Project on Religion and Human Rights, 88
pros hen ('towards one' or unity), 185
Protestant Reformation, 66, 68, 73
Pufendorf, Samuel V, 111
puraibashī, 171
Purdy, Michael, 14

QA. *See* Quality Assurance (QA)
Quality Assurance (QA), 131
Qur'an, 64, 77, 79–85, 89

Rahman, Fazlur, 81, 83, 93n10
Rawls, John, 7–8, 16, 19n3, 32, 47–48, 54–55, 59n7, 86–89, 93n11, 96, 121, 123
reciprocity, 3, 14
recognition, 14
reconceptualization, of *sharia* Islam, 80–84
Red Turban Rebellion, 120
Reformation, 66, 68, 73
relativism, 36–37, 137
religion/religious, 143–46, 149–58, 158nn1–2
religious conflict, 29
religious diversity, 155–56
religious freedom/religious liberty, 75, 78
religiously neutral, 105–6
religious pluralism, 120
Renaissance, 71
Republic of China, 100, 103
research ethics, 2

residential schools, in Canada, 51–52
Richmond, Jonathan, 127
Roosevelt, Eleanor, 95, 97, 102, 104, 108, 110, 122
Roosevelt, F. D., 95, 97

Scanlon, Thomas, 150
sceptical realism. *See* international scepticism
scepticism about a global ethic, 24
Schacht, Joseph, 79
Schmitt, Carl, 69
Schwab, Peter, 63–64, 73
Second Vatican Council, 69, 71
secularism/secularity, 72, 84–85
seken, 168–70, 172, 180; e-*seken*, 177–79; transformation of, 173–74
self, 143–44, 146, 149–53, 156–57, 172–73
self-sufficiency, 114
Sen, Amartya, 9–10, 34, 123
Senghaas, Dieter, 69
Shafer-Landau, Russ, 59n13
sharia Islam
conflict with human rights, 75–76; critical reconceptualization of, 80–84; pragmatic reforms in, 78–80
Shklar, Judith N., 113
Shue, H., 33
Singer, Peter, 25–26, 31, 60n15
Smith, Adam, 11
social liberalism, 32, 34, 121
social media, 177
social norms, of communication privacy, 171–72
socio-economic aspects of nations, 190
sociolinguistic characteristics, of Japanese communication, 164–68
Sophocles, 66
soto (outside), 167–71, 174, 180
source story, 28, 29
Stanley Chang, 99–100, 102–4, 107–8, 111, 118, 124n1
stoicism, 63, 65–67, 74

The Stoics, 27
stolen generations of aborigines, in Australia, 51–52
Stout, Jeffrey, 120
Sunna, 64, 77, 81–82
survival lottery, 50–51
Svensson, Marina, 103
Syllabus Errorum, 69
sympathy for others, 108, 112, 120–22

Taha, Muhammad, 80, 82
Taiping Rebellion, 120
Talbi, Mohammed, 84
tanin, 169–70, 177–79
Taskhiri, Ayatollah, 77
tatemae (courteous) speech, 170–71, 174, 176
teaching ethics, 45, 49–51, 53, 56–57
Thailand, critical thinking in, 130–35
Thales, 126
theology, 28
A Theory of Justice (Rawls), 32, 47
Thirty Years War, 39
Thomism, 105
Thomson, Judith Jarvis, 49
thought experiments, 50–53, 59n7
Tibi, Bassam, 64
ticking bomb scenarios, 52–53
tolerance, 79–80
tradition, 5, 9
traditional knowledge, 13
transboundary obligation, 23, 26, 29, 31, 33, 36, 38
transcend/transcendence/transcendent, 143–46, 149–54, 156–58, 158n2
Treaty of Westphalia (1648), 39
TRIPS agreement (Agreement on Trade-Related Aspects of Intellectual Property Rights), 12–13
Troeltsch, Ernst, 66, 68
trolley cases, 48–50, 56
trolleyology, 54, 60n15
Truth and Reconciliation Commission, 52
Turban Rebellion, 120

Tutu, Desmond, 14
Twitter, 163, 177–79

Ubuntu, 14
uchi/soto model, 167–71, 174, 178–80
UDHR. *See* Universal Declaration of
    Human Rights (UDHR)
ultimate reality, 144–45, 149–53, 155–
    56, 158n1
underrepresentation of women and
    minorities, in philosophy, 43–44,
    58–59n4
UN Human Rights Council, 89
Universal Declaration of Human Rights
    (UDHR), 8, 16–17, 75, 77, 89,
    95–123, 139
universal/universalism, 63–93, 125, 137,
    143, 146–47, 150, 152, 155, 158;
    culturally sensitive, 37;
    values and norms, 23, 24, 26, 27, 28,
    30, 31, 32, 33, 34, 36, 37
Upanishads, 157
utilitarianism, 26, 28, 30–31, 36

value colonialism, 181
virtue ethics, 11

wago, 165
Warring States period, 132
watashi (individual self), 168
well-being, 29, 30, 32, 33, 34, 37, 38,
    39, 40, 41
West/Western civilization, 63–75, 90,
    92
Western values, 9
Will, Pierre Etienne, 119
Williams, Bernard ("Jim and the
    Indians"), 56–57
women's rights, 75, 78, 80, 82–84
The World Association of Reformed
    Churches, 71
World Parliament of Religions, 25, 28
World Trade Organisation (WTO), 13,
    40
WTO. *See* World Trade Organisation
    (WTO)

yōgo, 165

Zakaria, Fouad, 85
zakat (alms), 8
Zen Buddhism, 166
Zhou En Lai, 99

Notes on Contributors

Maren Behrensen has a PhD from Boston University and is a lecturer at the Centre for Applied Ethics at Linköping University, Sweden. Her research focus is on the ethics of migration, ethics of technology, and the philosophy of sexuality and gender. She has recently published on biometry, identity documents and personal identity, gender testing in professional sports, and polyamory. Her publications include articles in *Journal of Information and Communication in Society* and *Sport, Ethics, and Philosophy*.

Heiner Bielefeldt is a professor of human rights and human rights politics at the University of Erlangen-Nürnberg in Germany since 2009. His research fields include the theory and practice of human rights, political intellectual history, philosophical ethics, legal philosophy and intercultural philosophy. Besides his academic position, he is also acting as United Nations Special Rapporteur on Freedom of Religion or Belief. He has published *Symbolic Representation in Kant's Practical Philosophy* (Cambridge University Press 2003) and a number of articles in various journals.

Göran Collste is a professor of applied ethics at Linköping University, Sweden. He coordinates an international master's programme in applied ethics and was 2011–2015 president of Societas Ethica (European Society for Research in Ethics). His research focus is on global justice and ICT ethics and his publications include *Global Rectificatory Justice* (Palgrave Macmillan 2015), *Is Human Life Special?* (Peter Lang 2002) and articles in *Global Policy*, *Ethics and Global Politics* and *Public Health Ethics*.

Nigel Dower is an honorary senior lecturer in philosophy at the University of Aberdeen. His main research interests are in the field of global ethics. His publications include *World Ethics - the New Agenda* (Edinburgh University Press 1998/2007), *Introduction to Global Citizenship* (Edinburgh University Press 2003) and *The Ethics of War and Peace* (Polity Press 2009). He was the president of the International Development Association 2002–2006 and received an honorary doctorate from the Uppsala University in 2009.

Peter Gan is an academic at the School of Humanities, Universiti Sains, Malaysia. His research revolves primarily around the field of philosophy of religion, especially in the area of mysticism and the relation between religion and ethics. A very recent publication of his examines Evelyn Underhill's premier text on mysticism through the lenses of dialecticism and sublimity.

Soraj Hongladarom is a professor of philosophy at Chulalongkorn University in Bangkok, Thailand. He has published books and articles on such diverse issues as bioethics, computer ethics, and the roles that science and technology play in the culture of developing countries. He has edited *Computing and Philosophy in Asia* (Cambridge Scholars Publishing 2007) and his works have appeared in *The Information Society, AI & Society, Philosophy in the Contemporary World* and *Social Epistemology,* among others.

Kiyoshi Murata is a director of the Centre for Business Information Ethics and a professor of MIS at the School of Commerce, Meiji University, Tokyo, Japan. His research interest is in e-business, information quality management, knowledge management and information ethics in business organizations including privacy, surveillance, ICT professionalism and gender issues. He is an international research associate at the Centre for Computing and Social Responsibility, De Montfort University, Leicester, UK.

Yohko Orito is an associate professor of management information at the Faculty of Collaborative Regional Innovation, Ehime University, Matsuyama, Japan. She received her PhD in commerce from Meiji University, Tokyo, Japan in 2007. Her research interest is in information ethics in business organizations, particularly use of personal information in businesses and protection of the right to privacy and freedom.

Elin Palm has a PhD in philosophy from the Royal Institute of Technology in Stockholm and is research fellow at the Centre for Applied Ethics, Linköping University, Sweden. She heads the research group 'Ethics of Migration' and conducts research on moral responsibility for irregular migrants. Her publications include articles in *International Journal of Migration and Border Studies, Surveillance & Society* and *Health Care Analysis.*

Hans Ingvar Roth is a professor of human rights at the Department of Asian, Middle Eastern and Turkish Studies at Stockholm University. He has written on human rights, affirmative action, minority rights and multicultural education. He has also worked as a Human Rights Officer for OSCE in Bosnia and as a Senior Adviser at the Ministry of Justice in Stockholm, Sweden. He has published *The Multicultural Park* (Liber 1999) and a number of books in Swedish.